SOFTWARE METRICS

A Guide to Planning, Analysis, and Application

SOFTWARE METRICS

A Guide to Planning, Analysis, and Application

C. Ravindranath Pandian

AUERBACH PUBLICATIONS

A CRC Press Company
Boca Raton   London   New York   Washington, D.C.

Note: This book was previously published by Quality Improvement Consultants, Hyderabad, India.

Library of Congress Cataloging-in-Publication Data

Pandian, C. Ravindranath.
  Software metrics : a guide to planning, analysis, and application / C. Ravindranath Pandian.
    p. cm.
  Includes bibliographical references and index.
  ISBN 978-0-84931-661-6
    1. Software measurement. I. Title.

  QA76.76.S65P36 2003
  005.1'4--dc21   2003048174

Visit the Auerbach Publications Web site at www.auerbach-publications.com

---

● 2004 by CRC Press LLC
Auerbach is an imprint of CRC Press LLC

No claim to original U.S. Government works
International Standard Book Number 978-0-84931-661-6
Library of Congress Card Number 2003048174

Contents

Preface

This book is an attempt to simplify software measurement, elicit its usefulness, and make it a pragmatic tool for management. Ideas and techniques presented here are derived from best practices. These are field proven, down to earth and, above all, straightforward, making it a treasure for practitioners.

Highlights

The illustrated book helps to enrich your knowledge about measurements and analysis, to know about the best practices, to realize how ordinary analysis techniques can be applied to achieve extraordinary results, and to understand model building from metrics for decision making. When you are through with this book, you should be drawn to the fact that this is a volume of "tools and techniques," simple and easy to apply.

Why This Book Was Written

This book is the result of years of application and teaching of quantitative methods. It all began in the early 1980s with a small team entrusted with empirical research for product development. Computer modeling, supported by measurement and analysis, helped us develop new techniques in an exceptionally short time. The key to success was inferred to be in "statistical thinking," a concept to which this book is committed.

We continued to employ statistical methods in R&D, while many had assumed that only manufacturing organizations needed them. The lean of the software industry toward metrics propelled us to disseminate statistical methods through seminars across India and consultancy sessions with several software project teams. And we were led to fresh insights.

Then we undertook "metrics data analysis" as a service, to perceive the latent problems in metrics implementation. Our collaborative work with several QA managers was synergetic and fruitful. The struggle was to integrate a metrics program with project management, and breathe life into metrics, a potential tool.

We succeeded by creating models from metrics and applied them to decision making in process management, business management, and defect management. In a scenario where metrics are often considered a tool for process improvement, application of metrics in creating project information, constructing knowledge, and erecting decision models received warm acceptance.

Our seminars generated active participation from software professionals who loved to interact with data to create and run process models on the spreadsheet, and took us through cycles of refinement of the concept, driving the learning, with unwavering persistence, toward pragmatism.

This book is the sum total of all the cited understandings and experiences and is our humble presentation to the software industry.

Acknowledgments

I am grateful to several of our clients who invited us to work with them on metrics and quantitative methods. I thank the software professionals who participated in our seminars; their keen interest in metrics inspired me and helped me to fine tune the concepts. We are indebted to the QA managers in the following organizations for their support and encouragement in metrics research:

- BPL Software (Bangalore)
- Case Consultants (Trivandrum)
- Cognizant Technologies (Pune)
- Datamatics (Mumbai)
- Geometric Software (Mumbai)
- HCL (Chennai)
- Hewlett Packard (Bangalore)
- Honeywell (Bangalore)
- Hughes (Bangalore)
- IBM (Bangalore)
- Infosys (Bangalore)
- Infotech (Hyderabad)
- Intelligroup (Hyderabad)
- ITC Infotech (Bangalore)
- KPIT (Pune)
- L&T Infotech (Mumbai)
- Mastek (Mumbai)
- Oracle (Bangalore)
- Robert Bosch (Bangalore)
- Satyam Computer Services (Hyderabad)
- Siemens (Bangalore)
- Verifone (Bangalore)
- Wipro (Bangalore)

I thank Samuel Devaraj, who helped me in my first step toward software metrics. I thank Mr. Sreeshaila, Mr. Ashok, and Mr. Nagaraj, who provided the first opportunity to us to apply statistical thinking in software projects. I must mention the close support and guidance we received from Mr. Bhashyam and his colleagues in propagating metrics analysis to several project teams. With gratitude I remember the infectious enthusiasm of Mr. Venkatachalam in applying metrics to management and the joint work we have done in that direction.

For the in-depth study on metrics and for the way they approached metrics, I must thank Mr. Rajamanickam and Mr. Gopinath. I must thank Sangeeta Jayadevan for her focus on metrics, and in particular for the efforts she took in training project staff on metrics. I appreciate Sujaya Ranganath for the efforts she took to simplify metrics and align the same with project goals.

I remember with thanks the encouragement provided by organizations such as SPIN (Bangalore) and ERTL (Trivandrum) in promoting quantitative methods.

I thank V. Prasad, Director, and L. Sudhakar, Joint Director, CETE Hyderabad, for giving us QPM assignments.

Special thanks are due to Navyug Mohnot, QAI, who supported our QPM research and conducted national and international seminars. We are collaborating with QAI in developing a Web-based training system on QPM. This has helped to consolidate our research work and apply the results.

Throughout the development of this book, my colleagues V. Gowri Shankar, S. Suresh Babu, Vasu Valluri, M. Anand, Saravana Kumar, and Shadrach K. Suman did the supportive metrics research. A.S. Sri Lakshmi helped in upgrading the application chapters and put in special efforts to complete the manuscript. P.R. Sundar provided logistic support and helped in production of the book. I thank each one of them and many other friends and well-wishers who have contributed to this book.

C. RAVINDRANATH PANDIAN

Chapter 1
Software Measurement

A New Order

In the last ten years the software industry has witnessed great growth. The discipline, called software management, has experienced several innovations. Foremost among these seems to be the rediscovery of management science. There is a new emphasis on measurements, denoting a drive for precision in decision making. Empowered by measurements, the modern decision maker is able to free himself from the clutches of prejudice to observe reality.

Fresh learning from process measurement has now tempered the established theories and practices; a new order has emerged.

In this new order, projects are now managed quantitatively with numbers. Intuition is enriched with empiricism, ushering in a new culture of managing by measurement.

To measure is to know, to learn, to understand. Measurement begins as recognition and is complete when we express our perception as numbers. Measurement reveals the architecture of our ideas, concepts, and models.

A common definition states that "measurement is a process by which numbers or symbols are assigned to attributes of entities of a software product, process, or project." The assignment of numbers must be governed by rules or theory. The formulation of rules can be done in several ways. Though several prescriptions exist, it is better that the rules are derived from decision models, as Cem Kaner suggests.

In the beginning many used measurements to monitor progress, particularly in critical areas. Further down the line, measurements are associated with improvements. The paradigm turned out to be "if you can't measure, you can't improve." Soon the industry realized that before improvement can be thought of, the current status had to be established. Measurements are used to assess the current status, and the improvement frameworks need this assessment because "if you don't know where you are, a map won't help."

1

Software measurement has influence reaching far beyond determining the present status and paving the way for improvement. Software measurement helps in creating indicators, building models for simulation, and decision making; it aids goal setting and deployment; above all, it liberates one from the constraints of ideologies and makes one recognize and respond to reality. Measurements have also made statistical thinking a way of life.

Measurement in Quality Thinking

Measurement and statistical thinking, symbols of new management, are not at all new. Historically, it began in the name of quality control in industries. But the first lectures on statistical methods by Shewhart in the 1920s were for engineering graduates, taught as a design methodology. Shewhart also recommended "statistical process control" to bring economy in production. Deming has indicated the need for managers to acquire "profound knowledge" by understanding variation in the process using statistical methods. Crosby, in addition to identifying "maturity levels" in the evolution of organizations, urges us to measure the cost of poor quality. Juran recommends a "trilogy," which uses control-chart representation of process improvement. Ishikawa ushered in a new revolution in Japan by creating "seven QC tools" for problem solving with emphasis on data collection and analysis. Taguchi applied "design of experiments" to build robust processes. Gradually, all these quality concepts and the associated measurement technologies have been acquired by software industries.

Humphrey, author of Capability Maturity® Model (CMM) and ardent proponent of process management, supports metrics both at the organizational level and at the individual level. He has developed a metrics-based framework, PSP (personal software process), for creating "software engineering discipline." IDEAL, a process improvement guideline from the CMM family of standards again emphasizes measurements for "process characterization" and diagnostics. ISO 9000:2000 focuses on measurement, analysis, and improvement. ISO 9126 gives a framework for measuring software quality. The Six Sigma movement, in one of its modern forms, is centered on the DMAIC principle: define, measure, analyze, improve and control.

After the numerous contributions by gurus and collaborative developments of systems (of which the previous two paragraphs capture only a set of representative examples), it may be seen that measurement has secured a permanent position in the quality management culture.

Precision in Expression

From the world of scientific inquiry to management, measurements have moved along an eventful path, redefining life along the way. Business systems adopted measurements (and the scientific spirit they represented) for defining performance standards, and tracking the actual performance against the standards. Soon an intrinsic worth of measurements was discovered in the ability of a measurement system to provide symbols for unambiguous communication. Managers began to express their goals quantitatively and publish results through numbers. Setting measurable goals became a leadership style that broke hierarchy and promoted understanding. In many instances this led to scaling down the goals to the capability levels of project teams, even changing those goals and aligning them toward customer needs.

Measurements helped managers achieve a precision that stood for knowledge. "When you can measure what you are speaking about and express it in numbers, you know something about it; but when you cannot measure it and when you cannot express it in numbers, your knowledge is of a meager and unsatisfactory kind," as Lord Kelvin put it. In particular, software estimation benefited from this influence. Supported by software measurements, estimation stopped being an imprecise guesswork, and emerged as a scientific forecasting system. The wave of precision swept across software engineering and influenced a whole spectrum of activities, from planning to review.

Representation of Reality

We see in projects what we want to see, until we look at data coming from measurements, which represents realities. This power of data lies in the fact that hollow theories and prejudices that hitherto dominated human thinking are replaced by validated concepts, empirical formulae, and ideas that work.

These data are used in building statistical models for developing management strategies, prediction, and risk assessment. These models achieve success in representing realities in convenient and concrete forms (such as the Monte Carlo simulation of project schedule) for decision making.

Lack of visibility is a well-known constraint in software project management. Software measurements bring visibility into processes. As the measurement capability improves, detailed process models can be constructed from data. The "vision" permeates into the processes, bringing in fresh certainty, transparency, and understanding. Correspondingly, risk comes down.

With the help of detailed measurements of process, it is now possible to set goals and performance standards at "micro levels" within the project, enabling process optimization.

Knowledge Creation

The corporate world has started recognizing intellectual assets as part of its inventory. It is now believed that data is the wealth of an organization.

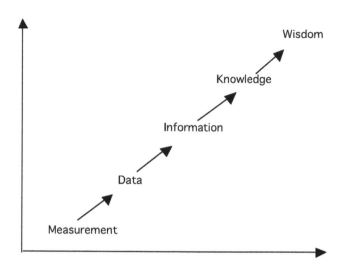

Exhibit 1. Quality of decision making.

Despite this significant recognition, the common scenario is that data remains not only locked in databases and lost in records but it is also difficult to access and to interpret; moreover, it remains incomplete and invalid. As a result, effective use of data is an elusive concept. What industry needs is the knowledge that is embedded in the data. One has to go beyond data gathering to unleash knowledge as a management support for decision making. Data remains in reality, a passive ore in dormant forms. Knowledge is not readily available from data; one has to mine it.

As shown in Exhibit 1, the first step is to create information from data by suitable methods; the next is to generate knowledge by processing information; and finally, to apply this knowledge for decision making. The integration of knowledge with decision making is wisdom. This is a road map from data to wisdom, consisting of a sequence of transformations, adding value every time.

The linear sequence is inspired and directed by goals, and supported by theoretical models en route. This sequence inherits its relevance from an organizational framework.

This data-to-wisdom route is the lifeline of modern decision support systems and knowledge engineering initiatives.

Measurement Technology

Is software measurement a separate discipline? Yes, it is a separate process area in Capability Maturity Model integration (CMMi). The core concepts in software measurements are based on the science of measurements or metrology. Proper understanding of this technology will make measurements look a lot easier than is believed. Improper understanding, on the contrary, complicates the matter and makes measurement look like an intricate process.

Measurement, as a process, exhibits an internal evolution and happens in three phases. The phases of measurement can be related to the concept of measurement scales well delineated in measurement theory. One can also identify measuring agencies or instruments, which are human-centric in software measurements.

These aspects of measurement technology are presented in subsequent paragraphs.

Measuring with the Mind: Cognitive Phase

The essential measurement is a mental process. We measure with the mind, the inward eye. In this context, measurement begins with perception. For example, measurement of risk in a project begins with perceiving risk elements, in the first place. Then, the probability of occurrence of each risk element and its impact on the project are guessed.

Measurement also involves judgment. One takes stock of a situation in the project and develops feelings or ideas that relate to and represent our assessment of the situation. This assessment or judgment is also an act of measurement.

In the cognitive phase of measurement, all the constituents of the mind, or whatever is represented by the word mind, are at play. For example, when a project manager estimates the size of a project based on "gut feeling" or experience, this estimation is an act of measurement.

Measuring with Words: Semantic Phase

In the next phase of measurement, semantic expressions are used to label or refer to the observation, which is known in measurement science as the nominal scale. Words can be used as signs denoting objects, experiences, or concepts in accordance with the referential theory of meaning.

Grouping similar objects together and giving the group a name or label is also measurement. For example, defects can be grouped or classified into various types. Each type can be given a unique name or label (GUI types — logic type). Such groupings and labeling may be seen as an attempt to bring order to an otherwise chaotic collection. Creating this order by naming paves the way for better understanding, a cardinal benefit of measurement.

Apart from serving as signs, words can be used to denote values, such as in grading productivity as high, medium, or low. Words now signify value, which is a product of culture, history, and convention. Using such value-level indicators is the most common and simple way of measuring.

5

Verbal expressions of value could trigger predictable responses within the same organization or society, due to the force of convention, but tend to be ambiguous during benchmarking across societies.

Measuring with Numbers: Quantitative Phase

Though observation with the mind and use of language help in measurement, the results are not highly reproducible. If the observations are expressed as numbers, this problem is solved, to a large extent. Hence, the more refined and precise process of measurement is quantitative measurement.

Numerical data completes a journey, which started with words and definitions. Flaws in the root concepts or erroneous definitions could severely damage the utilitarian power of numerical data.

The Three Phases Coexist

The three phases of measurement coexist, each one influencing the other two.

The cognitive phase is dominated by cultural symbols, paradigms, beliefs, and other impressions one has acquired from the life one has been living. This phase is also characterized by the creative ability to see beyond the rational border, the ability to act upon minimum clues, and the vision of a poet.

The semantic phase is marked by linguistic structures, which are used to articulate, disseminate, and propagate values and meaning. These structures have been deconstructed and rendered flexible by postmodern approaches, and have become more capable of coping with reality.

In the quantitative phase, numbers are used to indicate value, to represent quantities, and to denote levels. The quantitative phase permits construction of mathematical equations and advanced analysis. The quantitative phase is dominated by numbers.

These phases are not to operate in isolation. For best results, they draw upon one another. There exists an inevitable plurality in measurement methods. From this perspective, numbers are extensions of an existing system of observation, thinking, and communication. Numbers are not an "overhead" imposed on project economics but an elegant and natural superstructure that adds value as it grows.

Measurement Scales

Inside each measurement phase, the task of measuring reduces to the task of mapping attributes of real-life objects to numbers or symbols.

Exhibit 2. Measurement scales.

Cognitive Start	Consciousness
Nominal Scale Typological Scale	} Linguistic Scales
Ordinal Scale	
Interval Scale Ratio Scale Absolute Scale	} Numerical Scales

Almost naturally, we assume a "scale" while measuring, like in measuring human intelligence on a scale of IQ (with magnitudes ranging from 60 to 140). There are other scales available for measuring intelligence. We can exercise our choice while selecting a scale. Use of scales is very common in all fields of scientific pursuit, from economics to engineering.

The different types of measurement scales are listed in Exhibit 2.

Nominal Scale

Employing semantic expressions to represent objects (teams) for the purpose of identification (referential value) is known as nominal scale measurement. An example of nominal scale measurement is the assignment of ID numbers to bugs found. Another example of nominal scale is in how we recognize, define, and name software defects. Giving unique and unequivocal names to concepts and defining technical terms also belong to this scale.

Typological Scale

In the typological scale of measurement, we identify types or categories in entities that have been already recognized and named. Constructing risk taxonomy or classifying defects according to a well-defined framework like Orthogonal Defect Classification (ODC) could be examples for measurements done on typological scale, in which measurement is equivalent to categorization. This scale is also known as the nominal-categorical scale.

Ordinal Scale

Measuring in the ordinal scale amounts to assessing values in measured entities and rearranging them according to the order of value. Both value and order are expressed using words or symbols. For example, when defects are measured, their severity levels are described in semantic expressions such as high, medium, and low. CMM maturity levels, for instance, are in the ordinal scale.

Numerical Scales

Properties associated with numerical scales are magnitude, interval, and rational zero. When we graduate from semantic expressions to quantitative expressions of values, measurement becomes less ambiguous and more informative, and it allows numerical analysis.

Interval Scale. Interval scale is an arbitrary scale, used for perceiving increments, not ratios. There is no rational zero in this scale.

Gap measurement, where the interval between goal and current state is the judgment criterion.

Ratio Scale. Ratio scale is a more potential scale, which permits ratio calculation and equipped with rational zero reference point.

Absolute Scale. Absolute scale is a unique and unambiguous scale, like in counting lines of code.

The idea of scales of measurements has been applied to software by Fenton, Park et al., and several others, and is used by practitioners.

Levels of Measurements

Many tend to think that there is no measurement until quantitative expressions are used; as a consequence, the early phase measurements are ignored. But the different measurement scales permit different levels of measurements that reflect a progressive freedom from subjective errors and nearness to truth. (Scales of measurement in fact reflect levels of measurement.) The level can be chosen to suit the purpose at hand. It is desirable that the level of measurement matches the level of action. Let us not "measure with a micrometer, mark with a chalk, and cut with an axe." If organizations do not respond to lower levels of measurements — when problems written in the walls are not solved — the precision of higher levels of measurements appears as mockery to people with a bias for action.

In a business environment where decision-making skills are at play, practitioners learn to read ambiguous data and derive resolutions from imprecise clues. They do not await results with higher levels of precision (numbers) when results with lower levels of precision are available more readily and, perhaps, in time. Thus the utilitarian value of lower scales of measurements (costs less, easy to collect, easy to interpret) are incredibly large in a project life cycle. Exhibit 3 shows the ambiguity in measurement levels.

Measurement does not provide an absolute and final answer but yields in each level and results in varying degrees of precision.

Which is useful, the quantitative data or cognitive recognition? Both are valuable. Some feel that business prosperity springs from messages read off the lower scales of measurement.

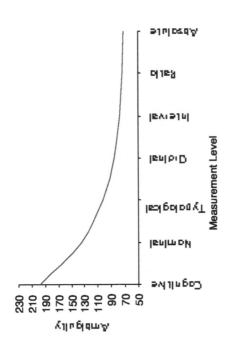

	Measurement Level	Ambiguity
7	Cognitive	198
6	Nominal	134
5	Typological	102
4	Ordinal	86
3	Interval	78
2	Ratio	74
1	Absolute	72

Exhibit 3. Ambiguity in measurement levels.

Intrinsic Nature of Measurement

The measurement process has been well understood and defined by measurement scientists (metrologists). To make the best use of measurements one must gain an understanding of the intrinsic nature of measurement.

Error, Accuracy, Precision, and Uncertainty

Measurement error is the difference between the measured values from the truth. Measurement accuracy is the tendency of the measuring device to get close to the true value. Measurement precision refers to the ability of the measuring device to reduce variation in observations in repeat measurements. Measurement uncertainty refers to the combined effect of all imperfections in measurements.

Noise

Classically, it is defined as unwanted or undesirable signal. Noise distorts the signal. For example, while measuring lines of code (LOC) to estimate defect density, the comment line count could become noise. (But the same comment line count is a desired signal while estimating intra-program documentation).

Sensitivity

It is the minimum increment that can be clearly identified by the measuring system. For example, we can relate this to the risk perception in software projects. Risk is perceived by someone whose mind has been sensitized by knowledge and experience. An ignorant or inexperienced person may fail to detect risk signals.

Calibration

Calibration is the process of comparing measured value with the true (actual) value. From this comparison a correction table is generated which can be applied during future measurements to predict true value from the measured value. In software engineering, estimation models (considered as measuring equipment) are calibrated before use.

Scale Shape

Some scale shapes are linear and some are nonlinear. Measuring cost, effort, and schedule uses linear scale shapes. Human response to motivation follows a nonalgorithmic scale. Another example of nonlinear scale shape is in measuring customers' satisfaction. Scale shape is the characteristic response of the sensor under given conditions.

Software Measuring Instruments

As evident from the discussion on phases and scales of measurements, it is the human mind that emerges as the basic measuring instrument. There are also certain software engineering processes that play the role of measuring, such as review and estimation. There are a variety of tools employed in software measurement. One can identify some standard instruments used for software measurement in the following list:

- Observation
- Cognitive recognition
- Estimation
- Tracking and monitoring
- Review
- Test
- Audit
- Data entry forms
- Data collection tools
- Log sheets
- Survey forms
- Checklists
- Assessment questionnaire
- Experiments

The measuring agency could sometimes be an automated system in whose environment the entire software development is carried out.

Measurement Continuum

Metrologists have added more scales of measurements to address special measurement situations, such as log-interval scale and cyclic ratio scales. We have difficulties in building measurement scales for complex entities, which are composed of multiple variables that cannot be independently measured. We also have problems in measuring volatile factors that exist in the dynamic and ever-changing environment in software projects.

However, instead of developing special measurement scales, the responsibility of representing complex realities may be transferred to a suitable metrics system. Metrics, derived from measures, can be used in turn to construct models. These models can be applied for decision making.

The journey is seen as a natural series represented by a measurement continuum known as measure-metrics-models (MMM) (Exhibit 4).

Despite carefully designed measurement scales, it is difficult to achieve perfect measurements that capture truth completely and accurately. The MMM approach proves to be a cost-effective alternative to the otherwise

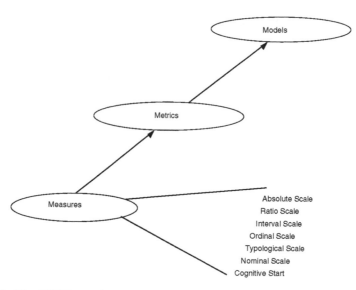

Exhibit 4. The MMM continuum.

costly and, many times, impractical methods that give accuracy in measurements.

Given the fact that metrics are themselves some sort of transformations of raw measurements and models that are constructed by a series of transformations on the metrics, the MMM package contains within itself a set of signal processing algorithms, one might say. It is well known that by using a signal processing algorithm we can achieve a better quality measurement in an economic way. Such processing, for instance, could filter out noise from measurements, achieve better accuracies, and get to know the truth very closely. A good signal processing sequence would give, in effect, a perfect measurement.

Thus, in the MMM approach sophisticated technical problems of measuring are handled at higher analytical levels rather than at the data-gathering level.

The Corner Stone

Measurements constitute the foundation of a new culture. The process of measurement, by its very being, establishes an environment of observation, and opens closed minds. With measurement begins innovation management, followed closely by improvement initiation. Applying measurements to project life is a discipline that creates knowledge, promotes realization, and remains the corner stone of engineering management.

Chapter 2
Software Metrics

Metrics Mapping

When measurements embrace a structure or system, they become more meaningful indicators called metrics. The structure could be a simple algebraic formulation or model. The structure behind metrics could be built on software engineering problems or business situations.

Moving from measurements to metrics is like moving from observation to understanding. Metrics are conceived by the user and designed to reveal a chosen characteristic in a reliable and meaningful manner. Then these metrics are mapped to ongoing measurements, to arrive at a best fit. The rules for mapping metrics to measurements depend on the problem one wants to address. The mapping rules could be tentative, and the metrics choice could be heuristics. The metrics–measurements mapping is shown in Exhibit 1.

Let us see how we can construct metrics from two common measurements, effort and time.

For tracking and control of projects we choose effort variance and schedule variance as metrics that are derived from the two measurements, effort and time.

In case we wish to build an advanced project simulation and forecasting model, we do not have to gather more measurements, but create a suitable model such as Earned Value Graph from just the two measurements. To build this model, all we need is a good conceptual structure and sound mapping rules but not more measurements.

Metrics are also indicators. Each metric becomes a natural element in the organization's business intelligence system or management information system. A well-structured metrics process would help in taking data-driven decisions in time.

Metrics List for Project Management

Thinking of metrics for project management makes one consider the project management structure that one is currently using or that one wants to use. That is the first step: to define the core structure — the bedrock — on which we build metrics. The structure could be based on a project manager's

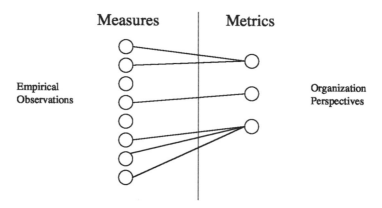

Exhibit 1. Metrics–measurements mapping.

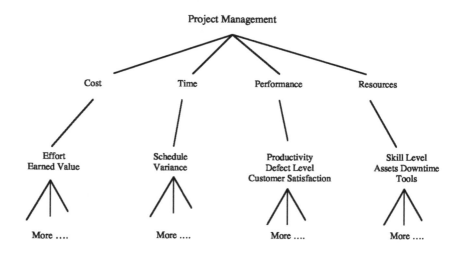

Exhibit 2. Project management metrics.

unwritten agenda of managing resources optimally. It could be based on the classical model from Kerzner, and focus on the structural elements of cost, time, performance, and resources. Or, it could have a Capability Maturity Model (CMM) orientation and regard people, process, and technology as the building blocks.

The management metrics we choose will certainly reflect the management system we settle for. The system provides sustenance, meaning, and context. Metrics provide supportive definitions, visibility, and feel. Management system elements cascade down to metrics, as illustrated in Exhibit 2. The management ideology is adapted from Kerzner, while the metrics are chosen from common practices.

14

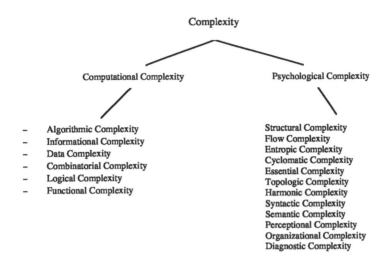

Complexity

Computational Complexity

Psychological Complexity

- Algorithmic Complexity
- Informational Complexity
- Data Complexity
- Combinatorial Complexity
- Logical Complexity
- Functional Complexity

Structural Complexity
Flow Complexity
Entropic Complexity
Cyclomatic Complexity
Essential Complexity
Topologic Complexity
Harmonic Complexity
Syntactic Complexity
Semantic Complexity
Perceptional Complexity
Organizational Complexity
Diagnostic Complexity

Exhibit 3. Software complexity metrics.

The success of metrics depends on the design of suitable structures and mapping rules but definitely not on mechanical collection of more and more data.

The influence of metrics on the structure is worth mentioning. In the first place, attempts to recognize, define, and measure structural elements bring about beneficial modifications in the structure. When metrics operate and data flows in, imperfections in the structure become visible, leading to additional improvements.

Structure and metrics have a master and tool relationship, and together characterize and superintend processes.

Metrics Choices: Build or Borrow

Many software practitioners build their own metrics. Working under project constraints, they solve problems related both to idea structure and metrics mapping as best as they can. Rigorous solutions require great effort and are beyond comfort levels — the result: ill-framed ideological structures breeding ill-suited metrics.

For example, developing a metric for complexity has been a scientific pursuit for decades. Solutions have been found and published by academicians but some practitioners are not enamored of them. They choose to deal with complexity just through the simple notion of size and remain content with the inadequate mapping it provides.

One can perceive complexity in so many ways, as presented in Exhibit 3, and pick a metric that will satisfy specific needs. Each complexity metric shown here is the result of careful application. Some of the complexity metrics are now supported with tools, to enable ease of application.

Simple Metrics

Plain Adaptation

A number of measurements can be seen directly in the organizational context, and hence can be taken as metrics. The effort taken to fix a bug is a simple example. This data is directly available in the log sheet or in the computer system if the job is done in an automated environment. As a metric, effort means cost to the project and indicates the cost of fixing the bug, which in turn will be seen in the light of financial implications, delivery time, and billing. In such cases the mapping rule is direct:

$$\text{Metric} = \text{Measured Value} \tag{2.1}$$

There are several such simple metrics which are plain adaptations of measurements without any further mathematical processing: time to finish a job, defect count, failure events per month, staff level, etc.

Comparison

Comparing a measurement with an estimate can yield a metric such as cost escalation obtained by taking the difference between actual and estimated values. The absolute value of escalation has special meaning in areas related to finance and reliability, for example.

Ratio

Ratios provide insight into processes and can work as very useful metrics, such as in the defect density shown in Equation 2.2. Here the ratio normalizes defect count by size, and in the normalized scale one can easily compare the quality of different software products. Mere defect counts alone, without normalization, do not support comparison or benchmarking.

$$\text{Defect Density} = \frac{\text{Defect Count}}{\text{Size}} \tag{2.2}$$

If the size of the software can be determined as lines of code without ambiguity, then one can establish a metric.

$$\text{Productivity} = \frac{\text{Size}}{\text{Effort}} \tag{2.3}$$

This definition is most common, and helps to set capability baselines of some practical use.

The definition can be carried to almost all processes. Expressions such as lines of code per day, function points per week, and pages reviewed per day are familiar to many. Some projects have used this ratio as a linear model for estimating effort once the size is known.

Complex Metrics

Metric from Six Measurements

A more detailed treatment of productivity is from Larry Putnam, who defines productivity in terms of a nonlinear function of multiple variables, namely, size, skill factor and experience, effort spent, elapsed time taken, and two influence factors. This is a very insightful combination where due importance to time as a factor has been given and the interplay between time, effort, and size has been brought out. His definition forms the basis for the Rayleigh model and has the power to govern the entire life cycle process, even in the maintenance phase.

Putnam's definition has a larger role to play as an estimation model in predicting effort, staffing pattern, and defect discovery profile, and in risk and trade-off analysis, the dynamic interplay of several influences, and recognizing nonlinearity of relationships.

$$\text{Productivity} = \frac{\text{Size}}{\left(E/B\right)^a T^b} \tag{2.4}$$

where:

E = effort
B = experience or skill factor
a, b = influence factors (typically the value of a = 1/3 and b = 4/3)
T = elapsed time

The above definition of productivity will be of special help when productivity is benchmarked across projects of different maturity levels. It may be noted that Putnam has included time in the calculations, and when used as an estimation model, we can predict both effort and time using this metric.

Which metric definition shall we choose: the simple ratio or the higher-order nonlinear function? Both have their uses, and both have their limitations. The choice depends on the complexity of productivity problem one deals with. Without adjustment for skill factors, productivity measurements and comparisons are unfair. Without the time element, productivity definition would lack customer focus and miss out on value earning. But managing a six-variable function instead of a two-variable formula would cost time and effort and specialist knowledge.

Exhibit 4. Function point table.

Item	Weighting Factor		
	Simple	Average	Complex
External inputs	3	4	6
External outputs	4	5	7
External inquiries	3	4	6
External files	7	10	15
Internal files	5	7	10

Metric from Structural Judgment

There are certain software engineering problems that consist of composite elements, all of which cannot be easily measured. Even if they are measured it cannot be done with the same level of precision. Such problems are decomposed into components and the components are measured on different scales. The measurement results are combined using a suitable algebraic equation, which yields the metric. An example is the construction of software size metric.

A well-known size metric is lines of code, developed some 40 years ago. For all its simplicity, its usefulness is on the decline because it could not meet emerging demands such as language independence and prediction capability. To meet these demands, metrics that use elaborate structures as well as multiple scales have been proposed. One such metric which is gaining currency is function point. Let us see how the function point metric handles the problem.

The function point of a software is the product of Unadjusted Function Count (UFC) and Value Adjustment Factor (VAF). UFC is the sum of all function counts for a given software component. Calculation of UFC involves physical counting of structural elements (on absolute scale) and choosing the weighting factors (on ordinal scale) according to the complexity level. The count and the weighting factor are multiplied to determine the function count. The format given in Exhibit 4 may be used for UFC estimation.

Calculation of VAF is first done by recognizing the factors having influence on the software under study, then these factors are evaluated on a scale (ordinal scale) that runs from 0 to 5, defined as follows:

0 = factor not present or has no influence
1 = insignificant influence
2 = moderate influence
3 = average influence
4 = significant influence
5 = strong influence

After the factors have been rated and summed, the total is converted to a Value Adjustment Factor, VAF, as shown in Equation 2.5.

$$VAF = 0.65 + 0.01 \, \Sigma IR \qquad (2.5)$$

where IR = Influence Rating. Now, Function Point of the software component is computed by the algebraic formula shown in Equation 2.6.

$$FP = UFC \times VAF \qquad (2.6)$$

where:

FP   = Function Point (Size Metric)
UFC = Unadjusted Function Point Count
VAF = Value Adjustment Factor

In the calculation of function point, it may be noted, despite the associated mathematical computations, the estimate has strong subjective elements such as recognizing value adjustment factors and judging the weighting factors. The metric is controlled by the structure and estimated more from cognitive judgment than from data collection.

This is a pragmatic way of defining metrics for a fairly difficult parameter. This is also an example of using multivariate models to measure true value of reality when too many factors govern the process outcome.

Metrics Are Organization Specific

The final choice of metrics has to be organization specific. Instead of fitting management systems to perceived metrics list, we better turn the table and look for fitting metrics choices. The true meaning of metrics is seen when measurements merge with the organization's culture. There is no universal metrics system that can be plugged into the project environment.

All roads to metrics begin with specific problems, issues, and objectives faced by the organization. A lot of tailoring and customization is required while adapting other plans. In some cases metrics evolve along with the organization, and mature along with the management system.

In this context, making use of the existing metrics lists and ideas is similar to using a quality system framework. Both have to be applied to the organization and translated into the organization's idioms.

Importance of Estimation and Planning in the Context of Metrics

There is a golden principle taught to students who begin measurements in laboratories: before you do an experiment, have a theoretical estimate of the expected results with ±10 percent, and do the experiment to find truth within ±1 percent.

Measurements without the support of a theoretical solution would prove to be less productive and even futile. This applies to all forms of metrics and can be extended to process improvement experiments. Before we measure a process outcome, we should know what is expected from the process under some conditions. Even ideal solutions are good starting points.

Beginning with prediction improves the effectiveness of measurements, motivates the observer, and creates value in the otherwise mundane task of data collection and processing.

The theoretical prediction is what estimation and planning stand for. Projects, as well as metrics, cannot afford to start without estimation and planning. Even a down-to-earth metric called effort variance depends on estimation, as the formula given in Equation 2.7 demands.

$$\text{Effort Variance} = \frac{\left(\text{Actual Effort} - \text{Estimated Effort}\right)}{\text{Estimated Effort}} \quad (2.7)$$

Effort variance indicates estimation capability as well as project implementation skills, and could contain signals in both directions. But the value of this metrics depends on the dependability of estimation and planning process. Poor estimation also makes the metric poor. Unreliable planning makes this metric equally unreliable.

Hence, effort variance metric derives its credibility from the planning and estimation environment of the organization.

Many organizations find that estimation emerges as the cardinal purpose of metrics during their metrics journey. Many of us look toward metrics to help us see and foresee a shade more clearly.

One has to achieve balanced progress both in estimation and metrics. One supports the other. Metrics are required to build estimation model. Estimation is required to breathe meaning into metrics.

Metrics Vocabulary

Years ago, very few software organizations used metrics, and whatever they measured related strongly to business priorities. With time, the list, scope, and reach of metrics have increased. Based on global surveys, several authors and consultants have published a commonly used metrics list. The number of metrics is so large that to comprehend them we use taxonomy — the tree diagram of metrics hierarchy.

There is value in looking at published metrics taxonomies. We get to know how others have named certain metrics. Of course, going one step further we appreciate how those metrics have been defined.

Those who wish to set up metrics in their projects would realize that the first step was to find the right name and then the right definition. A few organizations measure product quality as defect density but define it as defects per person month. Many organizations, on the other hand, use the same name defect density but define it as defects per kilo lines of code. Now, within the organization the local convention would hold true but when we wish to do benchmarking, we will be forced to redefine or rename our metrics. This mistake could have been avoided if a survey has been made of published metrics taxonomy, which will reveal global conventions.

Another benefit from metrics taxonomies is the semantic help they provide. As a language learner builds vocabulary, software engineering practitioners must acquire the metrics vocabulary.

A certain maintenance project manager was in a dilemma about setting up an estimation model for a bug-fixing effort. He could not find much guidance in the published literature. By looking at a complexity metrics list, he got some clues about how to characterize a software product and could extend the idea to bug fixing. He could directly borrow some of the complexity and, inspired, he could quickly figure out additional metrics. Metrics taxonomy here functioned as knowledge transfer mechanism as well as a semantic catalyst.

A useful metrics taxonomy (metrics lists with classification) has been presented by many researchers, including:

- Software Metrics Research Laboratory
- Karl E. Weigers
- Fenton
- Terence L. Woodings
- Reiner Dumke (http://irb.cs.uni-magdeburg.de)
- Center for Software Engineering of the University of Southern California (http://sunset.usc.edu)
- W. Humphrey

Guidelines from Quality Standards

ISO 9000 on Metrics

The ISO 9000 in its clause 4.20 suggests that all processes should use statistical techniques to measure process capability and product characteristics. ISO 9000:2000 edition introduces the MAI — Measure, Analyze and Improve methodology — establishing a noble purpose for metrics. It demands measurement of customer satisfaction in quantitative terms and also requires management to use metrics as an important input for planning, monitoring, and managing the project, and also for controlling the quality of the product.

Exhibit 5. Metrics application possibilities.

Maturity Level	Metrics Application Possibility
2	Project tracking
3	Defect tracking
4	Process capability study
5	Dynamic process models

Capability Maturity Model (CMM) on Metrics

In the CMM framework, as process maturity improves, metrics application possibilities improve, typically in a pattern shown in Exhibit 5.

Each Key Process Area (KPA) of CMM has measurement as an element and helps to increase the visibility. CMM serves as a guide for determining what to measure first and how to plan an increasingly comprehensive measurement program.

> *Metrics at level 2 focus on project planning and tracking, while metrics at level 3 become increasingly directed toward measuring the intermediate and final products produced during development. The metrics at level 4 capture characteristics of the development process itself to allow control of the individual activities of the process and at level 5, processes are mature enough and managed carefully enough to allow measurement to provide feedback for dynamically changing processes across multiple projects.*

Although CMM has established measurement as one of the enablers of process maturity, implementation trails behind vision. Aligning metrics with the maturity model is a slow process. A comparison between numbers of metrics planned and used, shown in Exhibit 6, points to this reality (in a typical scenario).

CMMi on Metrics

The Capability Maturity Model — Integrated Systems/Software Engineering (CMMi) has elevated measurements to a higher level of importance: it identifies Measurement and Analysis as a process area of the Managed Maturity Level (CMMi L2). Its purpose is to develop and sustain a measurement capability for supporting the management process. The goals are to align measurement with the organization information needs, ensure the availability of the measurement, and institutionalize the measurement as a managed process.

Measurement and Analysis supports all process areas by providing practices that guide projects and organizations in aligning measurement needs and objectives with a measurement approach that will provide

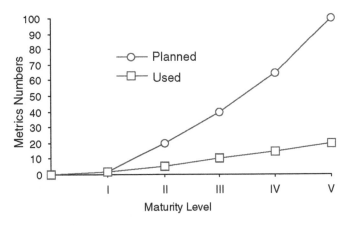

Exhibit 6. Aligning metrics with maturity model: reality.

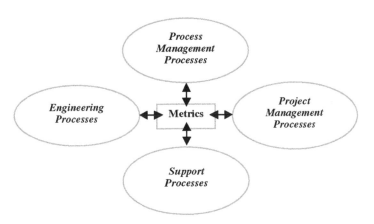

Exhibit 7. Metrics application model.

objective results that can be used in making informed decisions and taking appropriate corrective actions.

Applying Software Metrics: A Management Perspective

Several application models are available; however, we recommend a metrics application framework that focuses on four management areas illustrated in Exhibit 7.

Quantitative management of all the four areas is the objective of application. Metrics will help the manager see the management details in a structured manner, and move from somehow getting the results to optimizing resource utilization as well as performance. What was an unbroken black box, taking inputs and delivering outputs, now will be broken into

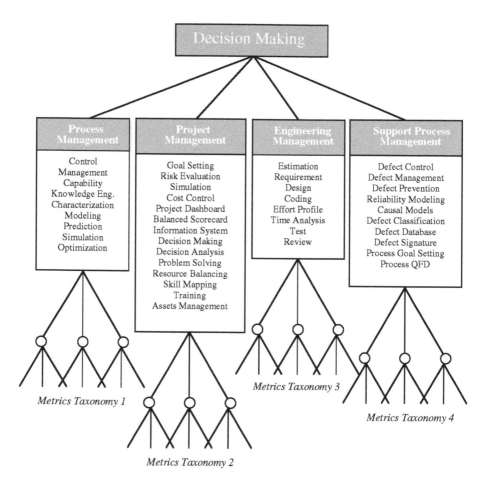

Exhibit 8. Metrics application structure.

micro projects within the project (or factories within the factory). Metrics exposes the hidden processes and brings in visibility to the degree and extent one desires and plans for.

In self-organizing systems, such as a committed human system, the moment of observation is also the moment of action. In such a highly pitched environment, metrics and the very act of creating metrics bring about process innovations.

When metrics penetrate into management areas, one can see an application structure evolving in each management area. The application structure consists of identified sub-areas and the associated metrics taxonomy, shown in Exhibit 8.

The complexity of the application structure increases when the associated metrics taxonomy sizes increase. After a few cycles, the application tree reaches and settles down at a critical size until the next phase change precipitates.

Benefits of Metrics

Metrics, by initiating observation, have led organizations (and individuals) to a process of self-discovery of goals, capabilities, and constraints. Quantitative expressions of the observations have brought in additional clarity and simplicity.

Metrics are seen as force multipliers in improvement initiatives and quality movements. On the one hand, the ability to improve is aided by the ability to measure (to see). By integrating knowledge and providing better communication, the resources are better utilized and efforts are better rewarded.

Structured thinking, a prerequisite for metrics, has paved the way for systems creation in unexpected areas. For instance, inspired by metrics data patterns, estimation models for bug fixing have been constructed and as a sequel the bug estimation task has been refined and redefined in many organizations.

Metrics data fills in human brains, gradually and almost imperceptibly. Over time, the personal thinking process gets enriched with fresh data and fresh learning. Beyond rational models, metrics also lead to cognitive intuitive models, perfecting a skill that comes naturally to human beings: vision. A map of benefits is given in Exhibit 9.

The most celebrated contribution of metrics is the decision-making support it provides. The first revolution metrics created is the information revolution. Over a period of time, information support has changed its style and moved from Management Information System (MIS) to Decision Support System (DSS), through the well-known phases of evolution.

Progress in metrics data analysis has created new and economic ways of creating knowledge assets in organizations. In that sense, metrics is a rudimentary knowledge engine. Constant interpretations of metrics inject a stream of values into the organization, some temporary, many more enduring. The learning process being what it is, experimental values and tentative knowledge structures all become part of the global repository of knowledge assets.

Problem-solving cycles have benefited from metrics in all the phases. All scales of measurement are useful here. Metrics are used for recognition and later for diagnostics of problems. Experiments are conducted to test ideas, true to the scientific spirit of metrics application.

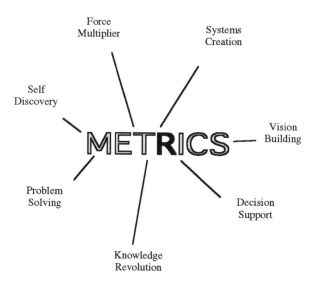

Exhibit 9. Metrics culture: map of benefit.

Chapter 3
Designing a Metrics System

Metrics System

Several rules have been prescribed to plan metrics in an organization. Methodologies have been developed to make effective use of metrics. In the past ten years there has been substantial progress in this direction. We applied these methodologies to several situations and worked with practitioners who have attempted implementation of their favored methodologies. Each time we tried an application, we realized its strong points and also encountered some difficulties.

We have studied metrics from a practical angle and identified factors that control the success rate of metrics implementation. What emerged from our findings is a new approach, which is presented here.

Metrics are best viewed as a system. We cannot design metrics in isolation from the environment. Metrics are connected to measurements by mapping rules. Metrics are connected to goals through decision rules. The architecture of metrics system is built around the information highway of organizations, which feeds decision centers. The objective of such a metrics system is to provide model-based decision support.

Designing metrics system architecture is the first step in metrics planning. The second step is to implement the system by working out a set of phased operational plans. Managing these two steps — design and implementation — is what metrics application is all about.

Information-Based Metrics Architecture

We propose a modern architecture in which metrics fulfills information needs in all the decision centers in an organization. The elements in metrics system architecture are

- Goal system
- Decision centers
- Models: knowledge capsules
- Metrics: indicators–signals
- Measurement: sensors

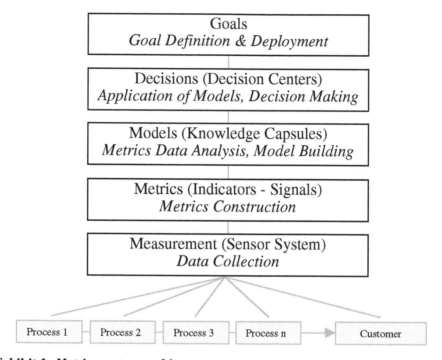

Exhibit 1. Metrics system architecture.

The architecture treats the organization as a network of processes delivering results to the customer. The concept of a value chain is used to identify processes for measurements. Processes that do not add value are not considered.

The metrics system architecture is illustrated in Exhibit 1. It may be noted that the system architecture is in agreement with the knowledge creation sequence discussed in Chapter 1, and moves data upwards. The architecture lives in an information environment, and can elegantly and naturally fit into MIS or decision support system (DSS) networks that exist in the organization.

Goals: The Drivers

It is well established that goals drive organizations. When we go into the details, we find that goals are translated and distributed across all organizational systems, decision centers, and problem-solving initiatives. Information systems need a "pull" from goals, human systems require goals for motivation and guidance, management systems use goals to define objectives, and goals are known to influence the very structure of all systems under their guidance. Decision making, at any level, depends on goals even more. Then, for problem-solving cycles, goals are the starting point and the

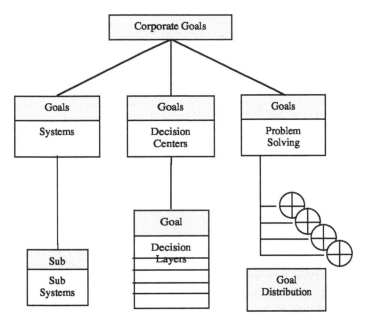

Exhibit 2. Goal tree.

very recognition of problems is achieved by comparing actual results against goals.

Now, systems have sub-systems and, correspondingly, goals have sub-goals. Decisions are made in organizational layers and, correspondingly, goals disperse into goal layers. Problem-solving cycles (as in Kaizen) are distributed across the organization, and we think of a suitable goal distribution. Placed together, all these constitute a complex goal system that can be modeled as a goal tree, shown in Exhibit 2. The metrics system architecture provides for an elaborate goal structure, as indicated in Exhibit 2. The design begins with defining goals. In reality, goal definition is a lengthy process; it happens in waves, each widening its reach.

Because the role of metrics is to support systems, decisions, and problem solving, when goals are not defined, metrics are futile because there is nothing to support.

When an organization launches its metrics program, it starts discovering its goals and perceives the goals with clarity. When the metrics culture sets in, goals are defined quantitatively.

The goals–metrics interaction is very dynamic and creative; each shapes the other. All known metrics initiatives, such as Basili's GQM paradigm and Park et al.'s adaptation called GQ (I) M, are goal-centered frameworks.

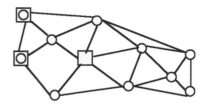

○   Process Center

☐   Knowledge Center

◨   Decision Center

Exhibit 3. The new organization.

The information flow shown in Exhibit 1 is directed toward goals. In organizations goals exist in multiple layers and are translated for "deployment." We recognize and strive for congruence among organization goals, project goals, team goals, and individual goals. Hence the complexity of a goal system can be seen.

Decision Centers: The New Organization

An organization is a network of processes. A few of the process centers also perform like decision centers, as shown in Exhibit 3. We look to the decision centers in an organization for metrics application. In this Information Age and era of the knowledge worker, the process-centric model of organizations, actively promoted by Total Quality Management (TQM) and business process reengineering (BPR) enthusiasts, is now superceded by the decision-centric model. The shift from process centers to decision centers occurs when the process is run by a dedicated "process owner," replacing mechanical and ritualistic "operators." A process center becomes a decision center when empowered with knowledge and decision-making freedom. There could be several process centers in an organization, but the number of decision centers could be dismally low. Decision centers shift constantly in unstable environments.

While the ritualistic process centers reject metrics, decision centers have a natural appetite for metrics. The rejection will then wrongly be ascribed to "failure of metrics."

We have to map the decision centers in an organization and trace them while developing a metrics plan. It is quite likely that the decision centers can be found in a hierarchical order and the metrics plan will inherit the hierarchy of decision centers, as shown in Exhibit 4.

Exhibit 4. Hierarchy in decision making.

Models: Knowledge Capsules

Models are abstractions of realities, which allow us to learn by inquiry as an economic alternative to trials. Models help in visualizing the process behavior. Models can be in the form of mathematical equations, graphs, and matrices that would represent real-world entities. They also help in forecasting, prediction, and what-if analysis.

Models are created using metrics, perhaps in knowledge centers. These models are consumed by all centers in the organization.

In decision centers, models meet with a special challenge, which arises from a very basic feature of decision making: search for alternatives. Decision analysis benefits from flexible, intelligent, and even interactive data presentations instead of frozen statistical predictions. Decision-making practices draw heavily from "management games" and probability assessment. Dynamic models can support decision making better than static models.

Based on the measurement scale employed, models can be in several forms: cognitive, iconic, semantic, visual patterns, quantitative structures, and, with the help of computers, artificial intelligence (AI). They can be built to address all process areas, as illustrated in Exhibit 5, mapping model building potentials to process areas. We can conceive a library of models, each an intellectual asset of immense value. The growth of software engineering can be traced to the discovery of new models for software quality, reliability, and estimation. From fixed assets management to knowledge management, all major disciplines have constructed and published models.

Published models need to be calibrated before use in an organization. Perhaps one has to choose between calibrating a ready-made model and constructing a new one. Calibration takes minimum effort, while construction is a project on its own merit. Both depend on metrics.

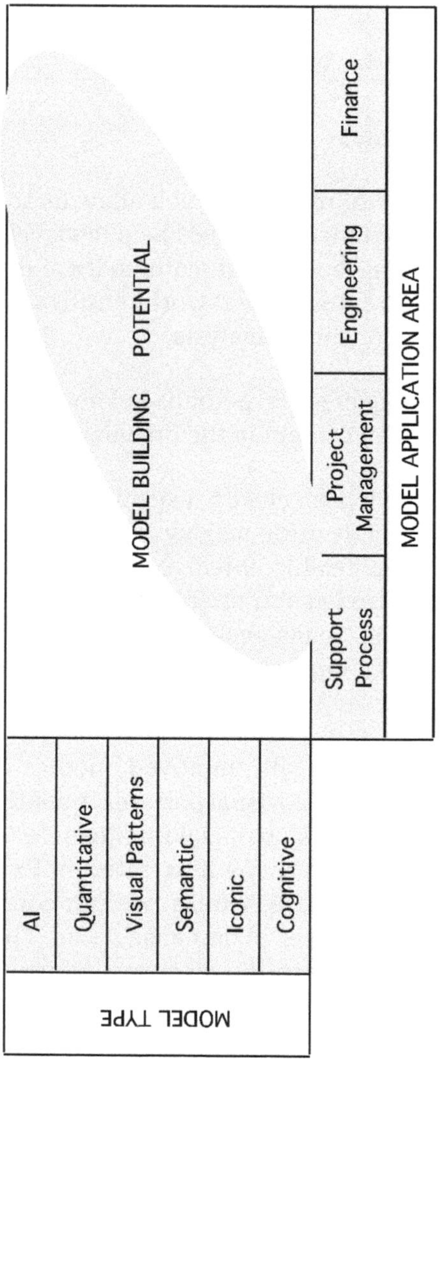

Exhibit 5. Model building potential.

Metrics: Indicators–Signals

The measurements–metrics–models presented in Chapter 1 become an integral part of the metrics architecture. To begin with, metrics are indicators, built from observations. Metrics are compared with goals, and the comparison provides the first level report. At the next level, models can be created.

That metrics support the subsequent information processes in the architecture is best seen from a communications system analogy. Well-designed metrics can play the role of corporate "signal generators," feeding information networks in the organization. The signal must emerge above noise and communicate messages clearly.

An example would help in appreciating metrics as origins of objective communications. Use of metrics in managing the training process is rather well known. Here is a common list:

- Rating of trainer
- Relevance of course
- Application potential of ideas presented
- Rating of training material
- Rating of environment (hall, light, video, audio)
- Rating of amenities provided (lunch, tea, water)
- Knowledge score before training
- Knowledge score after training
- Number of absentees
- Cost of training

In the example cited here, despite good monitoring of all the attributes of training process and presenting the reports quantitatively to the concerned managers and decision makers, one problem persisted. There were always absentees. All the nominated persons did not participate in the actual training. The training manager devised a new metric that better communicated the problem. He presented a new metric to the organization: cost of training per person per program. This metric may also be thought of as "dollar productivity" of the training process. Expressed in monetary units, the metrics caught the attention of senior managers, and an analysis revealed that the cost of training per person per program was almost double the budgeted cost. Had all the nominated people participated in the training, the budgeted dollar productivity would have been achieved.

The senior managers reacted to the messages provided by this metric, and the result was straightforward: it was communicated to all employees that if a nominated person did not attend training sessions, he would have to explain the reason to the management council in person. Attendance improved, as did dollar productivity of training.

While the earlier metrics set failed to represent and communicate the problem, the new metric effectively communicated the problem and resulted in organizational transformation.

Measurement: Sensor System

To measure is to observe or to sense processes, and hence measurement elements constitute a sensor system. The sensors planted at various stages of the process chain help in deriving the data. Locations of these sensors, the data collection points, are chosen to meet the information needs expressed in the form of desired metric and models.

The measurement system is distributed across the entire organization in a multitude of forms, ranging from automated tools to human observation. The characteristics of sensors vary correspondingly in consistency and bias.

The metrics system architecture integrates all measurements from a systems standpoint.

Data Collection

Collecting metrics data is perhaps the hardest part. Many a metrics program has failed on account of difficulties encountered in data collection. Hence, data collection systems must be carefully designed, avoiding the known pitfalls, and adopting lessons learned from metrics installations.

One sure thing is that we must design a metrics database. Different database technologies are available, including intelligent systems. The problem, however, is in the design of interfaces between the database and process centers.

In a common scenario, process owners tend to keep their personal databases. Project managers keep their data on a planning tool. Centralized metrics tools collect quality-related data but project data and some process data are not available. An integrated database seems to be an ideal beyond common reach. We may have to accept the reality of a heterogeneous and distributed database, as illustrated in Exhibit 6.

Implementing the Metrics System Architecture

Preparation

After designing the metrics system architecture, the task is to implement it. A good design is easy to implement, a poor design may demand a trial-and-error approach. The steps involved in the implementation address realizations of the elements of the architecture:

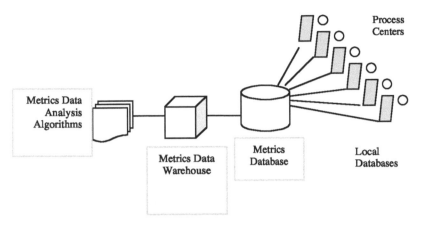

Exhibit 6. A heterogeneous and distributed metrics database.

- Recognize goals and define them.
- Recognize decision centers and list information needs.
- Build a suitable library of models.
- Define an economic metrics set.
- Define measurements.

Start with Small Scope

It is better to start a metrics plan with a small scope. One can limit the number of projects or take portions of the software life cycle. The most successful metrics system is evolutionary in style. The goals, decisions, models, and metrics are continually evaluated, and the metrics system changes to match the needs of the organization. Metrics and approaches are pilot-tested and discarded if inappropriate.

Begin with Lower Number of Metrics

Experience from successful metrics programs suggests that a minimal set of measures and metrics is usually adequate for beginning a program and sufficient to fulfill priority goals. If a single measure is sufficient to address the organization's goal, keep just one. It is not the number of metrics but what we do with them that is going to make a mark.

Phased Expansion

Many organizations begin measuring in the small, by applying measurements to a hot spot or difficulty, or by measuring to quantify the improvement in a process, product, or resource. Eventually, as staff becomes more comfortable with measurement, the small pockets of measurement spread to encompass most or all of an organization's software activities. This bottom-up approach to a measurement program is both popular and effective,

Exhibit 7. Goal–metrics correlation matrix.

	Metrics								
Goals	M1	M2	M3	M4	M5	M6	M7	M8	M9
G1	r_{11}	r_{12}	r_{13}	r_{14}	r_{15}	r_{16}	r_{17}	r_{18}	r_{19}
G2	r_{21}	r_{22}	r_{23}	r_{24}	r_{25}	r_{26}	r_{27}	r_{28}	r_{29}
G3	r_{31}	r_{32}	r_{33}	r_{34}	r_{35}	r_{36}	r_{37}	r_{38}	r_{39}
G4	r_{41}	r_{42}	r_{43}	r_{44}	r_{45}	r_{46}	r_{47}	r_{48}	r_{49}
G5	r_{51}	r_{52}	r_{53}	r_{54}	r_{55}	r_{56}	r_{57}	r_{58}	r_{59}
G6	r_{61}	r_{62}	r_{63}	r_{64}	r_{65}	r_{66}	r_{67}	r_{68}	r_{69}
G7	r_{71}	r_{72}	r_{73}	r_{74}	r_{75}	r_{76}	r_{77}	r_{78}	r_{79}
G8	r_{81}	r_{82}	r_{83}	r_{84}	r_{85}	r_{86}	r_{87}	r_{88}	r_{89}
G9	r_{91}	r_{92}	r_{93}	r_{94}	r_{95}	r_{96}	r_{97}	r_{98}	r_{99}

as staff buys into the value of measurement, one project or problem at a time.

In the horizontal expansion, the metrics program is implemented in more than one component of the software process or activities. In the vertical expansion, this metric is implemented in two or more software projects.

Goal–Metrics Correlation (GMC): Metrics Choice-Checking Tool

One can use a matrix structure to cross-check and analyze how the established goals and metrics go together, using the goal–metrics correlation structure presented in Exhibit 7. GMC seeks a correlation between goals and metrics but does not seek to trace out the reasons for choice. If GMC analysis discovers goals that are not correlated to metrics, these are orphan goals, left out of the renaissance in the organization.

If GMC shows metrics without correlation to goals, these metrics are lone rangers, drifting around listlessly. These can be dropped, of course. But our experience shows that the team, which introduced the particular metric in the game plan, was indeed addressing an unarticulated and hidden goal. Hence, the odd metric should be examined for its roots before any decision is made about its withdrawal from the plan.

Metrics Planning Approaches

Long-Term Plan: Core Metrics

Metrics have life cycles. They can become obsolete after the goals are attained. At least one can say that metrics acquire the life cycle of goals themselves, apart from acquiring other characteristics of goals such as hierarchy.

It feels good to operate on firmer ground and identify the core metrics that will be pertinent for a longer period. Core metrics have another requirement to fulfill. They must be relevant to all types of projects being executed in the organization, a constraint tougher than longevity. The most popular core metrics are schedule variance, effort variance, defect density, and productivity.

Short-Term Plans

By supporting the permanent core metrics we can identify short-term plans that can be rolled out across projects, capturing the specific business and process goals of the individual project. Technology-driven considerations would introduce metrics that are meaningful to categories of projects coming under technology umbrellas. Sometimes we use special metrics for special studies, such as in Six Sigma initiatives or Kaizen where the chosen problems may require metrics, which become useless after the study is over or the problem is solved. Separating the short-term from the long-term metrics has avowed benefits.

Metrics Planning Document Checklist

At the center of a metrics plan in an organization is the formal construction of metrics, which addresses the following details:

- Name
- Purpose
- Definition
- Example
- Data source
- Expected range of values
- Periodicity of data collection
- Format for data collection
- Metrics database structure
- Resources identified
  - Collection
  - Analysis
  - Reporting
- Model analysis

As a vehicle that carries organization data, the metrics plan is designed to pick out process intelligence with reliability and support the organization in decision making and process improvement. Metrics can yield benefits to the organization, as much as the plan will allow or provide for.

Chapter 4
Metrics Data Visualization

Data Analysis

Data analysis is an essential part of a metrics system. While the metrics data could be a process indicator, the hidden patterns are revealed only by analysis of data. Traditionally, data analysis is considered a tedious process dependent on rigorous statistical techniques. It is customary to brand data analysis as a "scientific method," not in the style of the practitioner. Furthermore, the cumbersome nature of some of the statistical techniques deters people. Data analysis can be made simple and interesting by using appropriate tools and an effective approach. The tool can be as handy as a spreadsheet with its statistical functions and built-in macros. There are several approaches to effective data analysis; we present here one such approach that reduces process behavior to three dimensions and has a strong bearing on visual techniques.

Visual Analysis

Before going to statistical techniques, we can analyze data in a much simpler and more effective way by using data visualization. Even if one chooses to do a complex statistical analysis, it is better to do a preliminary analysis of data using visual elements.

We may begin with viewing data in structured tabular forms and transform them to graphs and pictures to gain intuitive insights. One can also use exploratory data analysis (EDA) to reduce the amount of data by clustering and cut down the dimensions by mapping. EDA allows one to explore data as a precursor to more formal statistical analysis. Some view EDA as an integral part of statistical analysis. Such visual analysis reduces the complexity and provides a higher-level summary of the situation.

Rigorous Analysis

Rigorous data analysis brings to one's mind hypothesis testing, multivariate analysis, design of experiments, and similar sophisticated methods. We find that even with basic analysis such as histograms, control charts, and scatter plots, we can understand process behavior with sufficient depth. We can think of fruitful analysis of metrics data in the corresponding three domains: frequency, time, and relationship.

Graphical Analysis

A picture is worth a thousand words. Graphical forms have the potential to reveal the intrinsic patterns, otherwise hidden within the raw data. Visualization of data by the human mind is equivalent to execution of highly sophisticated analysis routines, albeit subconsciously. In the first place, data visualization requires creation of graphs, visual icons, and symbols, best done using the computer. It also requires human perception for the detection of patterns.

Data visualization as an emerging technology links the world's two most powerful information-processing systems — the human mind and the modern computer visual metaphors.

Creating graphs requires data and further processing such as:

- Data collection
- Data structuring
- Data cleansing
- Examination of data
- Creating graphs to visualize data

Perceiving patterns in a visual presentation is essentially a human process that involves the following cognitive elements:

- Active goals
- Motivation to find a solution
- Recollection of experience
- Application of knowledge
- Pattern discovery

Visualizing Data

Transforming data into a graph makes it easy to interpret. For example, Exhibit 1 presents productivity data from a bug-fixing process. The raw data columns are difficult to read even though they contain the basic information. Creating a line graph from this data, as shown in Exhibit 2, instantly makes it easy to see productivity, its variations, and trends. A pattern almost hidden in the data now emerges. Thus, the elementary but very useful application of graphs is reducing complexity and enhancing readability. This enables process analysis by the human mind.

Graphical Techniques

The spreadsheet supports many graphical tools for visualizing data. Exhibit 3 contains a list from MS Excel, which can be used to analyze most project situations.

Exhibit 1. Productivity data.

Work Package Ref.	Prod. Bug/PM	Work Package Ref.	Prod. Bug/PM	Work Package Ref.	Prod. Bug/PM	Work Package Ref.	Prod. Bug/PM
WP1	2.08	WP32	9.36	WP63	13.88	WP94	5.08
WP2	10.06	WP33	169.34	WP64	24.12	WP95	16.35
WP3	2.61	WP34	10.60	WP65	67.01	WP96	9.62
WP4	3.66	WP35	87.76	WP66	8.72	WP97	6.58
WP5	53.57	WP36	6.07	WP67	6.87	WP98	11.95
WP6	12.66	WP37	15.32	WP68	4.72	WP99	4.99
WP7	14.32	WP38	5.61	WP69	5.42	WP100	36.49
WP8	40.97	WP39	13.10	WP70	8.08	WP101	27.06
WP9	11.00	WP40	14.95	WP71	16.39	WP102	11.98
WP10	30.21	WP41	42.30	WP72	26.80	WP103	23.97
WP11	16.13	WP42	40.45	WP73	12.28	WP104	5.27
WP12	6.93	WP43	14.87	WP74	6.66	WP105	4.01
WP13	17.54	WP44	6.95	WP75	7.10	WP106	6.67
WP14	90.51	WP45	5.27	WP76	6.39	WP107	8.23
WP15	10.02	WP46	2.07	WP77	51.47	WP108	6.37
WP16	13.71	WP47	5.48	WP78	27.60	WP109	11.12
WP17	12.51	WP48	9.26	WP79	11.36	WP110	12.18
WP18	9.87	WP49	2.88	WP80	15.84	WP111	7.69
WP19	33.87	WP50	46.04	WP81	7.88	WP112	4.77
WP20	2.75	WP51	17.68	WP82	116.27	WP113	3.91
WP21	1.20	WP52	41.45	WP83	70.06	WP114	3.06
WP22	11.25	WP53	7.80	WP84	11.21	WP115	8.52
WP23	12.12	WP54	14.48	WP85	15.80	WP116	9.46
WP24	9.79	WP55	11.91	WP86	26.12	WP117	5.54
WP25	29.07	WP56	6.59	WP87	5.42	WP118	9.96
WP26	13.10	WP57	40.47	WP88	9.66	WP119	3.71
WP27	2.53	WP58	10.40	WP89	6.96	WP120	5.03
WP28	8.62	WP59	10.79	WP90	12.13	WP121	3.94
WP29	4.95	WP60	8.48	WP91	15.91	WP122	5.18
WP30	5.21	WP61	16.47	WP92	10.36	WP123	5.30
WP31	7.57	WP62	2.32	WP93	12.02	WP124	11.67

Pie Charts: Distribution Analysis

Pie charts have the inherent power to show distribution patterns. For example, distribution of rework cost among software products is illustrated in Exhibit 4. This chart gives us the picture of a problem at a glance, along with a sense of totality.

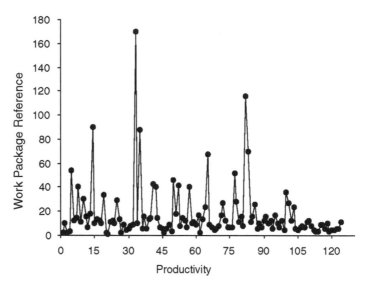

Exhibit 2. Productivity graph.

Exhibit 3. MS Excel graphical tools.

• Column	• Cone	• Floating bars
• Bar	• Pyramid	• Line column
• Line chart	• Area block (three-dimensional)	• Line column on two axes
• Pie chart	• B & White area	• Line on two axes
• Scatter plot	• B & W column (three-dimensional)	• Logarithmic
• Area	• B & W line timescale	• Outdoor bars
• Doughnut	• B & W pie	• Pie explosion
• Radar	• Blue pie (gradient)	(three-dimensional)
• Surface	• Colored lines	• Smooth lines
• Bubble	• Column area	• Stack of colors
• Stock	• Columns with depth	• Tubes
• Cylinder	• 3D cones	

Pie charts have unlimited application potential. They can be applied to almost any decision situation. Some of the common applications are

- Distribution of customer complaints
- Distribution of defects among components
- Effort distribution
- Market share analysis
- Defect discovery analysis
- Sales analysis
- HR analysis
- Downtime analysis

Project ID	Rework Cost ($)
A	3000
B	1500
C	2500
D	3000
E	1000

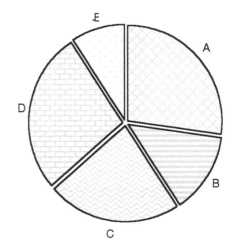

Exhibit 4. Distribution of rework cost among software products.

Mapping

Mapping is the process of displaying data as a projection into two- or three-dimensional space. During this projection the spatial separation between points represents "relations of the data." Data can be ordinal for the purpose of mapping. Thus, subjective assessments are allowed to be mapped without losing application potential. Also, mapping permits even nonlinear projections.

Mapping does not require that the measurement be done on a very precise and fully validated manner. Even ordinal scales of measurement, which could have subjective errors, can be used for mapping. Similarly, mapping accommodates nonlinear scales of measurement despite the inherent ambiguities. Thus, mapping as a method has a universal appeal and remains flexible.

The outstanding benefits of mapping are that it reduces the dimensionality of the dataset to a sufficiently small value to allow visual inspection.

Two patterns of people management emerge from Exhibit 5. The circles form a family of events that correspond to a "manage for results" approach. The squares form a different family that relates to a more-modern approach of "managing for results and people." Exhibit 5 is plotted from subjective evaluation of leadership styles in an organization. Despite its simplicity, it has a powerful revelation of two sub-cultures in the organization.

Profiles, matrices, and contours are some of the commonly used forms of mapping.

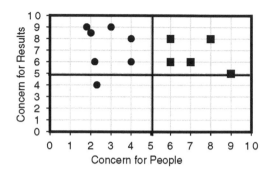

Exhibit 5. Management grid: map of leadership styles.

Life Cycle Profiles

Perhaps the most pertinent analysis in a software project is to view the life cycle of the project and to recognize process outcomes in life cycle phases. One can think of a series of life cycle phase analyses expressed in the form of profiles. Each life cycle profile (LCP) has the following benefits:

- It provides connectivity among phases.
- It arranges project events in a natural order in tune with the work-flow.
- It gives the complete picture of the project at a glance.

Apart from these common merits, there are additional advantages that can be derived from LCP, based on the metric chosen for the presentation. If the metric is defect, the profile gives clues about process maturity. If the metric is rework, the profile provides causal readings into cost control and could become an eminent problem definition for cost reduction initiatives. Risk can also be perceived from some profiles.

Effort Profile

Effort profiles for two projects are presented in Exhibit 6 and Exhibit 7. First, one can identify the following features in the profiles:

- The phase where effort peaks
- The share of effort devoted to requirements and design
- The share of effort given to testing
- The ratio of design effort to code effort
- The percentage of effort on project management

Perception of such features is the beginning of analysis. The mind delves into the recognitions aided by knowledge and motivated by expectations. Model effort profiles that have been reported in the past spring to the mind of the perceiver as baselines. One recalls effort profiles of design projects that used concurrent engineering and cut down defects 25 times and

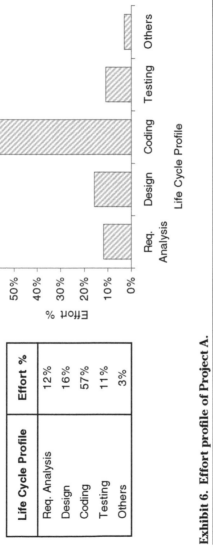

Life Cycle Profile	Effort %
Req. Analysis	12%
Design	16%
Coding	57%
Testing	11%
Others	3%

Exhibit 6. Effort profile of Project A.

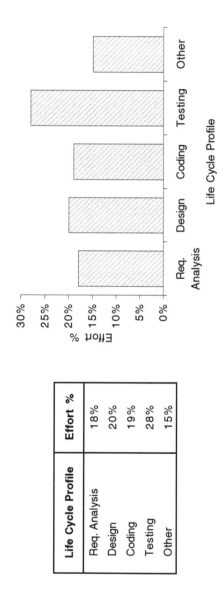

Life Cycle Profile	Effort %
Req. Analysis	18%
Design	20%
Coding	19%
Testing	28%
Other	15%

Exhibit 7. Effort profile of Project B.

reduced the "time to deliver" 4 times. These profiles recorded effort concentration in the early half of the project. One can also recall the Walker Royce finding of a similar trendy shift in effort profiles of modern software projects. Some may see the thrust on testing in Project B as a serious attempt toward the attainment of reliability growth, where operational profile testing continues well after system testing, costing a budget but cutting down postdelivery defects.

There are several possibilities when it comes to interpreting the effort profiles. During visualization, the mind runs through all known paths of visual analysis, almost in a jiffy, drawing from the vast storehouse of experiences, opinions, and knowledge units embedded in the viewer's personality.

When such effort profiles are constructed for all projects and compared with the business results attained by them, intuitive mapping rules emerge, which can be reapplied to new projects. The intuition derived from visualization gets one closer to forecasting the destiny of the project from data available from completed phases.

Almost certainly, the visual icon of effort profile will influence budgeting in the subsequent projects. It will also facilitate the project leader in setting phase-level process goals.

Process Compliance Profile

Measuring process compliance is done by auditing process centers against quality system elements such as capability maturity model KPAs or ISO 9000 clauses. The findings could be presented as a profile with compliance displayed on a scale of 0 to 10, as illustrated in Exhibit 8. This ten-level measurement has an element of subjectivity that depends on the auditor's experience and approach. Also, sampling methods might have been applied while collecting data, introducing additional possibilities of errors. The profile, however, succeeds in capturing the larger truth without much ambiguity. A profile is truer than an isolated point. By seeing the patterns of the strong and weak areas and their relative "distances," it is possible to understand what is wrong with the system. Such profiles display process landscape of organizations.

Responsibility Matrix

The matrix structure is a very convenient mapping tool, widely used in process analysis. The matrix structure is ideal to map relationship between two complex sets of data.

A good way to visualize responsibility allocation to project team members is to create a responsibility matrix, as shown in Exhibit 9. The header row represents team member ID, the header column contains responsibility

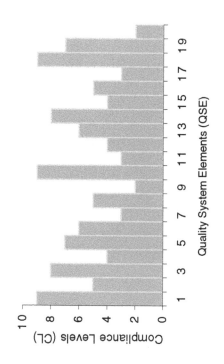

QSE	CL	QSE	CL
1	9	11	3
2	5	12	4
3	8	13	6
4	4	14	8
5	7	15	4
6	6	16	5
7	3	17	3
8	5	18	9
9	2	19	7
10	9	20	2

Exhibit 8. Process compliance profile.

Exhibit 9. Typical responsibility matrix.

				Team Member ID				
		A	B	C	D	E	F	G
Responsibility Levels	Requirements	10					5	10
	Design		10					
	Build			10	10			
	Review	10					5	10
	Test					10	5	
	Defect prevention	3						10
	Risk mitigation	3						10
	Project management							10
	Total	26	10	10	10	10	15	50

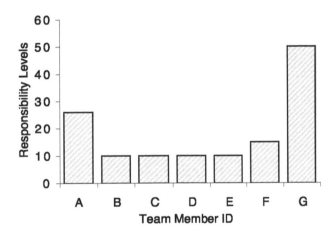

Exhibit 10. Responsibility allocation.

areas, and the cells contain the numbers that point toward responsibility levels.

We are able to first perceive the complex nature of two systems, the team, and the process, and then compare them in the matrix. Here complexity is reduced to one dimension, making it easy for visual comparison. The bearing of each grid element can be easily and conveniently read off from the headers. By encoding each grid element with color that represents the degree of relationship, we can quickly get a visual feel of interplay between two systems. Sometimes instead of color we use linguistic expressions: high, medium, and low, based on the user's preferences. If we choose to use numbers, even in an ordinary scale, further analysis is possible, as illustrated in Exhibit 10.

Exhibit 11. Responsibility matrix after reallocation.

Responsibility Levels	Team Member ID						
	A	B	C	D	E	F	G
Requirements	10					5	10
Design		10		5		2	
Build		3	10	10			
Review	10	2	2	2	2	5	10
Test				3	10	5	
Defect prevention	4	4	4	4	4	4	10
Risk mitigation	4	4	4	4	4	4	10
Project management		2	2	2	2	2	10
Total	28	25	22	30	22	27	50

Exhibit 12. Responsibility levels after resource balancing.

Resource Balancing

The responsibility matrix can be used for resource balancing. A graph can be created from a total responsibility quantum for each person. Exhibit 10 is such a graph, which visualizes responsibility distribution among people.

Exhibit 11 illustrates a typical scenario where people have narrow allocations of jobs. A few people share the bulk of the responsibility while others are waiting for better utilization of the skills. It may happen that, only after plotting the graph, people may realize the imbalance in resource utilization.

Where cross-functional teamwork and development of multi-disciplinary skills prevail, such imbalances could be minimized. Exhibit 12 illustrates a scenario after resource balancing.

Defect Code	Defect Level
CUST	2
REQ	5
DES	3
COD	8
PROC	1 2

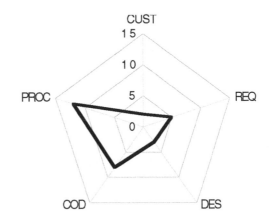

Exhibit 13. Quality contour.

Contours

A contour map is a top view of a terrain representing terrain features, which are otherwise hidden to a side view. Process contours, built from several metrics, provide a complete view in a similar manner. For example, quality contour graphs can be created to display product quality, as illustrated in Exhibit 13.

Quality is seen from several directions such as the customer perspective (CUST), requirement defects (REQ), design defects (DES), coding defects (COD), and associated process defects (PROC). It may be seen that each metric mentioned here has been captured in different phases of the project, using different detection techniques. Even the units of defect metric could be different. An attempt to define quality by a single metric is at any time a partial answer. Quality is seen as a continuum expression which starts from project inception and continues to implementation.

A product with poor history cannot suddenly become wonderful based on the final metric. A more practical view is to establish a connected view tracking the full quality history. Quality contours achieve this completeness of expression. Thus, quality contour redefines the meaning of quality.

Radar Charts: A Balanced View

Radar charts can present a balanced view of factors. For example, if a project has to support multiple goals, it is pragmatic to assume that all the goals may not receive equal attention at any given time. There could be competition among them. Fulfillment of goals could reflect the same situation. If you plot a radar chart for goal fulfillment with each goal in one polar axis, we get a diagram that will indicate balance in fulfillment. If one goal

51

dominates the scene the radar chart will look lopsided, visually indicating the problem.

In Exhibit 14 fulfillment of training needs in six chosen areas is plotted by a training manager. This graph helps us to visualize the learning tendencies of people gravitating toward technical training.

A radar chart can play the role of a rudimentary balanced scorecard in projects, based on the metrics chosen. The inherent ability of a radar chart lies in the fact that it can handle multiple variables at a given time and establish a visual relationship among them. A radar chart can be an ideal component in a project dashboard.

Dynamic Views

The visual elements can be made dynamic to interact with the viewer. The links between graphical presentations and the parent metrics database can be organized in a dynamic manner, instead of providing static images. While advanced data mining tools offer interactive facility, we can build on the spreadsheet macros that rearrange the data and feed the graphs with fresh choices of data sets. Pivot tables and data filters may be put to maximum advantage. To get the most out of graphs, we need to make them respond quickly to an inquiry. The changing views constitute "dynamic analysis" of process, almost a simulation run. Because graphs have a natural propensity to summarize data and run on the upper rungs of the information pyramid, these "simulation runs" appeal to the deeper recesses of human perception.

Clustering

A natural way of analyzing data is to group together, or cluster, similar data in accordance with some selected criteria. The clusters thus formed could be related to other clusters, forming a cluster tree. Huge amounts of data can now be reduced to colonies of clusters, which can be easily visualized.

Contrasting with cluster trees, sometimes dissimilar data is grouped into disjoint clusters. The clustering rules now tend to maximize the dissimilarities between clusters but minimize dissimilarities within each.

For example, maintenance project metrics data can be grouped according to the rules of priority ascribed to each bug. Clusters are formed around priority levels. Each cluster is characterized uniquely, still preserving and honoring the core precept that cements it.

Alternatively, maintenance events can be clustered around "cost" of bug fixing, if the clustering rule were cost. The high cost cluster may exhibit unique process characteristics, significantly different from low cost clusters.

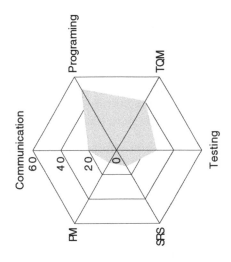

Training Needs	Fulfillments%
Communication	20
Programing	50
Total Quality Management	40
Testing	28
Software Requirement Specification	13
Project Management	10

Exhibit 14. Radar chart on training needs fulfillment.

The clustering reveals an inner order — a guide — which facilitates understanding of bug behavior.

There could be several such rules for clustering, such as cost and priority, each a vehicle for seeing the complete database from one perspective. Viewing the database from significant perspectives and clustering rules is a convenient form of data analysis.

Data Exploration and Visualization Tools

Data visualization tools in general provide highly interactive and dynamic graphics that helps the user to see multiple views of data. The graphics are designed to augment visual intuition so that we can better understand the data and see what the data has to say.

Many tools are compatible with the spreadsheet, benefiting business practitioners who use spreadsheets extensively.

Data visualization capabilities are commonly embedded in a wide range of software types, including tools for reporting, online analytical processing (OLAP), text mining, and data mining. Software tools for customer relationship management and business performance management also employ data visualization in the front end.

Data visualization tools are available suitable for stand-alone, embedded, or enterprise applications with several attractive features.

Features providing analytical support, particularly for interactive use, are listed here. These features show patterns on parameters or variable names (instead of defining data ranges and locations) that can be selected by the user with the click of a mouse.

- Interactive analysis
- Drag and drop
- Dynamic graphs (plots and tables)
- What-if simulation
- Multi-view graphics
- Linked plots
- Visual scalability
- Partition
- Data mining
- Animation to see patterns
- 3D images
- Nonparametric methods
- Drill down
- Cause-and-effect diagram

Exhibit 15. Data exploration and visualization tools.

S No.	Tool Name	Vendor Name	Site Address
1	PopChartXpress	CORDA Technologies	www.corda.com
2	Visual Insight	Bell Labs	www.bell-labs.com
3	Cviz	IBM	www.alphaworks.ibm.com
4	Dataplot	NIST	www.itl.nist.gov
5	Data Desk & Vizion	Data Description, Inc.	www.datadesk.com
6	JMP5	JMP	www.jmp.com
7	S-PLUS	Insightful	www.insightful.com
8	omegahat	Omega Project	www.omegahat.org
9	XploRe	Md Tech	www.explore-stat.de
10	Fathom	Key Curriculum Press	www.keypress.com
11	nViZn	illumitek	www.illumitek.com
12	MARS & CART	Salford Systems	www.salford-systems.com

Structural facilities, which allow convenient deployment, are discussed later. These facilities help in integrating the tools with business processes and related IT systems.

- Links to Excel
- Centralized application management (facility useful in multi-user environment)
- Inline analysis (facility to integrate our own algorithms)
- Direct data source linking
- Component library
- Data independence (ability to work with any kind of database)
- Web enabled
- Versatile deployment capability

There are a multitude of data visualization tool vendors offering a wide range of capabilities and facilities. We can pick and choose from the several models, based on our specific requirements. The proliferation of tool development indicates the growing demand. A representative list of such tools is presented in Exhibit 15.

Data Visualization: Emerging Technology

There is growing interest in data visualization in all disciplines, from engineering to management. Data visualization is used both in the initial exploration before statistical analysis and in the final display of results and model building.

In the preliminary run, attempts to visualize data will help the analyst go through an iterative process of data preparation improving the structure, quality, and suitability of datasets for higher-level analysis and model building. Elegance in visual design will reflect order in data, reinforcing the already-strong connection between visuals and data.

Applications such as the weather forecast use three-dimensional visualization to simulate cloud formations, cyclones, and rainfall based on parametric models that use as many as 16 variables. In software project management, similar opportunities for higher-end methods exist in visualizing many abstract phenomena, including:

- Organization behavior from 18 HR variables
- Skills inventory models for recruitment from demographic data
- Variable risk models (12)
- Cost models with 22 parameters
- Customer requirements models (10 parameters)
- Market forecast

With data visualization, metrics data analysis would be better, faster, and more creative. Before we resort to rigorous statistical methods, data visualization can be used as a convenient first-cut analysis with significant benefits.

Chapter 5
Metrics Data Analysis in Frequency Domain

Frequency Distribution: An Analysis Tool

All processes show variations that will become evident if a frequency distribution is drawn on the process metric. Understanding process variation, Demming observes, will lead to profound knowledge of the process. Frequency distribution also contains an indication about probability of occurrence of events. Analysis of metrics data in the frequency domain would result in empirical distribution curves. The shape and structure of these distribution curves represent a process signature. Analyses of distributions are usually based on several well-known probability distributions. We have selected two distribution types that find practical views in software projects: normal distribution and the Rayleigh distribution. All empirical distributions are referred to any one of these two for interpretation.

Normal Distribution

Normal distribution is considered nature's template, the most common pattern of process variation. A large number of project outcomes can be directly fitted to the ideal normal curve. For example, effort variance in a family of software projects has been analyzed to find that they have a mean value of 10 percent and standard deviation of 2 percent. From this analysis we can construct an ideal process model using a normal distribution curve illustrated in Exhibit 1. The equation to normal distribution is given in Equation 5.1.

$$f(x, \mu, \sigma) = \frac{1}{\sqrt{2\pi}\sigma} e^{-\left[\frac{(x-\mu)^2}{2\sigma^2}\right]} \tag{5.1}$$

where:

x = measured variable (time to repair)
y = probability density (frequency)
μ = mean
σ = standard deviation

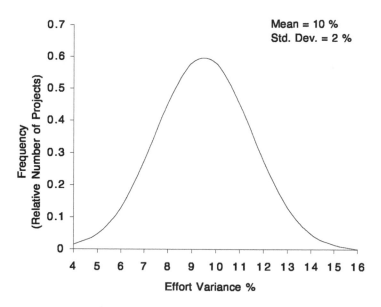

Exhibit 1. Frequency distribution of effort variance.

The process variation illustrated here makes us view software projects from a statistical standpoint. We now know from Exhibit 1 that during effort estimation, instead of considering one single value, we need to consider a range of possibilities within certain limits.

Bias: A Process Reality

Real-life process behavior may exhibit a bias. Such distributions lack symmetry and are skewed to one side. Also, these have a characteristic "tail," representing occurrences that have transgressed or strayed into unusual regions. The bias is characteristic of human systems that use intention or will to choose among several tactical opportunities. The long tail, such as in Rayleigh distribution, bears evidence to a fundamental but small propensity of nature to defy human design. This tail could be a symbol of machine failure in mechanical processes or estimation failure in project management. The tail of the schedule variance distribution presented in Exhibit 2 shows how "best-made estimates" have failed.

As a structure, the skewed Rayleigh distribution has been put to great use in software estimation by Putnam. Software reliability models use this structure to represent defect leakage into the field in the continuum of time. The Rayleigh curve can be expressed as given in Equation 5.2.

$$m(t) = 2 * K * a * t * \exp(-a * t^2)$$ (5.2)

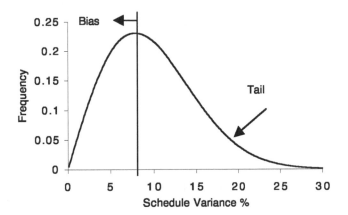

Exhibit 2. Schedule variance bias.

where:

$m(t)$ = manpower
K = total effort
a = constant (shape parameter)
t = time

Central Tendency of Processes

Central tendency in a skewed distribution, a more authentic representation of real-life processes, is difficult to establish. Nevertheless, it is conventional to refer to three measures of central tendency:

1. Mean
2. Median
3. Mode

The mean is the arithmetic average of all the observations. The median that divides a series of data arranged in the order of magnitude of their values so that an equal number of values is on either side of the center or median value. The median divides the distribution curve into two equal areas (A and B, as shown in Exhibit 3). The mode denotes the value that has the highest frequency of occurrence in the dataset.

If the distribution of the data is normal and not skewed, then the mode, median, and mean are equal.

It is customary to take the mean value to indicate the central value of a metric. It is convenient to think so, and many business models run on this simple assumption. But when the metrics data set contains outliers and extreme values, median could be a better choice because it presents a balanced picture. Mode is considered for setting process goals.

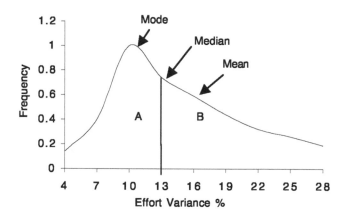

Exhibit 3. Central tendencies on skewed distribution.

Process Spread

Process results wander away from the mean value. The degree of wandering, or spread, is denoted by the standard deviation, sigma (σ), of process output values.

Frequency distributions are the most natural tools to study and analyze process spread.

In Exhibit 4, three models for effort variance are plotted, all with different standard deviations but a common central value of 10 percent. Process variations such as these indicate trouble. The larger the variation, the larger is the uncertainty. It may be noticed that as the spread increases, the number of "results on target" decreases. When the process deviations get closer to process boundaries or tolerance limits, the process tends to become unreliable.

Another example of process dispersion can be seen in how bug-fixing time (TTR, time to repair, in days), falls into three service levels, corresponding to simple, medium, and complex types of bugs. Fixing each type of bug is a process of its own, characterized by central tendencies and standard deviations. As illustrated in Exhibit 5, the distinction between these processes results in blur in some areas, and the maintenance project manager needs to use this information while setting goals and limits for delivery schedules.

Measures of Dispersion

Measures of dispersion describe how the observations in the dataset are spread out. Important measures of dispersion are

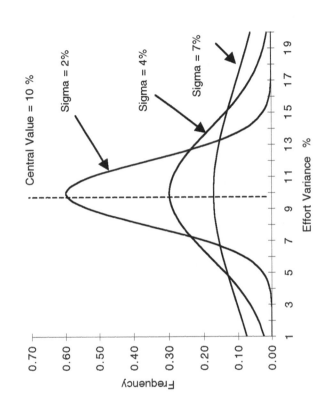

Bin	Sigma 2	Sigma 4	Sigma 7
1	0.00	0.02	0.07
2	0.00	0.04	0.09
3	0.00	0.06	0.10
4	0.01	0.10	0.12
5	0.03	0.14	0.13
6	0.08	0.18	0.15
7	0.19	0.23	0.16
8	0.36	0.26	0.16
9	0.53	0.29	0.17
10	0.60	0.30	0.17
11	0.53	0.29	0.17
12	0.36	0.26	0.16
13	0.19	0.23	0.16
14	0.08	0.18	0.15
15	0.03	0.14	0.13
16	0.01	0.10	0.12
17	0.00	0.06	0.10
18	0.00	0.04	0.09
19	0.00	0.02	0.07
20	0.00	0.01	0.06

Exhibit 4. Dispersion of effort variance: three models.

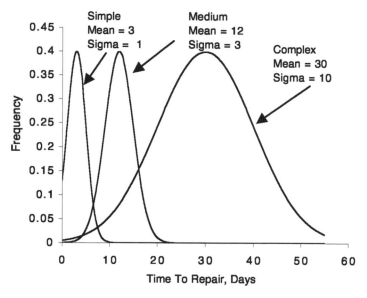

Exhibit 5. Three service models for bug fixing.

- Range
- Variance
- Standard deviation

Range is the difference between the highest and lowest values in a dataset. Variance measures the fluctuation of the observations around the mean. The larger the value of the variance, the greater the fluctuation. The standard deviation, like the variance, also measures the variability of the observations around the mean. Standard deviation is equal to the positive square root of variance. A standard deviation has the same units as the observations, and thus is easier to interpret.

Descriptive Statistics

Before we draw any inferences from data (using inferential statistics), we need to do descriptive statistical study. Hence, metric data can be first studied for its descriptive statistics, which includes estimation of the following parameters:

- Mean
- Standard error (of the mean)
- Median
- Mode
- Standard deviation
- Variance
- Kurtosis
- Skewness

- Range
- Minimum
- Maximum
- Sum
- Count
- Largest (#)
- Smallest (#)

Note:

- Skew means lack of symmetry.
- The skew can be positive (skewed to the left) or negative (skewed to the right).
- For a positively skewed distribution, the mean is greater than the median because a few values are large compared to the others.
- If a distribution is negatively skewed, the mean is less than the median.
- Kurtosis is a measure of the peakedness of the dataset. It is also viewed as a measure of the "heaviness" of the tails of a distribution.
- A tool for calculating descriptive statistics is available in Excel as a macro in the Analysis Tool Pak.

Deriving Frequency Distribution from Data

Basic Analysis

There are three ways of visualizing frequency distribution, ranging from mathematical to empirical. Each can be applied to a practical situation; each has its advantages.

Probability Density Function Curve. The first is to work from the mean and sigma to construct an ideal normal distribution curve, applying the equation to probability density function.

One can use the spreadsheet function NORMDIST and generate the graph by constructing an x,y table (and plotting an x,y chart) in accordance with the relationship given in Equation 5.3.

$$Y = 1.0 \text{NORMDIST}(x, \mu, \sigma, 0) \tag{5.3}$$

where:

Y = probability density (frequency)
x = measured variable (time to repair)
μ = mean
σ = standard deviation
NORMDIST = statistical function in Excel

This bell shaped curve is a classical way of getting a feel for the process.

Histogram. Next we can draw a histogram and study its shape. The bin intervals (or class intervals) are marked in the x-axis and the frequency in the y-axis. One can use a "tally" system to count the number of data points falling into each bin, or use the histogram macro on the spreadsheet and get the tally as well as the chart. Histogram will present details that had been ironed out in the normal curve.

Empirical Distribution Curve. Finally, we can transform the histogram into a "curve" by constructing a smooth line that passes through the tops of the histogram bars. Constructing such a curve, sometimes called the frequency polynomial, is not an attempt to find a mathematical expression for an empirical reality; it is an attempt to create a graphical pattern, as a model and a continuous representation process behavior.

For example, for a given set of bug fix data all three forms have been created and are illustrated in Exhibit 6. The first graph, the normal curve, can be called a "bug-fixing service model." The second graph, the histogram, reveals a healthy bias in the bug-fixing time and also exposes an outlier. The third graph, the empirical frequency distribution, shows the existence of a natural upper control limit, UCL, occurring well within the conventional 3σ point.

Frequency Scan

While arriving at empirical distribution curves, we stand to gain by doing alternative analysis by varying the bin sizes. One such analysis is "scanning," where we deliberately run a histogram on a large number of bins, although the number of data points may not warrant a large number of bins.

An example of schedule variance analysis with 32 bins is depicted in Exhibit 7. The frequency diagram scans the entire process range, like a spectral scanner, and finds occurrences in the right location in the metrics scale. Such an analysis highlights "bursts" of events, which stand far away in the frequency domain from the primary process modes. In the background, the best-fit normal curve built from the process mean and average is presented. It may be noted that the normal curve is very broad and shallow, indicating a widely varying process. The standard deviation is about 2.5 times larger than the mean, with the obvious consequences on the curve.

A frequency scan could make several discoveries in process behavior, including the following:

- Extreme deviations
- Process outliers
- Natural clusters
- Secondary modes

Data Time to Repair (TTR)	
1.7	9.5
3.9	1.5
7.9	15.3
13.1	1.2
9.4	1.1
17.2	23
3.1	0.7
2.5	4.1
14	4.9
4.6	10.5
2.8	6.9
5.4	1.6
1.3	10.7
3.9	5
12.4	2.8
11.1	1.8
6.4	1
0.9	8.3
9.9	5.2
15.3	7.5
12.4	6.4
6.3	4
15.9	#REF!

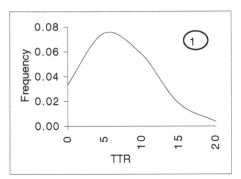

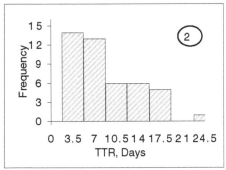

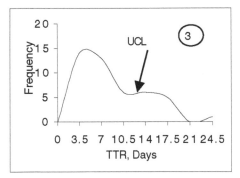

Exhibit 6. Deriving frequency distribution from maintenance project metrics data.

- Primary modes
- Zoom view of the significant modes

The Filter Effect: Getting a Smooth Overall Picture

We can obtain a smoother function, with the details ironed out, to show a broad picture of schedule variance, as shown in Exhibit 8. The desire here is not to prescribe discrimination rules or locate troublesome groups, but to get a sense of variation.

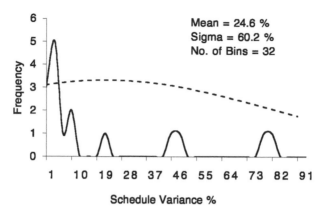

Exhibit 7. Frequency analysis with modified bins.

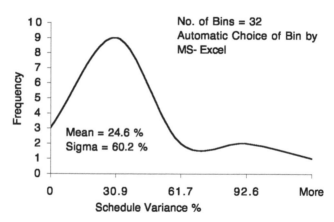

Exhibit 8. Frequency diagram designed to give the overall picture.

This choice is deliberately made because of the shift in decision-making approach from class discrimination to variation control.

The same process data, which was scanned in the previous figure, is now processed with less bin numbers, just 7 instead of the original 32. The result is a smoothened curve, which has muffled the fast variations, like a low pass filter, and indicates an overall picture.

One can vary the "filter characteristics" of a histogram to see different views of variation, and develop an insight from these many perspectives. It is like tuning in to different wavelengths, looking for signals.

Looking at Histograms

The histogram is known as the "voice of the process." On a chosen metric, histogram analysis can reveal process behavior such as stability and bias. The first-cut analysis is to look at the shape of the histogram and see the "process signature."

Standard types of histograms have been identified by Feigenbaum for manufacturing processes. The shapes and types could reveal the nature of the process from which the data points have been gathered. For example, a histogram truncated on both sides represented product behavior after the "out-of-tolerance components" have been removed. A histogram with the central portion missing can be traced to a population where the best components have been selected and removed, perhaps marked as a higher-grade delivery.

In software, too, we can identify histograms with telltale signatures. Three of these signatures are presented in Exhibit 9, along with their special meanings:

1. Comb structure
2. Right-biased structure
3. Left-biased structure

Many of the other figures furnished in this chapter contain real-life process signatures. Notable among them are the following:

- Bimodal distribution with equal peaks
- Bimodal distribution with a single dominant peak
- Multiple clusters
- Rayleigh type distribution with long "tail"
- Plateau structure (flat distribution)
- Spurs (in spectral scanning)

Projects can maintain histogram libraries and map them to the contributing process scenarios. This way, every organization can invent its own histogram types, as shown in Exhibit 9.

Process Capability from Frequency Distribution

Process Capability

A process that is under statistical control is said to be capable if it is able to satisfy the customer specifications or the goals of the process, in the event customer specifications are not available.

> *Process capability refers to the inherent ability of a process to repeat results for a sustained period of time under a given set of conditions.*

The frequency signature of a capable process has a few notable characteristics:

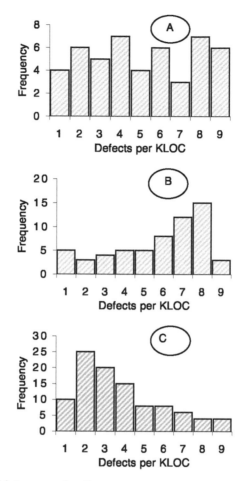

Exhibit 9. Defect histograms for three processes.

- Single mode
- Less variation
- Process peak tends to be closer to target

In the classical model of process capability computations, normal distribution is assumed, and numerical indices are calculated to quantify process capability.

Process Capability Index C_p

This index indicates the performance of the process by relating the natural process spread to the specification (tolerance) spread, as shown in Equation 5.4.

$$C_p = \frac{\left(\text{USL} - \text{LSL}\right)}{6\sigma} \tag{5.4}$$

where:

USL = upper specification limit
LSL = lower specification limit
σ   = standard deviation

Modifications of this basic definition are in use to account for the following special situations:

- Single limit
- Process drift

Such indices and their variants were originally designed for mechanical processes, based on well-established statistical models for process variation, defect occurrence, inspection, and sampling.

Calculating C_p for Software Projects

For software projects, can we apply C_p? There are several constraints. The beginning of the problem lies in the very nature of the process called project management or software engineering, each having process signatures different than that of mechanical processes. Next in line are the difficulties of prescribing control limits and specifications limits, which cannot be calculated based on old assumptions but require a deep understanding of statistical distributions of process parameters and defects.

An attempt is made here, as shown in Exhibit 10, to estimate C_p on effort variance in a simple project scenario. A few assumptions have been made in the computation of C_p:

- Two limits have been identified for effort variance.
- Mean and standard deviation are adequately representative of the true process nature.

The value for C_p turns out to be a mere 0.31. Good processes begin with a C_p of at least 1.33. For Six Sigma, the C_p should be 2.0 or better. However, most processes in software are operating with C_p values less than 0.1 for the existing practical goals. It may be borne in mind that when the goals shift, C_p values change.

Probability

The area under probability density function represents "probability" of occurrence. In Exhibit 11, the shaded area represents the probability that the upper specification limit of schedule variance may be transgressed.

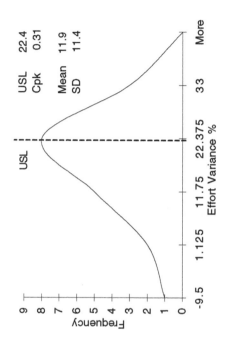

Bin	Frequency
-9.5	1
1.1	2
11.8	5
22.4	8
33.0	3
More	0

Exhibit 10. C_p calculation on effort variance.

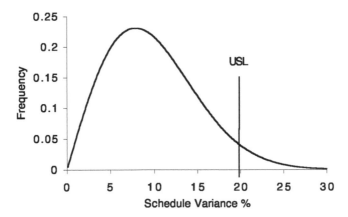

Exhibit 11. Probability calculation.

The exact value of this probability is obtained from the ratio given in Equation 5.5.

$$P(SV > USL) = \frac{\text{Shaded Area}}{\text{Total Area under the Curve}} \qquad (5.5)$$

The probability that the schedule target will be met corresponds to the unshaded area. The shaded area, lying outside the limit, constitutes what we can term as "process defects." The white area is the acceptable region. The areas are actually integral values of the probability density function, pdf, with the specified limits, and can be calculated by using the relationship given in Equation 5.6.

$$\text{Acceptable Output} = \int_{X=0}^{x=USL} \text{pdf} \qquad (5.6)$$

Probabilistic Expressions of Capability and Risk

Probabilistic models can be used to determine process capability and risk. Capability is defined as the probability of meeting the target and risk is the probability of missing the target. Capability and risk are like two sides of a coin. If a process is not "filled" with capability, the vacuum will be encroached by risk.

Exhibit 12 shows estimation of process capability and risk on effort variance. Capability is 66 percent while risk is 34 percent. Symbolically, these represent the resource management capability and effort escalation risk within a project. The entire perception here is influenced by what is set as

71

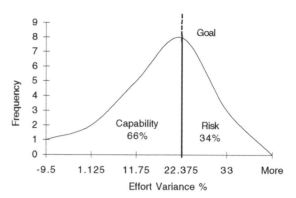

Bin	Frequency
-9.5	1
1.1	2
11.8	5
22.4	8
33.0	3
More	0

Exhibit 12. Process capability and risk based on probabilistic model.

goal. The target line, by dividing the process area into the twin components of risk and capability, also becomes the risk line.

A similar analysis can be done almost on all metrics, although the core metrics such as the ones in the following list are preferred choices:

- Schedule
- Productivity
- Defects

Analyzing Process Maturity

Process maturity can be analyzed using frequency distributions. Mature processes show slim frequency diagrams, with sharp peaks — the fat and the process wanderings having been eliminated. Mature processes show, decisively, a central value. The danger of secondary process intervention would have been eliminated to secure stability. The voice of the process will stand clear above noise from spurious performances, outliers, and strange isolated events.

Mature process peaks tend to drift toward customer satisfaction, resource conservation, and better performances. A productivity distribution, as the project matures in capability, tends to move toward higher values. The defect distribution peak, in a similar environment, will move to lower values.

A process behavior model is seldom static. It is highly dynamic, constantly shifting its location, and changing the shape. The process boundaries keep in tune and the process remains in a constant state of metamorphosis.

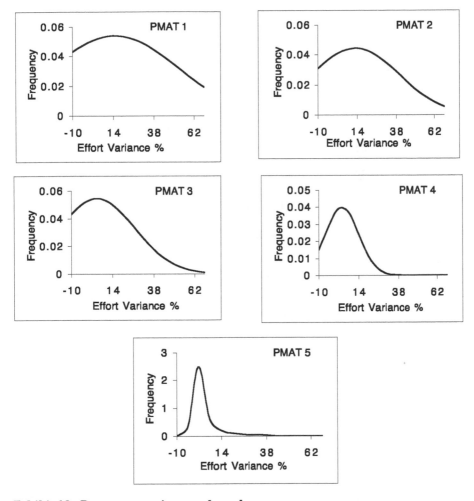

Exhibit 13. Process maturity storyboard.

The road to process maturity can be tracked using frequency diagram models of the process, and by arranging a process maturity storyboard or chronicler, which has now become an industry standard for visualizing "continuous process improvement."

Exhibit 13 presents a process maturity storyboard of an organization that is moving up the maturity grid as time passes. Approximately, the signatures correspond with capability maturity model (CMM) levels. The metric — the chosen indicator — is effort variance. If the organization's goals can be marked on these frames, one can easily perceive and estimate quantitatively resource management capability as well as effort escalation risk, and relate the findings to climbing maturity level. Apart from using process

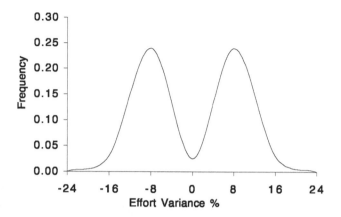

Exhibit 14. Bimodal frequency distribution in effort variance.

signatures to narrate a story in time, we can use them to compare business units within an organization or benchmark teams within a business unit.

We could also create a signature board to cover all primary metrics to see if there is balance in capability or how uncertainty and risk propagate into the deeper recesses of processes.

Process Diagnosis

Beyond Mean

Process baselines based on mean and sigma sometimes hide real problems, such as in the case study described here.

The effort variance in this instance shows a bimodal distribution, each mode on either side of zero. The arithmetic mean is almost zero; going by the mean one may think that the process is on target. Far from it, the process is severely unstable, toggles between two meta-stable states, as revealed in the frequency analysis shown in Exhibit 14. The project team recognized the problem, the first step in diagnosis, did a causal analysis, and spotted trouble in the estimation process, which was in its juvenile stage. Either effort was overestimated or it was underestimated. Where they had provided contingency cushions, it turned out that the expected risks did not attack. Where they had been optimistic, risks had surfaced eventually. More than estimation, the problem was in risk forecasting, and linking it with estimation. The team was trying to grapple with the problem and the struggle resulted in the twin modes.

Search for Natural Process Boundary

Higher-level metrics, such as effort variance, denote complex processes because they tend to capture the net result of several sub-processes.

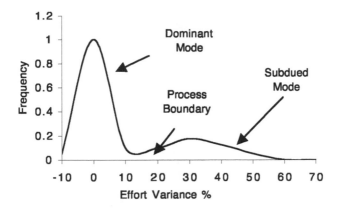

Exhibit 15. Natural process boundary.

Calculating process control limits in such cases is a tricky job. The exact distribution type of each sub-process may not be known, much less the way the sub-processes combine. Traditional control limits use mean and sigma-based concoctions. But we know the fallacy of blindly choosing the mean as a representative figure.

The questions emerge: What is the true process limit? What is going to be the decision threshold? Which is an outlier and which is the core? What control limits do we use in our control charts? We are looking for a natural process boundary that we can trust and use in decision making. The answer to the question lies in a frequency distribution study of the metric.

Typically, as illustrated in Exhibit 15, such an analysis would manifest a dominant mode, denoting a primary process, and a subdued mode, denoting a secondary process. The valley point is taken as the natural process boundary which can be used as the upper control limit.

Class Recognition: Productivity

Productivity in software development is a very complex area. Analysis of productivity using frequency distributions could give tangible benefits. Apart from the baseline normal curve, the empirical distribution derived with the right choice of bin intervals could reveal "productivity clusters," as illustrated in the following case study. In Exhibit 16, four modes have emerged during an organizationwide analysis of productivity data. These modes point to the existence of four distinct classes of projects; the discriminating factors could be complexity of job and skill grades of staff. There could also be interplay between other productivity drivers and barriers.

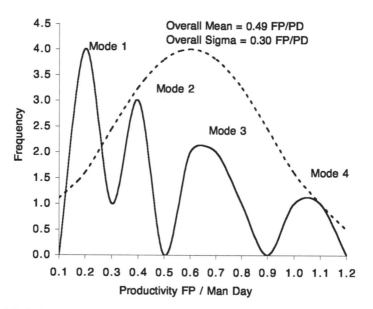

Exhibit 16. Software productivity classes.

This diagnosis establishes four productivity levels, and facilitates developing management strategies. It also provides a fair basis for performance measurement and comparison. The mistake of having and quoting one productivity figure for the entire organization can now be avoided.

The gaps in productivity levels provide a framework for improvement of performance levels, tools utilization, and better and more objective human resource management.

Benchmarking

A benchmark study using frequency distribution, in addition to the conventional comparison charts, could bring over more valuable information. Sometimes it is just a comparison of signature between successful projects and not so successful projects. Sometimes it can be a comparison of motivation level and commitment. It could also be technology-driven differences, such as the study of schedule variance shown in Exhibit 17. During a benchmarking study using frequency distribution, one can compare the following features:

- Process central tendency (dominant peak)
- Number of modes
- Natural process boundary
- Process capability (percent)
- Risk (percent)

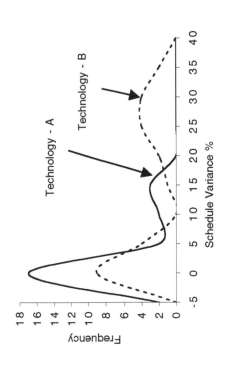

Bin	Freqency (FP)	
-5	0	2
0	9	17
5	4	2
10	0	2
15	1	3
20	2	0
25	4	0
30	4	0
35	2	0
40	0	0

Exhibit 17. Benchmarking.

- Outliers (percent)
- Extreme values (percent)
- Mean (overall)
- Sigma (overall)

Measuring the True Value

Software measurements can have ambiguities as large as 50 percent. The measuring process, such as review or testing, has its own sources of uncertainty, noise, and variation. The measuring tool and the measured process both vary simultaneously, making software measurements even more difficult.

In the presence of this ambiguity, histograms help in getting at the true value: the central tendency or the dominant mode. The histogram successfully points out the true value, even while presenting the details of variations. All modern measuring techniques and instruments use histogram analysis to detect true value. A case in point is defect measurement, fraught with uncertainties of high proportions.

Measuring Defects without Ambiguity. When it comes to defects, the measured value depends on the product of two factors, as shown in Equation 5.7.

$$\text{Measured Value} = \text{Actual Defect} * \text{Detection Effectiveness} \quad (5.7)$$

Detection effectiveness values could vary from 40 to 80 percent, depending on the review methodology used and the review capability of reviewers. Thus an uncertainty is associated with the review process. Measurement capability is inversely proportional to measurement uncertainty. The rule book of measurement says that the measuring instrument should have less uncertainty than the process variation the instrument is trying to measure. We have to measure defect variations of the order of 10 percent with measuring instruments such as review with an inherent variation of up to 70 percent.

The ambiguity in defect measurements can be overcome by using a simple signal-processing technique: defect histogram. The histogram peaks, such as those shown in Exhibit 18, take you closer to truth, and indicate the most likely values. In the presence of noise, the histogram improves the signal-to-noise ratio of measurement.

Comparison when Distinctions Blur

We go to statistics when we cannot make a judgment without its help. An example is the case study where it was called upon to compare two review methods. The first (DD) is a one-person method; the other is a group method (PI/DC). Defect detection probabilities looked very similar in both cases, and the raw data was confusing. Once the frequency distributions of

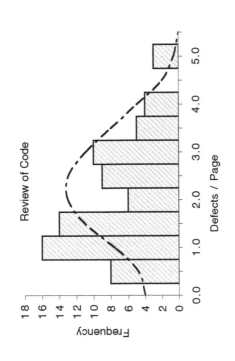

Bin	Frequency	
0	0	4
0.5	8	4.8
1	16	7.5
1.5	14	11
2	6	13
2.5	9	13
3	10	11
3.5	5	8
4	4	5
4.5	0	2
5	3	0.6
5.5	0	0

Exhibit 18. Defect histogram.

79

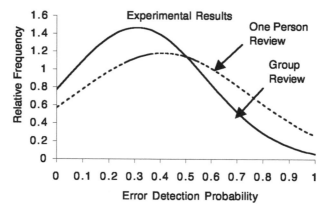

Exhibit 19. Review performance comparison.

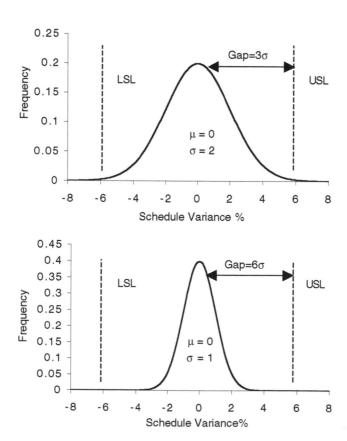

Exhibit 20. Six Sigma process model.

the findings were plotted, the bottom curves in Exhibit 19) emerged, and the whole picture could now be understood.

Six Sigma Model

Six Sigma concepts originally began with a process behavior model in frequency domain. The graphs shown in Exhibit 20 show a Six Sigma representation of process capability. Capability is measured by the gap — safety distance measured in terms of sigma — between the process tendency and performance limit. Graph A has a safety distance or gap of 3σ, and hence the process has 3σ capabilities. Graph B has a process peak that is 6σ away from the specification limit, and hence has 6σ capabilities. Defects in a Six Sigma process — those transgressions across the specification limits — account for a mere 3.4 parts per million (ppm) of the total events (even after allowing for some wandering of the process peak from the mean).

Chapter 6
Metrics Data Analysis in Time Domain

Viewing in Time

Metrics data, organized in the time domain in a framework, present a window into real world. Our purpose here is to see what the present holds out in the context of the past. We also wish to connect events, like a thread connects beads, and see meaningful patterns from which a future can be forecast. We will also be seeing how control charts can be devised to provide support in decision making. Because software projects run a predetermined path known as the life cycle, with a finite start and a finite end, time domain analysis proves to be only natural. Time domain analysis enables project teams to become sensitive to reality, responsive to situations, and self-organizing through continuous learning.

Temporal Patterns in Metrics

Plotting data in a chronological order, as in Exhibit 1, brings out the hidden temporal patterns. A causal factor for attrition, the motivational level of employees is measured here as a commitment index and gathered every quarter. We recognize first the simple linear trend, and later more intricate nonlinear trends. While the linear trend captures a broad, long-term behavioral pattern, the local characteristics are captured in increasing level of details by power, polynomial, and moving average trends. All of them are effective in suppressing noise but forecasting scope and efficiency vary. Each analysis offers an adaptive perception, different from the rest. The overall problem, of course, is a steady decline in commitment, but the pattern of decline, the seasonality, and similarity with known trends provide knowledge.

Time Series Forecasting

Using time series analysis, events can be predicted based on historical trends. The bug arrival pattern shown here is an important input for maintenance projects to decide the following:

- Work scheduling
- Human resource balancing
- Strategies for service quality assurance

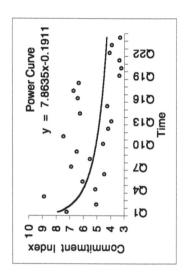

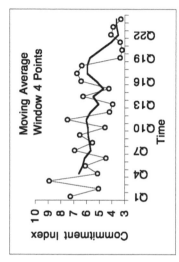

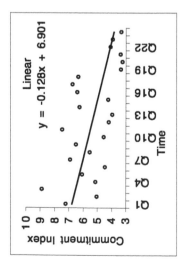

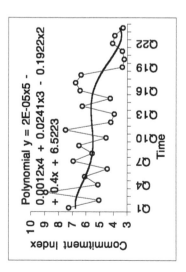

Exhibit 1. Measuring commitment trends.

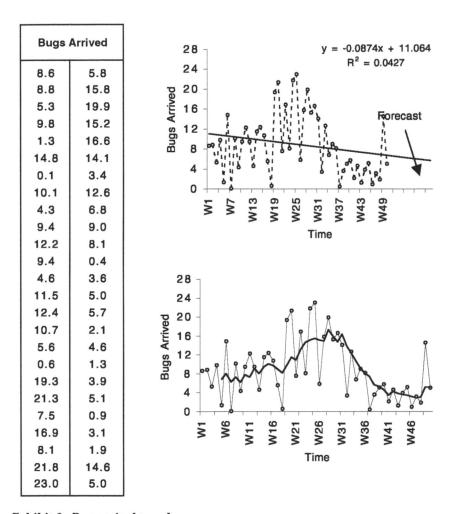

Bugs Arrived	
8.6	5.8
8.8	15.8
5.3	19.9
9.8	15.2
1.3	16.6
14.8	14.1
0.1	3.4
10.1	12.6
4.3	6.8
9.4	9.0
12.2	8.1
9.4	0.4
4.6	3.6
11.5	5.0
12.4	5.7
10.7	2.1
5.6	4.6
0.6	1.3
19.3	3.9
21.3	5.1
7.5	0.9
16.9	3.1
8.1	1.9
21.8	14.6
23.0	5.0

Exhibit 2. Bug arrival trend.

Forecasting requires that we identify structures in the data, which might repeat.

Software failure intensity data can be plotted and the trend can be used to predict failure, as indicated in Exhibit 2. In fixed assets and facilities management, assets downtime data can be plotted in time sequence, and the trend may be derived and used to forecast spare-parts requirements and manpower and tools requirements to fix failure events. With the information made available by forecasting, one stands to plan better and even avoid those marginal losses that are bound to be incurred without the benefit of advance information.

85

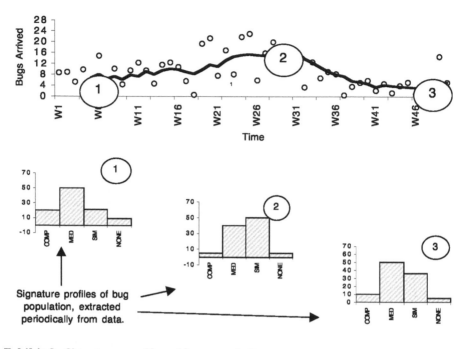

Exhibit 3. Signature profiles of bug population.

Signature Prediction

Beyond the bug arrival statistics, signatures of bug population are captured periodically, as illustrated in Exhibit 3, and used in prediction. The signatures become yet another dimension in forecasting. Here signature refers to a bar graph showing distribution of bugs among the known categories as percentages. The distribution pattern keeps changing. Risk tracking, risk exposure magnitude, and risk distribution may be carried out in a similar fashion. Defect magnitude and defect signature are known to have been tracked in a similar way by IBM in their ODC framework of defect management.

Prediction Windows

Prediction may be done by seeing patterns across projects or can be done locally within a project. For instance, customer satisfaction index may be tracked in an organization, as shown in Exhibit 4, project after project, and the trend may be used in decision making. The prediction window here is quite large and may run into years. Each project runs within a time window inside which predictions are made. Time to complete a project and cost at completion are both predicted from the earned value graph (EVG), which cumulatively tracks value and cost as a time series.

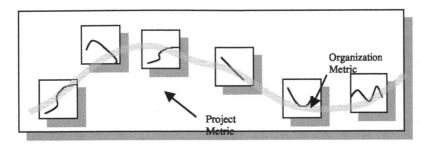

Exhibit 4. Prediction windows.

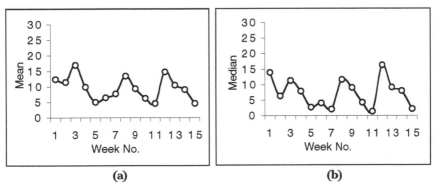

Exhibit 5. X-bar chart on TTR.

Within a project, there could be smaller process windows where very short time series curves operate. Reliability growth curve (RGC) tracks defects within the inspection window of the project. Failure intensity curve, being a reliability model, operates in a window that begins with in-process inspection but goes beyond delivery and penetrates into deeper time zones of alpha, beta, and acceptance tests and application runs.

Every metric operates in a time window, which also becomes the prediction window. The window patterns are eventually called models.

Process Characterization

Process Central Tendency Chart

A process behavior is characterized, in simple terms, by the mean value and the standard deviation. The first refers to the location of the process and the next represents variation of the process. The weekly average (X-bar value) of time to repair (TTR) bugs in a maintenance project itself is a good indicator of the process. Such a plot is called the X-bar chart, shown in Exhibit 5(a). When the process variations are quite large, central tendency is more meaningful with median values. Therefore, monitoring of

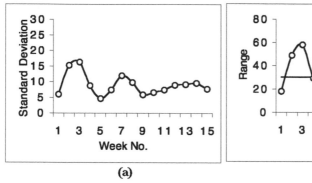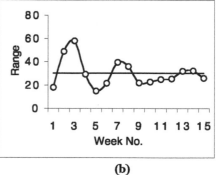

(a) (b)

Exhibit 6. Range–standard deviation chart.

process median charts is recommended in these conditions. Exhibit 5(b) shows the plot of median values for the same set of data.

Process Variation Charts

Process variation is represented by standard deviation. Exhibit 6(a) illustrates the weekly values for standard deviation, in the form of an S chart. There are occasions when process range is used as a measure of variation in place of standard deviation, which is represented in Exhibit 6(b).

Plotting Central Value and Variation Together

When accompanied by another chart showing how the range (maximum/minimum) varies every week, the pair is called X-bar–R chart, which has been very popular on the work floor. A simpler way is to plot the mean, minimum, and maximum values in the same graph and construct the MMM chart.

The weekly data set is known as sub-group (the sub-groups could stand for a group of projects, a group of components, etc.). In our example, the MMM chart is plotted for sub-groups, each corresponding to one week.

The chart could be modified to consider $(\mu + \sigma)$ and $(\mu - \sigma)$ instead of the maximum and minimum values to express variations.

In the MMM chart shown in Exhibit 7, we try to see the process central value and boundary and observe how they fall with time, showing a declining trend. The MMM format allows forecasting and pattern recognition.

Control Charts

Park et al., Fenton and Pfleeger, Adrian Burr and Mal Owen, and Thomas Thelin are among the earliest to have applied the traditional forms of control charts to software engineering processes. Many software development

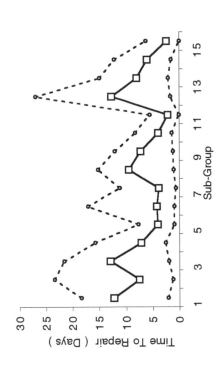

Max.	Mean	Min.
20.0	12.2	2.1
50.0	7.6	1.2
60.0	12.9	2.0
32.0	7.2	2.6
16.0	4.1	1.0
23.0	4.3	1.4
40.0	3.9	0.7
40.0	9.5	4.2
23.0	7.3	1.2
24.0	4.0	1.5
25.0	2.2	0.1
27.0	12.8	1.7
34.0	8.0	2.1
34.0	6.1	1.6
26.0	2.4	0.0

Exhibit 7. MMM graph.

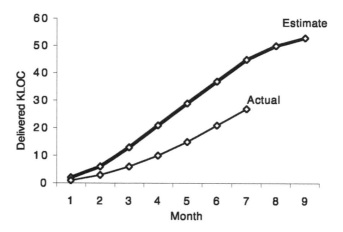

Exhibit 8. Tracking growth against point estimate.

houses have adapted control charts in one form or another. An established tool in manufacturing, the control chart is an emergent technology in software development.

In a control chart, process results are plotted in time and compared with an expected value. Examples for the expected values are

- Control limits set from experience
- Control limits calculated from data
- Specification limits drawn from process requirements
- Process goals set by benchmarking
- Improvement goals
- Estimated value
- Planned value

In Exhibit 8, the estimated value of cumulative lines of code is plotted against month, and the actually delivered lines of code are compared with the estimated. The perceived gap between the estimated and actual makes the process owner see the problem and do something to bring the process result back to the estimated value. Control here means adhering to a budget or a plan. The essential control chart is a decision support tool, an early warning radar that alerts the user.

Range in Expected Values

The estimated value, instead of being a point, could have a range, taking a clue from real-life process variations. Hence, there exists an upper limit and a lower limit for the estimated value, for a given confidence level. If σ represents the standard deviation and if the limits are estimated at 3σ, for instance, the associated confidence level is 99.7 percent.

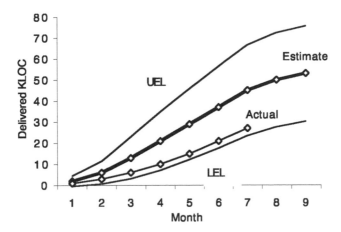

Exhibit 9. Tracking growth against interval estimate.

As shown in Exhibit 9, the actual values are plotted in the background of the estimated mean value and the limits. Now one sees a problem if the actual values cross the limits because we have already given a tolerance band to deviations from the expected mean value.

Those data points, which lie outside the tolerance band, are known as outliers. The first improvement one can think of is to prevent outliers, the next improvement being reduction of the allowed variation band.

Life Cycle Phase Control Charts

The acceptable limits (point estimates) on defect levels are marked in the life cycle phase control chart shown in Exhibit 10. The actual data is superimposed on the expectation levels. Perhaps this type of control chart is most natural for life cycle projects. One can plot the following metrics values in this control chart format:

- Effort
- Schedule
- Rework
- Defect found
- Defect leaked
- Review effort

These life cycle phase control charts provide an opportunity to disseminate process goals and deploy them phasewise. One can define the ranges around each estimate to be more realistic about goal setting. The expected values and process goals change with time and improve when the organization makes progress in its processes. There is perhaps no expected value that can be stationary and permanent.

Errors/KSLOC	Test	Errors/KSLOC	Test
4	UT	1	AT
3.5	UT	1.2	AT
5	UT	1.5	AT
4.1	UT	1.8	AT
5.7	UT	0.9	AT
2	ST	0.4	QP
1.5	ST	0.4	QP
1.75	ST	0.6	QP
1.8	ST	0.6	QP
3.5	ST	0.8	QP

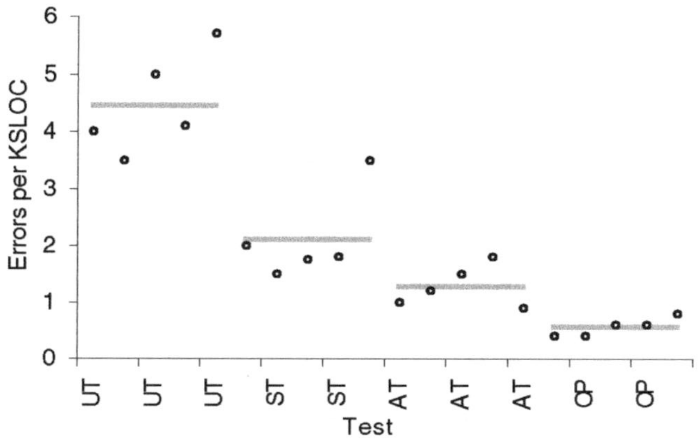

Exhibit 10. Defect profile control chart.

When Limits Blur

We must recall that uncertainties are associated with each measured value. Each data point is not a deterministic entity, but probabilistic in nature. If we plot the probability densities of measured values, as in Exhibit 11, each data point is not a single point but a distribution. Let us try to answer the following questions. Have distributions A, B, C, D, and E crossed the limits? Should we read red alert or early warning?

The answer: these are blurred crossings, not abrupt jumps. Statistically, they represent process diffusion.

We may relate control limits to the assumed confidence levels of judgment and appreciate the tentative nature of limits. We can move up or down the control limits and opt for yet another reference point as UCL. We can fix the UCL and LCL at chosen points on the process distribution curve and accept the corresponding confidence level for decision making. Crossing the limit is a question of degree, which depends on assumptions and perceptions and not so much on the seemingly rigorous mathematical expressions that are used to compute the limits.

Selecting Control Limits for Unknown Distributions

When the type of distribution is not known we can apply Chebyshev's theorem, according to which, for any population or sample, at least $(1 - (1/k)^2)$ of the observations in the dataset fall within k standard deviations of the mean, where $k \geq 1$. This is illustrated in Exhibit 12 as a relationship between standard deviation and the corresponding confidence level.

Chebyshev's theorem provides a lower bound to the proportion of measurements that are within a certain number of standard deviations from the mean. This lower bound estimate can be very helpful when the distribution of a particular population is unknown or mathematically intractable.

Because the software development process is totally a human process, one cannot expect a standard distribution pattern. Therefore, we should adopt an estimation method, which does not depend on data distribution pattern, and at the same time reasonably represent the actual situation. Therefore, depending on the confidence level required one could set the process capability baseline limits with 1.5σ, 2σ, or 3σ for 56, 75, and 89 percent confidence levels, respectively.

Control Limits for X m R Chart

When the sample data points are not available it is frequently impossible to construct an X-bar–R chart. In this case the only alternative available is to construct an X moving range chart. Here successive data points are grouped to form a sub-group.

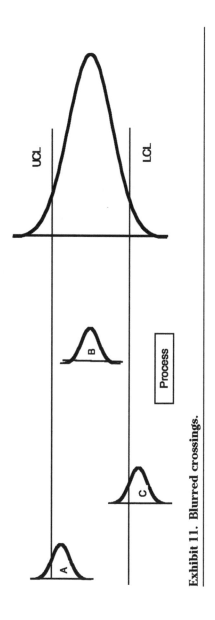

Exhibit 11. Blurred crossings.

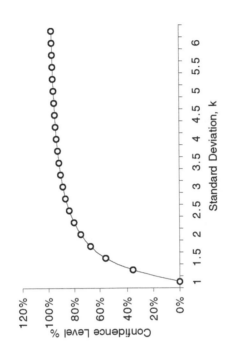

k	1-(1/k)^2	k	1-(1/k)^2
1.0	0.00	3.8	0.93
1.3	0.36	4.0	0.94
1.5	0.56	4.3	0.94
1.8	0.67	4.5	0.95
2.0	0.75	4.8	0.96
2.3	0.80	5.0	0.96
2.5	0.84	5.3	0.96
2.8	0.87	5.5	0.97
3.0	0.89	5.8	0.97
3.3	0.91	6.0	0.97
3.5	0.92	6.3	0.97

Exhibit 12. Selecting confidence limits for control chart.

Control limits for this chart are derived based on control chart constants. The limits are given in Equation 6.1.

$$\text{Lower control limit} = \text{X Bar} - E_2 * \text{R Bar}$$
$$\text{Center line} = \text{X Bar} \qquad\qquad (6.1)$$
$$\text{Upper control limit} = \text{X Bar} + E_2 * \text{R Bar}$$

where E_2 is 2.659 for sample size n is 2.

Let us consider an application of X m R chart for effort variance process. Because this data is less frequently available, at the project closure we can characterize this process and arrive at its baseline value through the application of X m R chart, as shown in Exhibit 13.

Process Capability Baseline Charts

Exhibit 14 shows the process capability baselines with popular control limits. If tighter control on a metric such as effort variance percent is wanted, one could choose 1.5σ limits; on the contrary, if the project manager does not want too many causal analyses to be made or if the process is in the inception stage, one could choose 3σ control limits, wherein nearly 89 out of 100 times the process value will be within the 3σ control limit.

Process Capability Baselines from Empirical Distribution

The process history, if available, can be used to set control limits such as demonstrated in Exhibit 15, where frequency distribution of historical data reveals the existence of natural process limits, the valley points dropping off the principal peak. UNPL refers to upper natural process limit and LNPL refers to lower natural process limit.

This approach allows us to use empirical frequency distributions, which are perhaps more relevant and accurate than the elegant assumptions made in the traditional computations of limits.

Statistical Process Control Chart

The Shewhart control chart, introduced in 1920, decomposes process variation into two components: random variation (predictable bounds) and systematic variation (anomalies). Random variations, when the cause system is constant, approach some distribution function, and hence remain predictable or statistically stable. Systematic variations are due to assignable causes, which are due to unusual causes, freak incidents, process drifts, and environmental threats.

Shewhart demonstrated how control charts could be used to identify and distinguish the two types of process variation, to achieve process efficiency, and ensuing economic benefits.

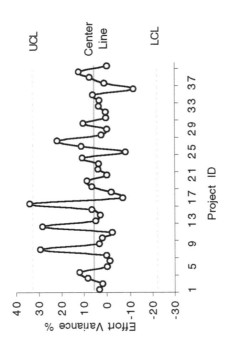

Effort Variance %		
3.20	2.81	0.39
1.81	6.46	0.46
8.37	34.20	3.45
11.99	-6.77	3.24
-0.14	-1.97	6.02
-1.36	6.51	-11.44
0.04	8.59	1.12
29.44	0.00	7.42
3.19	3.80	12.35
1.90	3.55	0.00
-2.27	10.84	21.97
28.51	-7.88	2.31
11.19	0.00	-
4.84	10.32	-

Exhibit 13. X m R chart on effort variance.

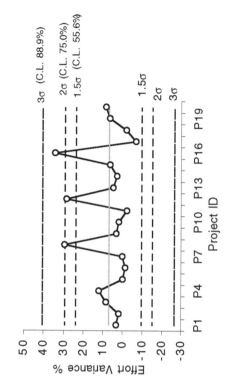

Project ID	Effort Variance %	Project ID	Effort Variance %
P1	3.20	P11	-2.27
P2	1.81	P12	28.51
P3	8.37	P13	4.84
P4	11.99	P14	2.81
P5	-0.14	P15	6.46
P6	-1.36	P16	34.20
P7	0.04	P17	-6.77
P8	29.44	P18	-1.97
P9	3.19	P19	6.51
P10	1.90	P20	8.59

Exhibit 14. Control chart with confidence limits.

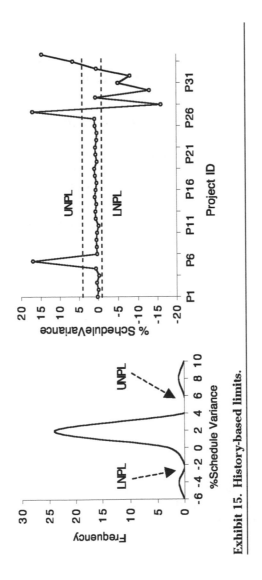

Exhibit 15. History-based limits.

Exhibit 16 shows how a training manager uses the Shewhart Control Chart to identify (and later solve) two problems: extraordinary cost for Training ID 7 and the average cost (μ) greater than the budget.

Armand V. Feigenbaum allows specifying control limits from past experience and guesswork in a pragmatic manner.

Tests for Control Charts

Tests for statistical control have been in use for a long time. The classical tests or decision rules to be applied while reading the control charts are presented in the following list, along with an illustration in Exhibit 17.

- *Test #1:* Any point outside one of the control limits is an indication of a special cause and needs to be investigated.
- *Test #2:* A run of seven points in succession, either all above the central line or below the central line or all increasing or all decreasing, is an indication of a special cause and needs to be investigated.
- *Test #3:* Any unusual pattern or trend involving cyclic or drift behavior of the data is an indication of a special cause and needs to be investigated.
- *Test #4:* The proportion of points in the middle-third zone of the distance between the control limits should be about two thirds of all the points under observation.

Control Chart in the Presence of Trend

If the metric shows trend, such as delivered defect density (DDD) in Exhibit 18, the control charts may be partitioned to make a clearer presentation of the problem. The trend line helps in forecasting and risk estimation. The baseline helps in process analysis, estimation, and setting process guidelines.

Dual Process Control Charts

Sometimes the metric is a product of two major components, each showing its own independent characteristics. Defects found by design review, for instance, are a product of defect injected and review effectiveness, shown in Equation 6.2.

$$\text{Defects Found} = \text{Defects Injected} * \text{Review Effectiveness} \qquad (6.2)$$

The UCL in the control chart of defect/KLOC, as shown in Exhibit 19, is more relevant to the designers, who have to keep defect level below the UCL. The LCL, on the other hand, appeals to the reviewers to find defects more than the UCL. In the defect control chart in Exhibit 19, the following references are marked for proper interpretation:

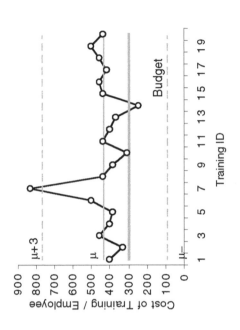

Training ID	Cost of Training	Training ID	Cost of Training
1	400	11	435
2	333	12	400
3	455	13	370
4	400	14	250
5	385	15	435
6	500	16	455
7	833	17	417
8	435	18	455
9	385	19	500
10	313	20	435

Exhibit 16. Controlling the cost of training.

101

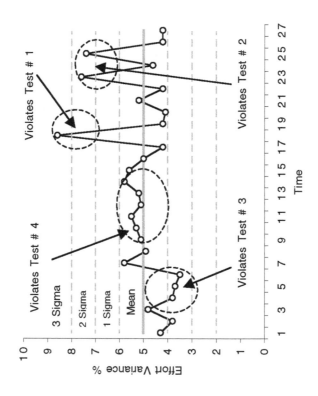

Effort	Variance %
4.3	5.6
3.8	5
4.8	4.2
3.8	8.6
3.7	4.2
3.5	4.1
5.8	5.2
4.9	4.2
5.1	7.6
5.3	4.6
5.5	7.4
5.1	4.2
5.2	4.2
5.8	-

Exhibit 17. Tests for Statistical Process Control (SPC) charts.

ID	Def. /PM	ID	Def. /PM
P1	4.75	P37	0.14
P2	0.28	P38	0.30
P3	0.22	P39	0.16
P4	0.79	P40	3.29
P5	0.05	P41	0.01
P6	0.74	P42	0.84
P7	0.01	P43	1.36
P8	0.02	P44	0.12
P9	0.43	P45	0.90
P10	1.13	P46	2.00
P11	0.21	P47	1.73
P12	1.49	P48	0.13
P13	0.27	P49	0.30
P14	0.07	P50	2.20
P15	0.03	P51	2.30
P16	0.40	P52	2.17
P17	0.10	P53	1.25
P18	0.40	P54	1.21
P19	0.73	P55	1.43
P20	1.07	P56	4.18
P21	0.88	P57	2.23
P22	0.08	P58	1.12
P23	0.78	P59	0.23
P24	0.04	P60	3.40
P25	0.49	P61	0.55
P35	0.30	P62	3.20
P36	0.20	P63	2.30

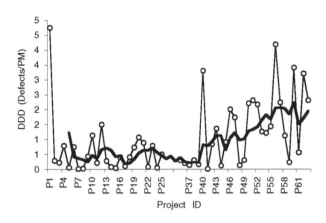

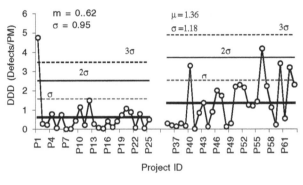

Exhibit 18. Trend and baselines.

- UCL ($\mu + \sigma$): for designer
- USL (based on customer specification): -do-
- Mean: for baselining
- LSL (based on benchmarking): for reviewer
- LCL ($\mu - \sigma$): -do-

From Dual Limits to Single Limits

The control chart in Exhibit 19 is cluttered, and one has to strain to read, analyze, and interpret the chart. When the chart is used to give process feedback, some process owners may mix signals, one demanding a minimum production of defects, another may demand just the opposite.

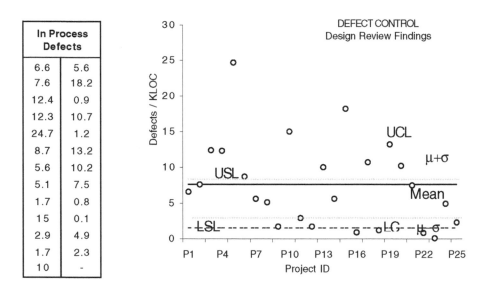

In Process Defects	
6.6	5.6
7.6	18.2
12.4	0.9
12.3	10.7
24.7	1.2
8.7	13.2
5.6	10.2
5.1	7.5
1.7	0.8
15	0.1
2.9	4.9
1.7	2.3
10	-

Exhibit 19. In-process defect control chart.

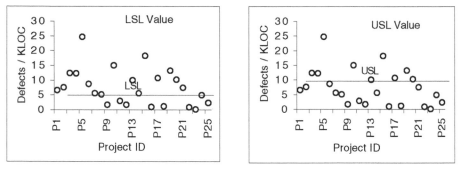

Exhibit 20. Splitting a double-side limit into two single-side limits.

This problem may be solved and effective presentation may be made to the process owner, if only we could construct two separate control charts, each delivered to the process owner with the appropriate control limits, as indicated in Exhibit 20. After the split, the new control charts look simple and clear, with just one decision rule marked. The process owner, the designer, or the reviewer, gets a clear signal. The process defects are marked as circles in both cases. With defects clearly marked and the goal (specification limit) clearly specified, each process owner can go into causal analysis of process violations and initiate corrective measures. The purpose of this control chart is to provide effective feedback and facilitate corrective action.

104

Control Charts Types

There are several control chart forms in use, including the ones we have used so far. Below is a brief list for a quick reference. The exact formulas for computations may be found elsewhere.

When we have a large number of data points that can be organized as sub-groups according to some real-life order, and when the sub-group sizes are used in determining the control limits, the following charts may be useful.

- X-bar chart with UCL and LCL
- X-bar – R chart with UCL and LCL
- X-bar – S chart with UCL and LCL
- p Chart (percentage defectives) with UCL and LCL
- u Chart (defects per unit size) with UCL and LCL
- c Chart (defect counts per module) with UCL and LCL

If instead of sub-groups we have just an individual data point for every process delivery, we can artificially create a sub-group by selecting data points from a moving average window, and plot a graph with control limits calculated in the traditional way.

- Individuals chart (X m R) with UCL and LCL

When all we desire is to characterize the process and generate some performance baseline on a chosen metric, the following forms may be used. These forms can be used across life cycle phases or across sub-groups.

- MMM chart
- M, $\mu + \sigma$, $\mu - \sigma$ chart
- Life cycle profiles with $\mu + \sigma$, $\mu - \sigma$

If we wish to compare actual values with estimates, then the following may be used:

- Cumulative graphs with point estimates
- Cumulative graphs with interval estimates
- Run charts with estimates shown as USL, LSL
- Life cycle profiles with USL and LSL
- Run charts with baseline values (history) marked

Special Forms

Most performance models are constructed this way. A few of them are illustrated in this section.

Performance Comparison Chart

The design review process of each individual can be tracked using the metric called number of pages reviewed per hour. The bar graph in Exhibit 21 shows the individual's review performance against the average group performance and with respect to maximum and minimum performance.

Multi-Process Tracking Model

A simple way to take a holistic and balanced view of processes is to track all related process metrics on a radar chart, marking the target values and the achieved values. Cost drivers, performance drivers, and defect drivers in software development can be plotted on the radar chart for effective process control. Tracking of multiple goals, all competing for resources, is presented in the radar chart format in Exhibit 22. The following is a list of metrics used to represent and measure goals:

- Customer satisfaction index (CUST SAT)
- Productivity index (PROD)
- Employee satisfaction index (EMP SAT)
- Right first time index (RFT)
- Defect removal effectiveness (DRE)
- Training need fulfillment index (TNF)

All these are measured quantitatively on a 0 to 10 scale (ratio scale). Targets and achievement in each direction are plotted. This is a control chart because it compares reality with expectation and allows one to see deviations. It gives deeper meaning and allows one to visualize a balanced picture or model on goal achievement.

Dynamic Model: Automated Control Charts

Control charts in modern times have taken a totally new form. They are embedded in metric databases and analysis modules, which perform dynamic functions.

A defect-tracking tool uses a defect database as the platform and tracks bug closure. If the time taken exceeds a preset limit, the software generates a message to the tester. Even if the bug lives long after the message, the software escalates the issue and the message is now flashed to the project manager. The tester or the manager does not see a physical control chart but gets the results.

The limit setting can be a choice from the manager, where his experience and judgment prevail. Or the limit setting can be done by the software logic, which will use an appropriate decision rule and raise an alarm. The decision-making algorithm can be simple algebra or a sophisticated knowledge engine that learns and works with intelligence.

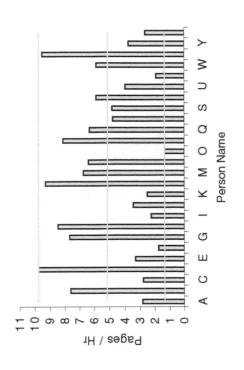

Person	Pages/ hr.	Person	Pages/hr.
A	2.8	N	6.4
B	7.6	O	1.3
C	2.8	P	8.1
D	9.8	Q	6.3
E	3.3	R	4.8
F	1.8	S	4.9
G	7.7	T	5.9
H	8.4	U	4.0
I	2.3	V	1.9
J	3.5	W	5.9
K	2.5	X	9.5
L	9.3	Y	3.8
M	6.8	Z	2.7

Exhibit 21. Review performance comparison.

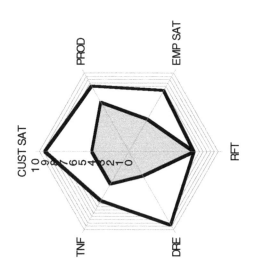

	Target	Achieved
CUST SAT	9	4
PROD	8	6
EMP SAT	7.5	4
RFT	7	7
DRE	9	3
TNF	6	4

Exhibit 22. Goal control radar.

The graph is printed, on demand, as a report from the tool along with other statistics. In a similar way, metrics data analysis tools can generate dynamic control charts on all metrics. These charts can be published in the monthly process capability baseline reports.

Control Chart for Effective Application

There are many forms of control charts but they all must be structured well for effective application. Here are some suggestions.

On any metric we can plot a control chart. Choose the metric that communicates better. For instance, a training manager can choose cost of absenteeism instead of number of people who are absent because the former makes senior management look at the control chart seriously.

The data should be in chronological order. Most software development processes follow the learning curve, both first order and second order. Before process stability is achieved, the learning curve is encountered. Chronological order gives control charts the vital meaning and power.

A decision rule must be provided to enable problem recognition. The rule could be expressed in the following ways:

- Control limits
- Specification limits
- Baseline references
- Estimated values
- Process goals
- Process constraints
- Benchmark values
- Expected trend
- Zones

The reader must be made familiar with the rules for interpretation. The chart must be designed with the most likely readers in mind, and every effort must be made to make the chart provide effective communication to a human system (biofeedback).

Provide support data as annotations for significant data points. For example, a defect distribution pie chart can be provided as a companion to a defect control chart.

Annotate identified hot spots or trends with causal analysis findings. We learn from such annotations. Wherever possible, suggested corrective action may be indicated.

Modernism in Process Control: Decision Support Charts

Metrics data, when presented in time series, offers a new form that helps to understand the process.

A well-structured time series chart could emerge into a model once it captures a pattern that can be applied as a historic lesson. The time series analysis for trend or process control is also a time series model of the process, inasmuch as it can increase one's understanding of the process behavior and forecast.

What-If Analysis

But the outstanding issue in software projects is whether a process goes according to a plan or estimate. The need for statistically derived, self-organizing goals, should it arise, is only secondary. The term *control chart* may then be replaced with the term *decision support chart.* The concept of control limit will be substituted with the concept of decision thresholds. What-if analysis can be done on a control chart by shifting the limits and seeing each time how many events are picked up and earmarked for investigation. The problem set will shift according to the location of the threshold line.

Clues, Not Convincing Proof

There are reasons why metrics control charts end up issuing suggestive clues but not convincing proof about process problems:

- Data errors
- Ambiguity in measurement scale
- Process having nonnormal distributions
- Nonavailability of defect propagation models

But all a project manager is looking for is a set of clues, not final proof. A decision support chart can coexist with ambiguity but the classical control chart cannot.

If It Is Written on the Wall, Do Not Draw Control Charts

If known problems are not solved, nobody wants to use a control chart to detect new problems. If trouble can be spotted without having to use a control chart, avoid control charts. Going one step further, if without the aid of control limits we can spot outliers using the naked eye, let us not draw control limits.

The connection of control charts with action is now legendary. The best control chart is the one on which somebody acts.

Chapter 7

Metrics Data Analysis in the Relationship Domain

A Fertile Domain

Processes are interdependent, forming a network. The interplay between process parameters has been the subject of several studies in software engineering, leading to understanding of the hidden process dynamics. The interactions that exist in the process network can be symbolically represented as a map of relationships between metrics. The symbolic world of relationship between metrics is a new domain, which mirrors the real world of processes and the influences they exert on one another.

The analysis of an individual metric in the frequency and time domains enhances the indicative abilities of the metric and allows us to see patterns. In the new domain, we expand our view angle, look at the neighborhood around each metric, spot more metrics (which seem to be connected), and focus on capturing the interrelationships. The relationship domain brings in a pragmatic perspective. In the real world, processes do not work in isolation and, as a consequence, complete truth cannot be represented by isolated metrics. Analysis in the relationship domain complements analysis in the other domains.

When processes work as interconnected systems, the interrelationships may follow an order or rule. This may be just a local discipline governing a narrow range of process events. Or it may be a global order, with universal influence. The order may change from time to time when processes shift from one phase state to another. When we analyze metrics data in the relationship domain, we use metrics "snapshots" of the process, to try to arrive at formulas that depict the order, rule, or discipline by which the process runs. The formulas could be local or global, following the characteristic of the process order. Some are ephemeral while others are everlasting. Some are reversible, some are irreversible. Some are reproducible while others are not. We search for all. The relationship domain is a fertile hunting ground.

Studying relationships among metrics with existing data is one approach. Making special observations under controlled conditions or conducting experiments is another approach. The choice between routine observation and experiment is decided by the proposed degree of rigor in the intended analysis and cost. We proceed with the first choice, studying naturally available data without incurring the expenditure of experiments. We believe that in a project environment there is a lot to learn from available data and a lot of improvement can be made from the study results of such data before the need arises to commission experiments.

The relationship between metrics and the expression of the same as a formula or equation can be presented graphically. In fact, we begin with graphical analysis and then arrive at empirical formulas.

Search for Relationships

Relationship between metrics is a mirror of interplay between processes. Now we wish to analyze metrics in search of relationships.

In principle we can suppose a relationship between any two metrics. For example, let us look at the relationships between six core metrics selected from a project:

1. Skill level
2. Productivity
3. Review effectiveness
4. Defect density
5. Effort variance
6. Size

A relationship map of these six core metrics is displayed in Exhibit 1. The connecting lines denote possible relationship. Any two metrics, an ordered pair of them, provide an opportunity to conceive a relationship. There are 15 ordered pairs of metrics and to match there are 15 relationship lines in the map. Not all the supposed relationships are meaningful. Some are merely mechanical constructs, just unreal mathematical possibilities. In others, we do have expectations to uncover relationships of practical significance.

Pairing metrics is a limited, simple step, useful within the limits. We can see a complex set of relationships if we connect one "driven" metrics to five "driver" metrics. This way we are applying a cause-and-effect relationship or predictor–response model. We take defect density as the effect and can imagine that it is driven by the remaining five metrics, establishing a one-to-five multivariate mapping. Considering the simultaneous influence of five predictor metrics on one response metrics is a more complete and more rigorous approach.

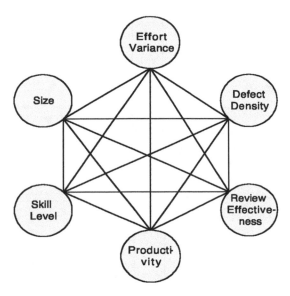

Exhibit 1. Relationship map.

Exhibit 2. Relationships revealed in a scatter diagram.

Type 1	Strong	Positive
Type 2	Strong	Negative
Type 3	Weak	Positive
Type 4	Weak	Negative
Type 5	Weak	No Relationship

Perceiving Relationships

Let us consider metrics in ordered pairs — two at a time — and take a look at the possible types of relationships that can exist between them. Relationships may be perceived by plotting scatter diagrams. One of the two chosen metrics will be treated as the dependent variable (y-axis), the other as the independent variable (x-axis). The scatter diagram may reveal relationships, which can be among the five types mentioned in Exhibit 2.

Perceiving the type of influence between metrics allows us to see the interplay between process elements. In Exhibit 3 the five types of influences, or relationships, are illustrated.

113

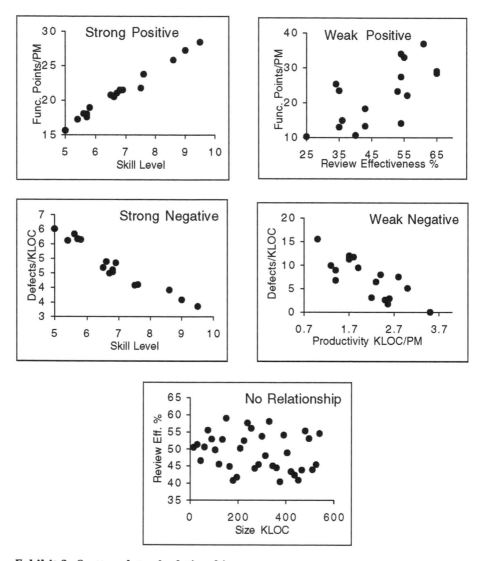

Exhibit 3. Scatter plots of relationships.

Strength of Relationship: Correlation Coefficient

We may begin the relationship study between two variables by estimating the correlation coefficient (r), which is a statistical measure of the degree of linear relationship between the two variables. It lies between +1

Exhibit 4. Productivity: skill level data.

Observation No.	x Skill Level	y Productivity
1	5.0	15.7
2	5.7	17.6
3	7.5	21.8
4	9.0	27.2
5	6.9	21.5
6	9.5	28.4
7	5.8	18.9
8	6.6	20.5
9	5.7	18.0
10	5.4	17.2
11	4.8	15.7
12	8.6	25.8
13	6.7	21.0
14	6.8	21.5
15	5.6	18.1
16	6.8	21.5
17	7.6	23.8
18	6.5	20.8

and –1 depending on whether the relationship is positive or negative. The strength of the relationship is expressed by the absolute value of the correlation coefficient.

Let us consider the metrics Skill Level and Productivity as x and y variables for a correlation study. Metrics data obtained from a project is given in Exhibit 4. The correlation coefficient r is defined in Equation 7.1.

$$r = \frac{\Sigma(\delta x)(\delta y)}{\sqrt{\Sigma(\delta x)^2 \Sigma(\delta y)^2}}$$

(7.1)

where:

$\delta x = x - \text{mean}(x)$

$\delta y = y - \text{mean}(y)$

Computation of r using Equation 7.1 yields a value of 0.993 for the correlation coefficient. The computation is shown in Exhibit 5.

Exhibit 5. Calculation of correlation coefficient.

Observation No.	x Skill Level	y Productivity	δx	δy	$(\delta x) * (\delta y)$	$(\delta x)^2$	$(\delta y)^2$
1	5.0	15.7	−2.6	−8.1	21.1	6.8	65.8
2	5.7	17.6	−1.9	−6.2	11.8	3.6	38.3
3	7.5	21.8	−0.1	−2.0	0.2	0.0	3.9
4	9.0	27.2	1.4	3.5	4.9	2.0	12.1
5	6.9	21.5	−0.7	−2.3	1.6	0.5	5.1
6	9.5	28.4	1.9	4.7	8.9	3.6	21.9
7	5.8	18.9	−1.8	−4.8	8.7	3.2	23.4
8	6.6	20.5	−1.0	−3.3	3.3	1.0	10.8
9	5.7	18.0	−1.9	−5.8	11.0	3.6	33.3
10	5.4	17.2	−2.2	−6.5	14.4	4.8	42.6
11	4.8	15.7	−2.8	−8.0	22.5	7.8	64.3
12	8.6	25.8	1.0	2.1	2.1	1.0	4.2
13	6.7	21.0	−0.9	−2.7	2.5	0.8	7.5
14	6.8	21.5	−0.8	−2.3	1.8	0.6	5.2
15	5.6	18.1	−2.0	−5.7	11.4	4.0	32.6
16	6.8	21.5	−0.8	−2.3	1.8	0.6	5.3
17	7.6	23.8	0.0	0.0	0.0	0.0	0.0
18	6.5	20.8	−1.1	−3.0	3.3	1.2	9.1
Mean	**6.7** Mean (x)	**20.8** Mean (y)	**Sum**		131.1 a	45.3 b	385.5 c

$$\Sigma(\delta x)(\delta y) \qquad = a \qquad\qquad = 83.2616$$

$$\Sigma(\delta x)^2 \qquad = b \qquad\qquad = 30.5094$$

$$\Sigma(\delta y)^2 \qquad = c \qquad\qquad = 230.5248 \qquad (7.2)$$

$$\sqrt{\Sigma(\delta x)^2 \Sigma(\delta y)^2} \quad = \text{SQRT}(b*c) \quad = 83.8641$$

$$r = \frac{\Sigma(\delta x)(\delta y)}{\sqrt{\Sigma(\delta x)^2 \Sigma(\delta y)^2}} = a/(\text{SQRT}(b*c)) = 0.9928$$

The correlation analysis shows that there is a good correlation between productivity and skill level. We need not go through all these time-consuming steps to do a correlation study. Excel and similar spreadsheets lend support with built-in statistical functions.

Causal Relationship and Statistical Correlation

There is a difference between correlation and causal relationship. Correlation between metrics suggests that they are associated; a change in one follows approximate changes in the other. However, mere association does not assure causal relationship. Correlation could be superficial. The variables keep pace perhaps by coincidence. In a feeding experiment with pigeons, food was dropped in a random manner. However, some pigeons happened to see food drop when they raised their heads. A coincidence, indeed. These pigeons moved their heads up when they needed food and expected food to drop from the feeder. Other pigeons thought sideways movement caused food drop. The pigeons soon settled in a self-devised superstition on the basis of apparent correlation. Expectation (or estimation) based on the strength of mere correlation might be misleading.

Likewise, if the linear correlation coefficient is zero, we cannot come to a conclusion that there is no relationship at all. Other forms of relations might still exist, invisible because they are "buried" in the data. Sometimes, linear correlation studies may not be able to grasp highly nonlinear or cyclic patterns.

One should be careful while making correlation studies; correlation can degenerate into scientific superstition if invalidated.

Relationship on the other hand goes beyond statistical correlation and coincidence. Usually a relationship is conceived before data analysis, based on some fundamental assumptions or well-known, time-proven concepts. Sometimes a new relationship is proposed based on theoretical reasoning, which awaits validation.

Linear Regression

We will now move from correlation coefficient, which measures the strength of relationships between two variables, to regression analysis, which determines the mathematical expression of the relationship. In the simplest form of regression, the dataset is fitted to the equation $y = a + bx$, where y is the dependent variable and x is the independent variable. The values of x are assumed to cause or determine the values of y. $y = a + bx$ is known as the regression line to which the data points regress. This is also taken as a regression model, which estimates y from x.

Error Sum of Squares

The difference between the estimated value and the true value is called the error of estimation or residual in regression. For a proposed regression model, one can find error sum of square by Equation 7.3.

$$\text{Error Sum of Square (ESS)} = \Sigma(y_{\text{true}} - y_{\text{estimated}})^2 \qquad (7.3)$$

The Principle of Least Squares

The best fit regression model, built according to the principle of least squares, is the regression line that achieves a minimum value for the error sum of squares. This is done through a process of iteration, where the error sum of squares converges to its lowest value.

Standard Error of Estimate

Standard error of estimates measures the variability or scatter of the observed values around the regression line. It is also a measure of reliability of the regression line as an estimation equation. It is calculated using Equation 7.4.

$$\text{Standard Error (SE)} = \sqrt{\frac{\text{ESS}}{n-2}} \qquad (7.4)$$

Total Sum of Squares (TSS)

This is the total of the squared observations between each sample observation and the sample mean, as shown in Equation 7.5.

$$\text{Total Sum of Square (TSS)} = \Sigma\left(y_{\text{true}} - y_{\text{mean}}\right)^2 \qquad (7.5)$$

Coefficient of Determination R^2

Coefficient of determination is defined as a measure of the proportion of variation in y that is accounted for by regression on x.

$$R^2 = 1 - \frac{\text{ESS}}{\text{TSS}} \qquad (7.6)$$

Linear Regression: Example

We present an example of regression analysis on the relationship between Review Effectiveness (RE) and Defect Density (DD). The independent variable is Review Effectiveness, and the dependent variable is Defect Density.

We expect a relationship between DD and RE. We believe that increase in RE will make DD come down. However, we do not know whether the relationship will be nonlinear, weak, or strong; we wish to find from the regression analysis.

A typical regression analysis using the Excel tool yields outputs that include the following results:

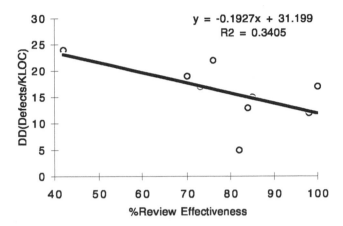

Exhibit 6. Regression line plot.

Exhibit 7. Regression analysis results.

% Review Effectiveness (x)	DD(Def/KLOC) (y true)	Predicted Value (y estimated)	Residual
42	24	23.11	0.89
70	19	17.71	1.29
73	17	17.13	–0.13
76	22	16.56	5.44
82	5	15.40	–10.40
84	13	15.02	–2.02
85	15	14.82	0.18
98	12	12.32	–0.32
100	17	11.93	5.07

- Regression line
- Regression table
- Residual plot
- Regression statistics

The first output, the regression line, is shown in Exhibit 6. The equation to the regression line and the coefficient of determination are also printed in a textbox next to the regression line.

The regression results are presented by the tool in a tabular form as shown in Exhibit 7. This table presents the predicted values (y estimated) and the observed values (y true). The difference between them is presented as residuals. The residuals provide important information for judging the adequacy of the regression analysis. One way they can be used is in a plot of the residuals versus the independent variable. If the residuals do

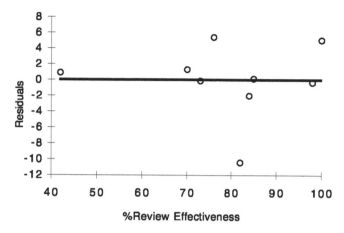

Exhibit 8. Residual plot.

Exhibit 9. Regression statistics.

Multiple R	0.58353385
R Square	0.340511755
Adjusted R Square	0.246299148
Standard Error	4.930198016
Observations	9

not appear to be randomly scattered above the horizontal line, it may indicate a problem with the regression analysis.

Perhaps a straight-line relationship is not appropriate, or the assumptions of normality or constant variance are not reasonable. A plot of the residuals is shown in Exhibit 8.

Regression statistics includes the estimation of coefficient of determination (R^2) and the standard error, as in Exhibit 9.

Outliers in Relationship

A special graph showing the sloping lines (1 SE and 2 SE) that run parallel to the best fit line indicating outliers is given in Exhibit 10. Those data points that lie beyond a threshold of 1 SE slopes are considered as results of process violations, and marked for study and examination.

The graph in Exhibit 10 is known sometimes as a sloping control chart. Here the control chart raises a trigger when a process changes its inner dynamics. This trigger is regarded as more proactive than the conventional control charts.

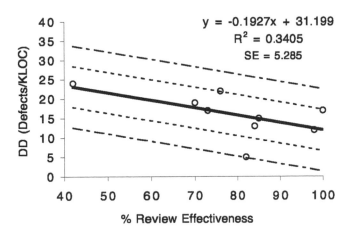

Exhibit 10. Reliability of regression line.

Departure from expected relation is the decision criteria, and, not the magnitude of defect density. For example in Exhibit 10, the outlier has the least defect density, and for all practical reasons it represents a good job done by the developers. However, we wish to question why the relationship with review effectiveness has changed. This unexpected change in relationship could mean that:

- A new complexity has arrived in the development process.
- Factors other than Review Effectiveness have contributed to defect reduction.
- The intended relationship (DD = −0.1927 RE + 31.199) has failed to govern this outlier for reasons not known to us.

Nonlinear Regression Models

In nonlinear regression the dataset is fitted to nonlinear curves, again using the principle of least squares. Where linear relationships are absent, there could be nonlinear relationships that we must verify.

Nonlinear regression analysis is an iterative approach. We try different modeling equations; if one equation does not describe the data, then we try a different equation. The dataset must be carefully examined before the iteration begins. If the data is not enough in "critical ranges," it is safer to wait until more data is collected in the region.

If the data is too scattered, nonlinear fittings could give unstable results. If possible, collect more data to make sure that the wide scatter (suggesting weak relationship) is not a mistake but a reality we have to deal with.

Simple data transformations or normalization may be tried to see if the data scatter can be narrowed.

Exhibit 11. Data used for nonlinear regression.

Actual Size (FP)	Productivity FP/Month	Actual Size (FP)	Productivity FP/Month
5152	16.89	840	9.13
5635	17.55	5180	20.08
805	8.05	5775	13.18
3839	12.03	10577	27.69
2119	9.06	3983	13.78
2821	15.17	3164	10.01
3913	16.44	3542	11.58
7854	30.21	4277	9.06
2422	20.88	7252	25.36
4047	15.21	3948	8.73
9051	35.08	3927	18.97
2282	21.73	6405	22.47
4172	18.71	5922	14.66
4977	14.47	2620	5.25
3192	31.92	2174	18.42

Nonlinear Regression Analysis of Productivity

Software development productivity in the simplest definition is size/effect. Productivity is a heavily loaded metric, and is very complex in the sense many factors determine its value. Productivity tends to be fundamentally nonlinear in nature.

Studies have been made in mapping productivity drivers to productivity estimates. We will pick size from the potential drivers and study its relationship with productivity.

Metrics data has been collected for size in function points (FP) and effect as person months (PM). Size is the predictor variable or independent variable, x. Productivity itself is the "response variable" or dependent variable, y. The data is presented in Exhibit 11.

Nonlinear Regression Analysis

We will use the following nonlinear equations for regression analysis of a typical productivity dataset given in Exhibit 11. Excel has been used to generate the regression curves that correspond with the following six nonlinear equations:

1. Nonlinear regression logarithmic equation
2. Nonlinear regression polynomial-degree 2
3. Nonlinear regression polynomial-degree 3
4. Nonlinear regression polynomial-degree 4
5. Nonlinear regression power equation
6. Nonlinear regression exponential equation

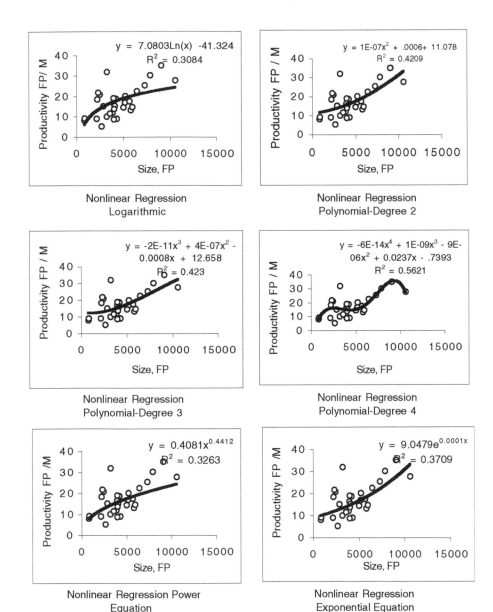

Exhibit 12. Nonlinear regression.

Goodness of Fit

The regression curves are shown in Exhibit 12. It may be seen that the coefficient of determination, R^2, which represents the quality of fit, is different for different regression equations. The lowest value is 0.3034 for the logarithmic curve and the best value is 0.5621 for the fourth degree polynomial

123

Exhibit 13. Results of forecasting.

Regression Model	x Size, FP	y Productivity FP/M
Logarithmic	15000	26.76
Power	15000	28.4
Exponential	15000	40.54
Polynomial deg 2	15000	42.58
Polynomial deg 3	15000	23.16
Polynomial deg 4	15000	−1337.74

curve. R^2 gives an indication of closeness of data points to the regression equation in a statistical sense. This helps in making a first order judgment on regression.

Monotonicity

However, choosing the regression curve must consider the other requirements of curve fitting. The regression curves must be monotonic and stable. A look at the six models in Exhibit 12 shows that one model — the fourth-order polynomial — shows a curve, which reverses its trend in a few places. Physically, trend reversal means larger program costs less in those regions of reversal — an absurdity.

Stability of Nonlinear Regression Curves: A Comparison

The forecasting ability of nonlinear curves has to be assessed while choosing regression models. Let us formulate a forecasting problem and examine how the six nonlinear regression models fare.

The forecasting problem we have taken is to predict productivity value (y) for a given size of 15000 FP (x). It may be noted that the current data range is 0 to 11000 FP. This means that the regression curve has to be extrapolated up 4000 FP and reach an estimate.

The results of forecasting are illustrated in the figures given in Exhibit 13. The fourth-order polynomial predicts a deeply negative value, while all other models predict productivity in the range between 23 and 43 FP/PM. Negative productivity is a physically meaningless number, and magnitude of the negative value indicates a complete failure in forecasting. The forecasting performance of the fourth-order polynomial is shown in Exhibit 14, along with the power curve. It is seen from these results that the polynomial curve has collapsed to negative values of productivity. Hence, it is a poor and unreliable estimate. The power curve, however, behaves better and predicts a value that is realistic.

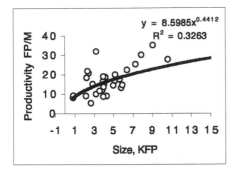 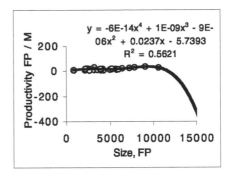

Exhibit 14. Forecasting nonlinear regression model.

Multiple Linear Regression

So far we have been looking at relationships between one dependent variable (y) and one independent variable (x). But in many studies we need to consider the influence of several independent variables. In multiple linear regression, the mean of the dependent variable is a linear combination of the independent variables, as shown in Equation 7.7.

$$y = a + b_1 x_1 + b_2 x_2 + b_3 x_3 + b_4 x_4 \ldots + b_k x_k \qquad (7.7)$$

Linearity

If the linearity assumption is not met, sometimes we can transform one or more of the x variables, like taking the square root, and get a linear dependence.

Interaction

If interactions between the independent variables are to be included in the model, then additional cross products, $x_i x_j$, have to be included in the model.

Surface Plot

We will consider a case study for multiple linear regression with two independent variables. The dependent variable is Defect Density (y), measure in Defects/KLOC. The independent variables are Skill Level (x_1) and Review Effectiveness (x_2). A surface plot of the linear model is shown in Exhibit 15. The planar Defect Density surface indicates how quality of the software work product is influenced by two variables. The surface gently slopes towards the high performance point with the following coordinate values:

Skill Level	=	10
Review Effectiveness	=	50
Defect Density	=	2

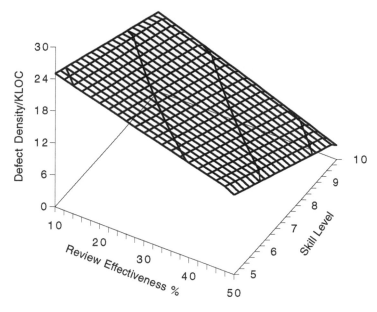

Exhibit 15. Surface plot.

This surface, being a plane, does not offer optimum points but only indicates the general direction of process improvement.

Regression Model Application

Regression models have huge application potential in software engineering and management. They support the creation of a wide variety of knowledge products from simple visual display of relationships to estimation equations. They can reflect real situations in different degrees of detail, ranging from simple two-variable models to complex multiple variable models. They can capture process nonlinearity and allow us to exploit this knowledge, either in optimization or in risk avoidance. A few regression model examples built using Excel on practical data are presented in the remaining part of this chapter.

Application 1: Process Optimization

Controlling effort variance (EV%) is of paramount importance in projects. We study the process for factors which cause effort variance.

Such a study begins with the search for relationship between potential predictors (independent variables) and effort variance (dependent variable). For regression analysis we consider requirement effort data along with effort variance for nine projects. The data table and its regression analysis are shown in Exhibit 16. It may be seen from the results that effort

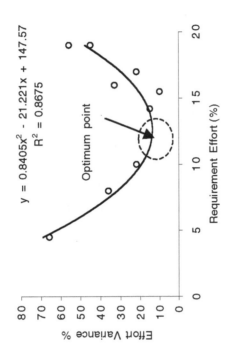

Req. Eff. %	Effort Variance %
4.5	66
8	36
10	22
14.2	15
15.5	10
17	22
16	33
19	45
19	56

Exhibit 16. Optimization of the requirements effort.

variance depends on requirement effort according to a parabolic equation. The curve shows that there is an optimum value for requirement effort, where the effort variance takes minimum possible value. On either side of this optimum zone, effort variance increases. The confidence level in prescribing the optimum zone is given by the R^2 value; in this case it is about 86.75 percent. Because the confidence level is more than 75 percent, this optimization rule can be considered as an input for decision making.

This knowledge of existence of an optimum value for requirement effort helps in effort budgeting in the beginning of the project for optimum performance. It also helps to set process goals based on objective understanding.

The conventional cost functions are usually complex and require special data. However, in this example we have demonstrated an empirical cost function, which is derived from commonly available data.

Application 2: Forecasting Product Quality

It is a well-known principle in software engineering that product quality depends on design quality. Regression study will help in determining how much the dependence is. It will also yield an estimating equation connecting these two factors. If we can obtain an estimation equation, then forecasting product quality becomes possible from the effort spent on design.

First we must decide on the metrics that indicate product quality and design quality. Product quality is measured as defect density, while design quality is considered proportional to design effort%. These two metrics have been collected from a few projects and given in Exhibit 17. Regression analysis of the dataset is presented alongside the data table.

Observation supports the theoretical expectation that defect density comes down when design effort increases. But the confidence level available in this linear model is 53.42 percent. Even if this is taken at face value, without model refinement, the message is clear and cannot be ignored.

This case study is in agreement (as with the PSP studies by Humphrey) with the almost-universal finding that spending more effort in design yields better quality. This is an input for strategic planning of software projects.

Application 3: Defect Correlation

Defect forecast is the business of software reliability studies, an avowedly cumbersome area of research. Reliability models are used for accurate prediction of defects. If the objective is not accurate prediction, but a broad understanding of defect leakage to the field, then we can use a simple method such as defect correlation and regression model.

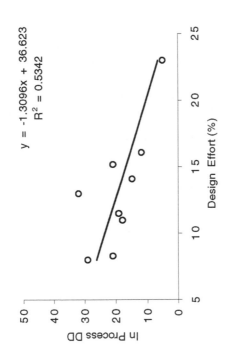

Design Effort %	In Process DD (Def /KLOC)
8.3	21
16.1	12
15.2	21
11.5	19.2
13	32
14.1	15
11	18
23	5
8	29

$$y = -1.3096x + 36.623$$
$$R^2 = 0.5342$$

Exhibit 17. Forecasting product quality from design effort.

In-process defects and customer reported defects data from a software project (at low maturity level) is presented as a table in Exhibit 18. The regression line shows a strong relationship with a good quality fit. The statistical dependence of field defects on in-process defects is not a surprise, and in fact is expected. But the magnitude of field defects is alarmingly high.

With 91.32 confidence level, we can foresee field defects even when in-process defects are uncovered. That gives us the rest of the project life cycle for doing something to prevent leakage of defects. For example, a special reliability enhancement program can be announced. The regression model now plays the role of an early warning system in the project.

Apart from this benefit, this model indirectly represents inadequacies in testing, arguing a case for process improvement there.

Application 4: Causal Analysis

Regression models are naturally poised for causal analysis application. The *x-y* relationship is a cause–effect relationship (in the predictor–predicted sense).

The regression analysis discussed here makes use of productivity data. requirement effort% has been chosen as the independent variable. The data and the nonlinear regression line fitted to the dataset are shown in Exhibit 19.

The association rule for causal analysis demands a good R^2, and we get a value of 64.34 percent. The extraneous data and outliers can be put aside and we can focus on the regression line to do causal analysis. Logic tells us that software productivity should improve with better requirement capturing (and a direction for causal analysis is set this way). The regression model (nonlinear, logarithmic) shows asymptotic rise in productivity, and we can see a shoulder on the curve after which it becomes flat. Requirement effort affects productivity up to a point, then either other factors take over or further investment on requirement does not yield return.

Application 5: Demonstrating How Review Makes Customers Happy (Indirectly)

The beneficial effects of review are increasingly recognized in the software industry. A regression model can demonstrate the effect quantitatively, lending credibility to the belief.

First, the choice of representative metrics is restricted to what is available and on going. Postdelivery defect density is taken as customer satisfaction index and Review Effort% is taken as the engineering variable.

Development Defects by Component	Usage Defects by Components
0	0
3	24
7	4
17	2
19	15
28	18
52	18
74	24
128	46
262	76
293	126

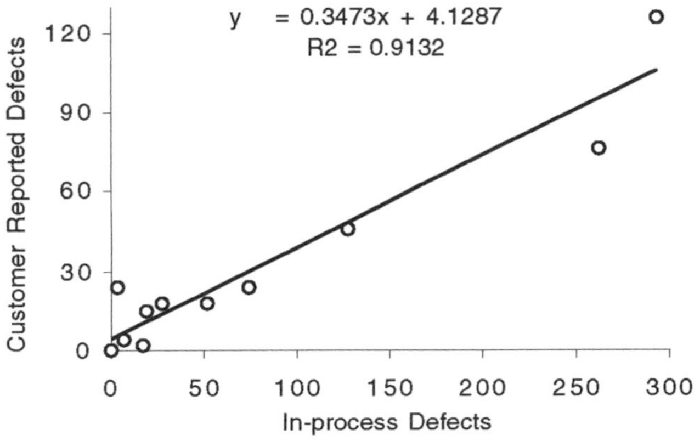
y = 0.3473x + 4.1287
R2 = 0.9132
Customer Reported Defects
0
30
60
90
120
0
50
100
150
200
250
300
In-process Defects

Exhibit 18. Forecasting field defects from in-process defects.

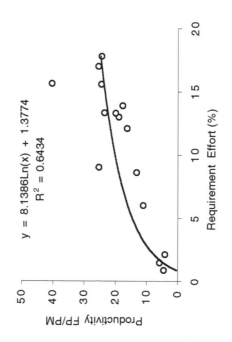

Requirement Effort	Productivity (FP/PM)
0.88	4.45
1.47	5.76
2.13	4
6.03	11
8.64	13.2
9.04	25.3
12.11	16.22
13.01	18.9
13.9	17.7
13.32	20
13.33	23.6
15.59	24.55
17.01	25.5
17.8	24.5
15.64	40.3

Exhibit 19. Influence of requirement analysis effort on productivity.

In many projects the correlation between these metrics is weak because of inadequacies in the defect measurement system and defect database management. Carefully collected data are presented in Exhibit 20, along with a nonlinear regression curve of 73.38 percent R^2.

The power equation shows the law of diminishing return, indicating the presence of many other factors affecting postdelivery defects. The curve begs the question, "is the minimum required effort spent on review?" so that the initial advantages are not lost (some projects register no relation at all between these metrics, where questions arise about the effectiveness of review, defect measurement capability, and defect discovery patterns).

Application 6: A Myth Breaks

Many of us have the habit of thinking in reflex that quality initiative cut into productive hours. We also think speed kills quality, and frame the familiar question "productivity or quality?".

The productivity data shown in Exhibit 21 has been drawn from life cycle projects, manned by freshly trained staff on the initial stages of their learning curve.

The regression analysis shows just the opposite of conventional thinking: productivity does increase quality (or perhaps quality should have the driver variable!).

It is one thing to hear stories about how organizations discovered this law and publicized it; it is quite a different matter to "realize" this with our own project data and see this truth established in our own lives.

There is overwhelming evidence to this model in many projects that the author has worked with. Similar curves have been obtained from projects with highly capable people, projects with different technology types. This data is used in setting productivity and quality goals for the organization.

Application 7: The Crossover

In maintenance projects speed of response is taken as the primary requirement. The service level agreements are to be adhered to satisfy customers. A regression model for quality, shown in Exhibit 22, has an important message.

The dependent variable, productivity, is measured as the ratio of number of defects per person month of effort. The independent variable, quality, is measured as the number of resulting bad-fixes per month.

The regression equation is nonlinear, a second-degree polynomial. Goodness of fit is a mere 26.1 percent, the data has wide scatter. The data points include different categories of bugs. Right now no distinction is

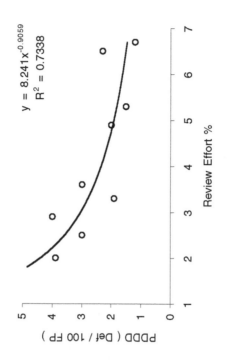

Review Effort %	PDDD (Def / 100 FP)
5.3	1.5
2	3.9
3.6	3
4.9	2
6.7	1.2
2.5	3
3.3	1.9
6.5	2.3
2.9	4
1.8	6.2

Exhibit 20. Review effort controls postdelivery density.

$$y = 8.241x^{-0.9059}$$
$$R^2 = 0.7338$$

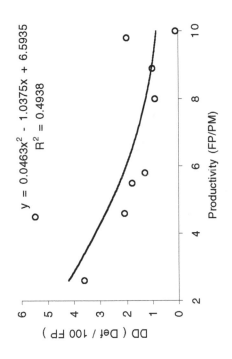

Productivity (FP / PM)	Defect Density (Def / 100 FP)
8	0.9
9.8	2
5.8	1.3
4.5	5.5
8.9	1
5.5	1.8
4.6	2.1
10	0.1
2.6	3.6

$$y = 0.0463x^2 - 1.0375x + 6.5935$$
$$R^2 = 0.4938$$

Exhibit 21. Productivity vs. quality: life cycle projects.

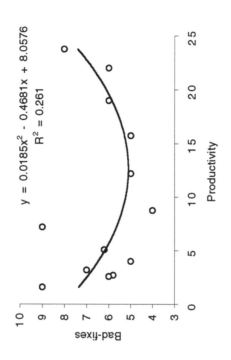

Productivity	Bad-Fixes
5.1	6
19.0	6
12.2	5
4.0	5
23.8	8
8.8	4
1.6	9
2.7	6
7.2	9
2.6	6
15.8	5
22.0	6
3.2	7

$y = 0.0185x^2 - 0.4681x + 8.0576$

$R^2 = 0.261$

Exhibit 22. Maintenance project.

made between these, and that is one of the reasons for the lack of association. The noise levels are low in these measurements and can be ignored.

Productivity, or bug fixing speed, seems to drive quality to start with. Soon it reaches a turning point, and any further increase in speed affects quality. In this example, the organizational goal was to fix 24 bugs a month; the "constraint" equation suggests an optimum of about 15 bugs a month as possible goal. The choice depends on whether we optimize on speed or optimize on quality. (We can show this constraint model to the customer, and if he agrees, the goal can be readjusted to the optimum value.)

Application 8: Optimum Team Size?

That there exists an optimum team size has been much discussed and widely quoted. But what are the facts? A regression model of team size on productivity reveals the real picture.

Team size productivity data is shown in Exhibit 23, and the graph shows the nonlinear regression curve, a power equation, which fits to an R^2 of 42.28 percent.

According to the regression model, when the team grows away from the organic small size, its productivity decreases exponentially. The nonlinear model does permit optimization of team size; it imposes a constraint equation on software projects. Choice is made not based on the intrinsic demonstration of best among the lot prediction but based on other factors. For example, a strategic limit on minimum productivity would dictate the team size limit.

In those cases, where a larger team size is chosen based on other considerations, from the model we know what would be the corresponding loss in productivity, and take appropriate counter measures.

This model would also help in breaking work packages to smaller units and operate the project with the proverbial small teams.

Application 9: Detecting Hidden Problems

In this application example, the regression model exposes a hidden process problem. Size and quality data of software components are presented in Exhibit 24. The regression line is nonlinear, with an extraordinary sharp decrease in defect level as size increases from 1 KLOC to 10 KLOC. Afterward, the improvement in quality is slow.

The regression model makes us think about small and big projects, the transition occurring around 10 KLOC. It would also have us propose a hypothesis that smaller projects have poor quality level, and larger projects are better.

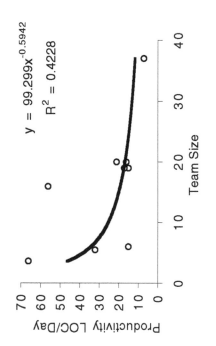

$$y = 99.299x^{-0.5942}$$
$$R^2 = 0.4228$$

Team Size	Productivity LOC/day
6	15
3.6	66
37	7
19	15
19	17
20	21
5.5	32
16	56
20	16

Exhibit 23. Team size constraints on productivity.

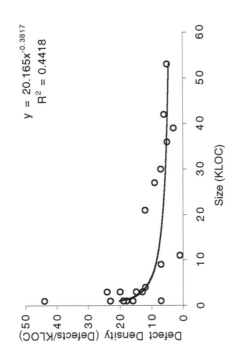

$y = 20.165x^{-0.3817}$
$R^2 = 0.4418$

Size	Defect Density	Size	Defect Density
1	7	3	24
1	16	4	12
1	18	9	7
1	44	11	1
1	19	21	12
1	23	27	9
3	20	30	7
3	13	36	5
3	15	39	3
3	24	42	6
4	12	53	5

Exhibit 24. Size vs. defect density.

This model is a common experience in several software projects. Those who have normalized defects by effort and expressed quality as Defect Injection Rate also have experienced a similar trend.

Many reasons have been proposed by practitioners to explain this "anomalous" behavior:

> *Larger works never get fully tested. Smaller projects never get their engineering right, there is never time. Reuse in larger projects could change the metric. Larger projects benefit from the learning curve.*

And so on.

Use of this regression model as an estimator of defect level has been questioned. But this model has been an eye opener to many; it has made people examine and reexamine their engineering practices.

Application 10: Analysis of Defect Discovery Economics

Economics in defect discovery has remained a focal point of software engineering. Creating mathematical cost models for defect discovery is by no means a small task. It has been known that such a cost model for defect discovery contains in it software reliability functions too. That doubles the significance of defect discovery cost model. The financial metric helps in cost reduction in the first place; it also helps in reliability management.

By regression, we can create an empirical cost model of defect discovery as derived from the following metrics data:

- Review effectiveness (RE)
- Cost of fixing bugs discovered by review (RC)
- Cost of fixing bugs discovered by tests (TC)
- Total cost of fixing bugs

Based on effort log sheets, the cost of bug fixing has been estimated in some projects and presented in relative units as well as a normalized function in Exhibit 25. Along with that regression analysis of cost of bug fixing as a function of review effectiveness is also presented. The model is non-linear (logarithmic) and agrees with the expected trend: the cost of bug fixing decreases when review effectiveness increases. This confirms the view that tests are costlier than reviews, eventually.

Reliability Hinterland

When the review effectiveness increases, reviews capture more and more bugs, leaving less bugs for tests to discover, and as a consequence, the bug lifetimes becomes shorter and shorter. There is a precept that the less time bugs live in software, the more reliable the software is. While interpreting this regression line, the reliability hinterland may be remembered as a background scenario.

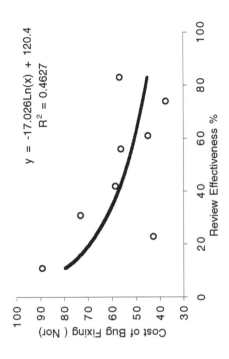

y = -17.026Ln(x) + 120.4
R^2 = 0.4627

Review Effectiveness	Cost of Bug Fixing	Normalized Cost
11	625	89.29
23	300	42.86
31	512	73.14
42	411	58.71
56	395	56.43
61	315	45.00
74	262	37.43
83	399	57.00

Exhibit 25. Nonlinear regression model (normalized cost of bug fixing).

Exhibit 26. Theoretical estimates of "normalized cost of bug fixing."

RE%	Cost of Defect Fixing		
	(TC/RC) = 10	(TC/RC) = 6	(TC/RC) = 4
100	10.0	16.7	25.0
90	19.0	25.0	32.5
83	25.3	30.8	37.8
80	28.0	33.3	40.0
74	33.4	38.3	44.5
70	37.0	41.7	47.5
61	45.1	49.2	54.3
60	46.0	50.0	55.0
56	49.6	53.3	58.0
50	55.0	58.3	62.5
42	62.2	65.0	68.5
40	64.0	66.7	70.0
31	72.1	74.2	76.8
30	73.0	75.0	77.5
23	79.3	80.8	82.8
20	82.0	83.3	85.0
11	90.1	90.8	91.8
10	91.0	91.7	92.5
0	100.0	100.0	100.0

Note: RE = Review Effectiveness; TC = Testing Cost;
RC = Review Cost.

Goodness of Fit

To qualify as a cost model we need to improve the goodness of fit from the present 46.27 percent to higher values. Statistical transformation of the data is one way of achieving a better fit used by data analysts often.

Theoretical Limits

We wish to refine the model by imposing theoretical curves for cost and remove data points that do not lie within the bounds set by logical expectations. To do that, we create theoretical cost function that is based on the ratio of cost of bug fixing by testing (TC) and the cost of bug fixing by review (RC). The ratio TC/RC has been studied by many, and the values vary. Most practical observations (in the type of projects from where data has been collected) of this ratio, range from 4 to 10. Theoretical cost functions for this scenario are presented in Exhibit 26 and superimposed on the regression line in Exhibit 27.

142

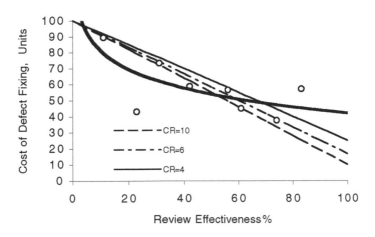

Exhibit 27. Finding outliers (superimposition of theoretical estimate curves on regression line).

Refining the Model

The theoretical boundaries shown in Exhibit 27 provide a rule to detect and remove outliers. The data points, which are far away from the theoretical limits, require special analysis, but right now we have enough reasons to keep them out of model building.

Refined Model

With the outliers removed, the dataset now shows better regression, as illustrated in Exhibit 28. After refinement, the regression model has become linear and the goodness of fit is 97.15 percent. The model now has agreeable qualities.

Standard Error vs. Theoretical Boundaries

Detecting process outliers based on a statistical approach will lead us to the sloping control chart, explained earlier in Exhibit 10. Standard errors-based limit lines were used to locate outliers.

But using theoretical models, as in Exhibit 27, to locate abnormalities is preferred. At the end of model building, we now have a validated theory and strengthened our knowledge. Without theoretical analysis, the whole exercise is merely statistical, which takes much longer and much later to learn the complete meaning.

Application 11: Building an Effort Estimation Model

Predicting effort from size has been a favorite game for several researchers. They go by the name of cost models and estimation models (some are illustrated in Chapter 8).

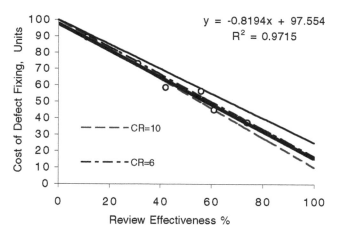

$$y = -0.8194x + 97.554$$
$$R^2 = 0.9715$$

Exhibit 28. Refined regression model (after removal of outliers).

Exhibit 29. Effort data.

Size (FP)	Effort (Hrs)	Size (FP)	Effort (Hrs)	Size (FP)	Effort (Hrs)
305	5152	92	840	514	19894
321	5635	258	5180	308	6699
100	805	438	5775	505	14987
319	3829	382	10577	259	4004
234	2149	289	3983	311	12824
186	2821	316	3164	145	2331
238	3913	306	3542	204	5817
260	7854	472	4277	188	2989
116	2422	286	7252	135	3136
266	4047	452	3948	342	14434
258	9051	207	3927	157	2583
105	2282	285	6405	177	2520
223	4172	404	5922	143	1603
344	4977	499	4620	300	2800
100	3192	118	2174	588	9520

Our objective here is to apply regression modeling to design an effort estimation model from data commonly available in projects, namely, effort and size. Some practical data is provided in Exhibit 29.

Expectation

The metrics used here are effort in hours and size in function points. Size is taken as the independent variable. The expected relationship, based on several experiences, is a power equation of the form

144

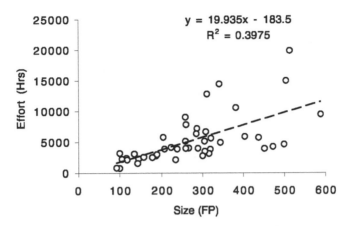

Exhibit 30. Effort estimation from size: the first regression.

$$\text{Effort} = a\ \text{Size}^b \qquad\qquad (7.8)$$

where a and b are constants.

We also expect complications in regression model building. Size measurements can have errors, which will interfere with regression.

Analysis

Regression analysis of the dataset is shown in Exhibit 30. A linear regression line appears with goodness of fit 39.75 percent, a poor value for an estimation model. There is a large scatter of data. The model requires improvement.

Presentation of such scatter plots sometimes invites criticism. Lack of clear trend makes people give up and lose interest in analysis. They conclude that "if you have enough data you can prove any theory." The problem is quite basic. The step that had been missed in data collection is "categorization," a discipline lower in the rank of measurement scales but which could bring in clarity.

Clustering

By examining the scatter plot in Exhibit 30 we may notice that there is a possibility for clustering, regrouping data according to some logical rule, and try separate regressions for each cluster. The exploratory data analysis indicates a natural divide in the data, worth finding.

Now we know that there must be logic for regrouping which is based on some physical reasoning, such as types of projects, nature of technology,

Exhibit 31. Clustered data.

	Cluster 1				Cluster 2		
Size (FP)	Effort (Hrs)	Size (FP)	Effort (Hrs)	Size (FP)	Effort (Hrs)	Size (FP)	Effort (Hrs)
100		266	4047	100	805	266	
92	840	223		92		223	4172
143	1603	472	4277	143		472	
234	2149	499	4620	234		499	
118		344	4977	118	2174	344	
105	2282	305	5152	105		305	
145	2331	258		145		258	5180
116	2422	321	5635	116		321	
177	2520	438	5775	177		438	
157	2583	204		157		204	5817
300	2800	404	5922	300		404	
186	2821	285		186		285	6405
188	2989	308		188		308	6699
135		286		135	3136	286	7252
316	3164	260		316		260	7854
318		258		318	3192	258	9051
306	3542	588	9520	306		588	
319	3829	382		319		382	10577
238	3913	311		238		311	12824
207	3927	342		207		342	14434
452	3948	505		452		505	14987
289	3983	514		289		514	19894
259	4004			259			

and even year of completion. Histograms can be used to test for existence of strong clusters.

The data was grouped into two clusters. The regrouped data is shown in Exhibit 31.

New Regression Models

The new regression lines, obtained after clustering, are shown in Exhibit 32. The goodness of fit figures is 83.44 percent for one and 67.63 percent for the other. Regression quality is far better than what we had in the first run. This is an example that emphasizes the need for iterative runs in model building.

We can continue the iteration with further clustering, transformation, partitioning, or other means of model refinement. We can also search for better equations. Of course, we can go to multiple linear regressions and achieve better and better models. It is a process by itself. The quest is

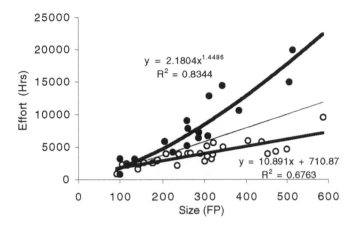

Exhibit 32. Regression after clustering.

brought to an end, when we have a reasonable model which will have reasonable confidence level and which agrees with common sense.

Important Lesson

This application proves one principle: estimation models predict better within their own families. Each estimation model represents a narrow world, inside which it operates best. There is no universal estimation model.

Hence, even if we have just a few data points, better to build our own estimation model, one for each family.

Application 12: Calibration of Intuitive Models

Calibration: Ascertaining Prediction Errors

Calibration is one of the major applications of regression modeling. All estimation models require calibration. The idea of calibration is normally associated with measuring devices. Measuring equipments have errors and calibration is a process by which the errors are determined by comparing the readings with real values. After calibration, the error table can be used to predict the true value from the value indicated.

We have already seen how estimation can be regarded as a form of measurement. In this sense, the estimation model can be equated to the measuring device.

Instead of an error table, we look at the relationship between the estimated value and the actual value for calibrating the estimation model. In this context, the regression line, which represents this relationship, is known as calibration curve.

147

In good estimation, the actual value and predicted values agree very closely. In most cases a linear regression line captures this close relationship, in which case the slope of the regression line is nearly equal to one. The coefficient of determination R_2 in this case indicates "estimation capability" of the model used for estimation. It is common to come across R_2 values greater than 95 percent in full life cycle projects. If reestimation is done in the project after the requirements are understood better, the R_2 value has been increased to 98 percent. In maintenance project, R_2 value falls to about 65 percent in many practical cases. This indicates a shortfall in the estimation capability in such projects due to well-known reasons: Estimation of bug fixing is done in a hurry and also validated models are not available.

Building a calibration model is easier and certainly less expensive than building our own estimation model. But it must be made certain that if the estimation model changes then the calibration model should be reestablished.

Regression Analysis

Calibration of quantitative estimation models is statistically rigorous exercise, where measurement errors, bias, frequency distribution characteristics of data, and noise will have to be determined before we begin calibration.

We are now dealing with intuitive models, like what is used for estimation of bug fixing effort in a maintenance project. In Exhibit 33, we present maintenance project data on bug fixing effort.

The planned and actual values are plotted as scatter diagrams and regression analysis is made. It is found that linear regression fits well. Two kinds of linear equations have been tried. The first one has a y intercept, the second one does not have (passes through origin), as shown in Exhibit 33.

Fantasy Factor

The second model gives a thumb rule by declaring that the actual bug fixing effort will be 1.2419 times the estimated value. The slope of the equation also becomes the multiplication factor. Bill Hetzel estimated this factor to be around 1.22 and called it the "Fantasy Factor." For reasons best known to mankind, we have been underestimating all our jobs by a predictable factor. This factor can be used to predict true values.

Estimation Quality

The R_2 values, which express goodness of fit of the calibration curves, can also indicate the estimation quality. In life cycle projects, calibration

148

Est. days	Actual Days	Est. days	Actual Days
1	5	14	20
3	4	15	15
3	5	15	15
3	9	15	21
3.5	4	16	22
4	4	17	23
5	7	18	24
6	12	20	25
10	8	20	30
10	16	21	24
11	13	21	32
11	16	24	50
12	12	25	30
12	18	25	31
13	15	28	29
13	19	28	30
14	12	28	31
14	15	33	46
14	19	40	38

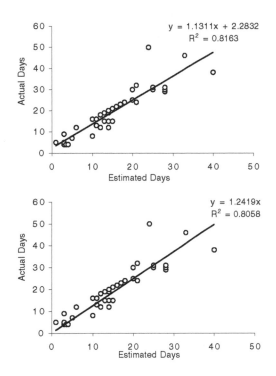

Exhibit 33. Calibration curves.

curves usually show confidence levels higher than 95 percent. In maintenance projects, where estimation is a quick assessment, the present values 81.63 percent and 80. 68 percent for the two models are considered good. Still, the industry is gearing up to come out with better estimation processes in maintenance.

Evaluating the Estimation Model

Partitioning. The data is split into two ranges, creating a partition between the small and large bugs. The result is creation of two ranges which tests the performance of the estimation model by regression analysis.

The partitioned dataset is given in Exhibit 34. Calibration curves in the two ranges, small and large bugs, are also shown in Exhibit 34. Goodness of fit in the two ranges is 70.12 and 47.81 percent, respectively.

This partition analysis exposes a problem: estimation quality in the case of larger bugs is inferior and requires improvement. Analysis of the entire data as a whole could not reveal this nuance.

Range I		Range II	
Est. days	Actual Days	Est. days	Actual Days
1	5	15	15
3	4	15	15
3	5	15	21
3	9	16	22
3.5	4	17	23
4	4	18	24
5	7	20	25
6	12	20	30
10	8	21	24
10	16	21	32
11	13	24	50
11	16	25	30
12	12	25	31
12	18	28	29
13	15	28	30
13	19	28	31
14	12	33	46
14	15	40	38
14	19	-	-
14	20	-	-

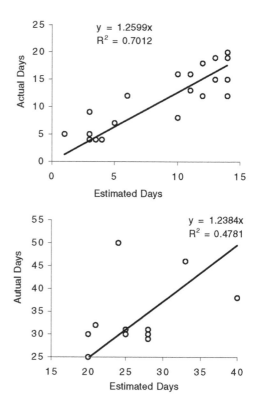

Exhibit 34. Calibration curves with ranges.

Performance of Calibrated Estimation Model. The final test is to see how the intuitive estimation model behaves after calibration. After applying the correction factors derived from the regression model shown in Exhibit 33, the revised estimates have been computed and plotted in Exhibit 35.

The regression line shows a new calibration curve where the actual value is equal to the estimated value. It may be noted that the confidence level, however, remains the same at 80.58 percent.

More Applications

There is no limit to the application possibilities of regression. With the help of tools it is so simple and perhaps the most natural form of analysis. There is no doubt that the best value of metrics is realized by regression analysis. We have presented a few representative examples in this chapter, but there are many more possibilities.

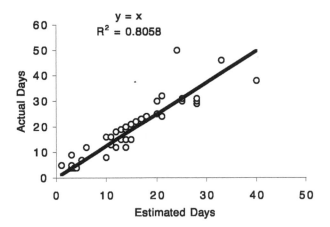

Exhibit 35. Calibrated estimation model.

Chapter 8
Process Models

From Analysis to Systems Thinking

Systems thinking is to move from metrics analysis toward synthesis, from single-variable perspective to multi-variable perspective, from single-dimensional consideration to multi-dimensional considerations. Systems thinking involves creating process maps and process models for interactive decision-making, keeping system goals in mind all the way.

A higher-level map is to be created before designing process models. For creating the map, the following four categories of processes in software development may be considered:

1. Project management processes
2. Process management processes
3. Engineering processes
4. Support processes

All these processes work as a system to make deliveries to the customer. Inputs may be taken from suppliers. The idea of a process map expands to include both the customer and supplier processes. A hierarchy of process models now can be envisaged to represent the selected processes or sub-processes. In the systems approach, the process metrics are applied to build an integrated whole, which relates to business goals and results.

Model Building: Knowledge Consolidation

A model is a representation of the real world. We break a complex problem into manageable parts and use a model to describe how they are linked together. The power of the model is not in the complexity of the mathematics, it is in the way the problem is broken down and organized into a structure.

Each model addresses and hence remains relevant to definite goals, such as decision making or problem solving; each model is based on several assumptions. Due to practical reasons, a model is often built from a local perspective of a global situation. The scope of model application is correspondingly approximate, limited in reach, and local in perspective.

Models are of great practical use, although they are imitations of the real world. Process models are known to be supportive of the following activities:

- Process management
  - Process capability study
  - Process control
  - Process improvement
  - Process optimization
- Project management
  - Strategic management
  - Technology management
  - Knowledge management
  - Uncertainty management
- Forecasting
  - Prediction
  - Risk analysis
  - Estimation
  - Planning
- Learning
  - Process characterization
  - Process simulation
  - Decision analysis
  - Problem solving
  - Training and learning

Models are knowledge structures created in convenient forms that allow use and reuse by the authors and others. Without model building, the vast array of knowledge elements — scattered across the organization, embedded in the memory cells of humans, present as fragments in records — run the risk of being lost to posterity. Models are legacies from history, extracted from experience waves, created by process innovators. They are also process learning centers.

Theoretical Models: The Soul

The soul of models lie in the conceptual framework which had originally inspired model building, helped in the selection of parameters, influenced the choice of functions, and in the case of discrete modeling helped in deciding on the discrete levels. Theoretical models represent an expected behavior and can be expressed in several forms, including:

- Verbal description
- Table
- Flow chart
- Diagrams
- Graphical presentation
- Simulation methods
- Linear programming
- Equation
- Computer algorithm

Process metrics will be used to denote variables while constructing mathematical models. Semantic measurements are used in other models. Both bring out the inner order of processes.

Basic Empirical Models

Empirical models are built from data. They do not aim to explain but predict process behavior. A combination of exploratory data analysis methods and statistical techniques can be used to build empirical models from metrics data. The value (and complexity) of a model increases with the number of metrics it uses.

Models Using Single Metric (Analytical Models)

Single metric models result from data analysis in time and frequency domains. The most common application of these models lies in establishing baselines and probability curves such as the normal and Rayleigh distributions. These models help very much in process control and process capability analysis. Design of analytical models, interpretation of them, and pattern recognition possibilities from these models have been outlined in Chapters 5 and 6.

Models Using Two Metrics (Regression Models)

Two metrics models — regression models — result from analysis in the relationship domain. In their simplest form, these are scatter plots. We can fit regression curves to these data and generate rigorous models, linear and nonlinear, if needed.

Visual Models

Visual models such as the Radar chart or Pareto chart have the inherent power to present multiple metrics data in one window, more for understanding, and less for prediction. The matrix structure is another form that allows analysis of complex relationships between two sets of variables; matrix cells can be filled with semantic expressions or numeric values, making the matrices either merely visual models or rigorous numerical models. Matrices can switch their levels of rigor and mathematical power.

Decision Support

The basic empirical models fulfill their intended purpose of supporting decision making; examples are listed in Exhibit 1.

Higher-Level Empirical Models

Higher-level empirical models deal with real-life complexities more earnestly. The multivariate treatment of cost by a Constructive Cost Model

Exhibit 1. Examples of analytical models for decision making.

Model Name	Decision Support	Number of Metrics Used
Effort profile	Strategic budgeting	Single
Defect profile	Indicates process maturity	Single
Defect signature	Helps in expecting defects	Many
Matrix	Multivariate modeling	Many
Radar	Influence balancing	Many
Pareto chart	Prioritization	Many
Control chart	Identifies outliers, creates baseline	Single
Trend chart	Forecast	Single
Moving average	Detect seasonal fluctuations	Single
Histogram	Process tendencies	Single
Empirical frequency distribution	Risk prediction, goal setting	Single
Regression line	Creates estimation models, calibration curves	Two

(COCOMO), presented in Chapter 8, is a noteworthy example. Building such a sophisticated and powerful model requires a great deal of scientific effort, a great deal of data collection and analysis, and a rigorous approach. Building such a model is like building a tool, the project must be sponsored and the cost shared by users.

We wish to consider those higher-level models which practitioners can build with ease. We need models that can be constructed within project life cycles by project team members. Pragmatism would drive us to parsimonious approaches to model building. This is an area where continuous innovation is in progress. New forms are discovered every day somewhere in some projects. We are glad to present a few examples of such an approach.

Approaches for building parsimonious empirical models at the higher level, which are illustrated in this chapter, are

- Descriptive statistics on multiple metrics
- Multiple analysis of single metrics
- Three analytical dimensions
- Process diagnostic panel
- Analytical summary of single metrics
- Global summary of metrics system
- Correlation matrix
- Multiple scatter plots
- DOE

Pragmatism, economy, and simplicity have been achieved in these models by relying on visual synthesis of analysis results instead of attempting complicated mathematical treatments.

Descriptive Statistics on Multiple Metrics

Descriptive Statistics

A basic but comprehensive treatment of metrics data is achieved by descriptive statistics. Following is a list of estimates presented as descriptive statistics summary by Excel:

- Mean
- Standard error
- Median
- Mode
- Standard deviation
- Sample variance
- Kurtosis
- Skewness
- Range
- Minimum
- Maximum
- Sum
- Count

This descriptive statistics model examines, by means of its components, several key aspects of process behavior including:

- Central tendency
- Variation
- Bias

In all, these statistics characterize a process and can be called a single-variable rudimentary model. The nuances and anomalies in process behavior seen through a single metric window is brought out in this model.

Building a Multiple Metrics Model

To build a multiple metrics model, we need to choose a set of metrics that we think will characterize the process chosen for modeling. For example, let us see how we can build a process model of the descriptive statistics kind using available core metrics.

We begin with a goal of characterizing the business process using the following critical factors selected and presented here:

- Growth
- Customer satisfaction
- Profit

- Excellence in software engineering
- Human resource
- Productivity
- Quality
- Fixed assets performance

Business performance involves eight factors, the first three representing results and the remaining five denoting what causes the results.

Then we will proceed to select metrics that capture each of the critical factors. We may have to design new metrics if we do not already have the required metrics. A practical method is to choose from the existing metrics plan. In this example, the following metrics have been selected from a running metrics system:

- Market share%
- Customer satisfaction index (scale 0 to 10)
- Rework
- Effort variance%
- Schedule variance%
- Size variance%
- Review effectiveness
- Absentees%
- Productivity
- Defect density
- Downtime of assets

One can map these metrics to the goal factors and ensure that the right metrics have been selected. Sometimes we cannot find perfect mapping; some metrics may be weakly coupled to the goal factors. Then we have to balance the cost of defining a new metric and collecting additional data against the benefits.

We can get descriptive statistics for each metric. Only seven statistics have been chosen for this modeling. If these 7 statistical estimates can be compiled for all the 11 metrics and shown in the format given in Exhibit 2, then we build a higher level model. This model gives an 11-metric snapshot of business performance and makes it easier for the user to make judgments. Seeing all the metrics statistics in a single framework promotes strategic views. Snapshots of the previous years can be compared with the present. Cognitive perception of the multi-metrics data may yield clues to strengths and weaknesses.

Similar models can be created for different levels of the organization. There is a possibility of building an exclusive model for each of the support processes, supplier processes, engineering processes, etc. Hierarchy in such models follows hierarchy in the metrics plan.

Exhibit 2. Multiple metrics model using descriptive statistics.

Metric	Descriptive Statistics						
	Mean	**Median**	**Mode**	**Std. Dev.**	**Max.**	**Min.**	**Range**
Market share							
Customer satisfaction index							
Effort variance							
Schedule variance							
Size variance							
Defect density							
Review effectiveness							
Productivity							
Rework							
Downtime of assets							
Absentees (percent)							

Multiple Analysis of Single Metrics

In this model, we take a single metric and perform multiple analysis to understand and illustrate a complex process behavior. Let us consider measurement of effort in software components. From this measurement alone, we can develop the most commonly used metric called effort variance% by calculating normalized deviation from budgeted effort. If we choose to analyze this metric in the time domain, we can perform at least the following four analyses, instead of stopping with the control chart:

1. Run chart
2. Linear trend
3. Moving average trend
4. Control charts with UCL and LCL

Each analysis presents a certain view of the process in time domain. Exhibit 3 illustrates a pack of four time series analysis graphs. The run chart reveals a broad process behavior. The linear trend chart captures a heavily averaged process trend, useful in strategic forecasting. The moving average trend chart registers the slow local variations, and cautions if any systematic trends exist. The control chart serves dual purposes. On one hand, it serves as a baseline from which one can expect process performance; on the other hand, based on the defined LCL and UCL, it points to outliers for root cause analysis and corrective action.

159

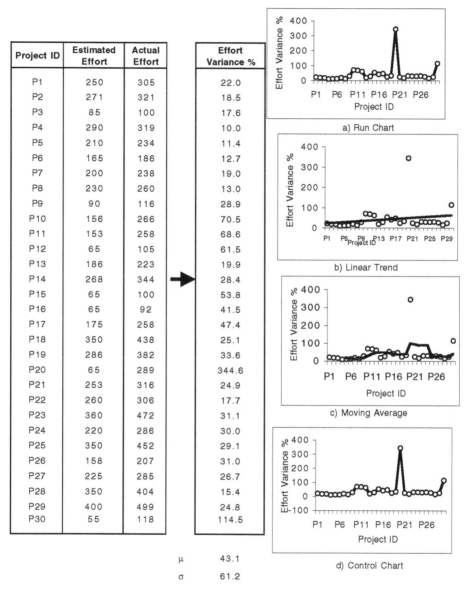

Project ID	Estimated Effort	Actual Effort		Effort Variance %
P1	250	305		22.0
P2	271	321		18.5
P3	85	100		17.6
P4	290	319		10.0
P5	210	234		11.4
P6	165	186		12.7
P7	200	238		19.0
P8	230	260		13.0
P9	90	116		28.9
P10	156	266		70.5
P11	153	258		68.6
P12	65	105		61.5
P13	186	223		19.9
P14	268	344		28.4
P15	65	100		53.8
P16	65	92		41.5
P17	175	258		47.4
P18	350	438		25.1
P19	286	382		33.6
P20	65	289		344.6
P21	253	316		24.9
P22	260	306		17.7
P23	360	472		31.1
P24	220	286		30.0
P25	350	452		29.1
P26	158	207		31.0
P27	225	285		26.7
P28	350	404		15.4
P29	400	499		24.8
P30	55	118		114.5

μ   43.1

σ   61.2

a) Run Chart

b) Linear Trend

c) Moving Average

d) Control Chart

Exhibit 3. Time series analysis graphs.

Seeing the Meaning

For good interpretation, effort values are assumed to be expressions of project cost, having a strong bearing on human resource utilization. The effort variance metric, seen through the four graphs, therefore emerges with the following meanings:

- Resource utilization
- Budget
- Estimation accuracy
- Implementation commitment
- Organizational learning

In the first place, we expect a learning curve. Events after events are passing by, and the most natural process in a human system is experiential learning by repeatedly doing things. Learning is expected in financial control and estimation capability. Both these expectations demand a trend where effort variance steadily falls with time.

The possibility of seasonal variations also catches our eye from the moving average model. A point to be considered before dismissal, possibly.

The control charts bring to our attention the outliers that have crossed the border — the threshold limits. We question whether the organization has seen and responded to the extreme deviations. We also wonder whether proper goals have been set at the process level, and the disadvantages of not meeting the goals have been communicated with clarity.

Creating Additional Metrics from the Same Data

Additional metrics can be created from the same data, at no extra cost of data collection. In the current example, instead of normalizing effort variations by the estimated effort, we can compute the absolute value of effort escalation (or cost escalation).

Percentage variation is one thing, absolute escalation is another. Large percentages in small amounts may be less significant than small percentages in large amounts. Creating a second metric as a cost function in Exhibit 4 presents a completely different picture. The outliers are different, the warning signals occur at different points of time. The cost function (absolute value of effort escalation) shows a serious financial problem that is not highlighted in the traditional metric.

If such a thing as creating the second or third meaningful metric from the same data were possible, by all means we should extend the model to include the new perspective.

Exhibit 3 and Exhibit 4 illustrate two different approaches in creating multiple analysis graphs from the same data.

Three Analytical Dimensions

Process behaves in three dimensions: frequency, time, and relationship. Process is to be felt and sensed in the three orthogonal dimensions, shown in Exhibit 5. This is a fundamental concept in process analysis. Seeing in a single

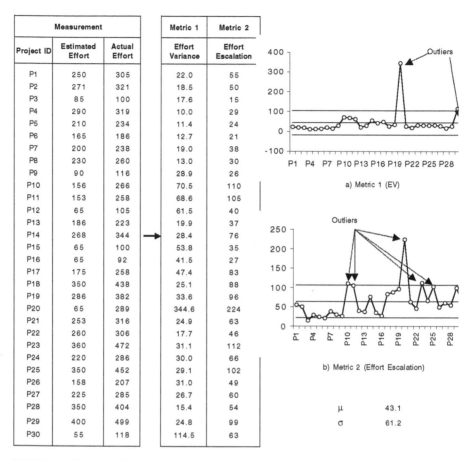

Measurement			Metric 1	Metric 2
Project ID	Estimated Effort	Actual Effort	Effort Variance	Effort Escalation
P1	250	305	22.0	55
P2	271	321	18.5	50
P3	85	100	17.6	15
P4	290	319	10.0	29
P5	210	234	11.4	24
P6	165	186	12.7	21
P7	200	238	19.0	38
P8	230	260	13.0	30
P9	90	116	28.9	26
P10	156	266	70.5	110
P11	153	258	68.6	105
P12	65	105	61.5	40
P13	186	223	19.9	37
P14	268	344	28.4	76
P15	65	100	53.8	35
P16	65	92	41.5	27
P17	175	258	47.4	83
P18	350	438	25.1	88
P19	286	382	33.6	96
P20	65	289	344.6	224
P21	253	316	24.9	63
P22	260	306	17.7	46
P23	360	472	31.1	112
P24	220	286	30.0	66
P25	350	452	29.1	102
P26	158	207	31.0	49
P27	225	285	26.7	60
P28	350	404	15.4	54
P29	400	499	24.8	99
P30	55	118	114.5	63

a) Metric 1 (EV)

b) Metric 2 (Effort Escalation)

μ   43.1

σ   61.2

Exhibit 4. Control charts: two metrics derived from same data (different messages).

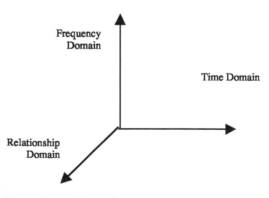

Exhibit 5. Three dimensions of metrics.

ID	Effort PM	Size DSLOC	Productivity DSLOC/PM
1	1.0	300	300.00
2	2.3	450	195.65
3	0.9	200	222.22
4	0.2	24	120.00
5	1.2	232	193.33
6	1.2	435	362.50
7	0.2	22	110.00
8	0.6	56	93.33
9	0.5	43	86.00
10	1.0	124	124.00
11	1.1	321	291.82
12	1.0	345	345.00
13	1.3	455	350.00
14	2.0	645	322.50
15	4.0	1002	250.50
16	3.8	945	248.68
17	2.7	730	270.37
18	0.8	230	287.50
19	1.1	435	395.45
20	1.1	354	321.82
21	1.0	322	322.00
22	0.8	244	305.00
23	1.0	343	343.00
24	1.0	321	320.00
25	3.9	945	242.31
26	0.9	349	387.78
27	1.2	284	236.67
28	1.4	463	330.71

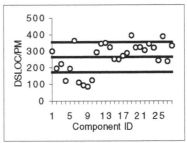

a) Time Series Baseline

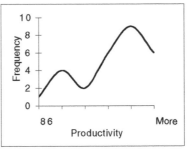

b) Frequency Distribution

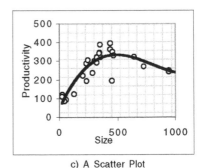

c) A Scatter Plot

Exhibit 6. Composite view from three analytical dimensions.

dimension lacks depth and misses out on many precious details. In the experience of the author, there is no process problem that lies outside this three-dimensional analytical universe. Dimensions of even the most complex problem can be reduced to just these three meaningful sets. For example, software productivity, defined in the simplest possible style as the ratio of effort to size, is analyzed in three dimensions, and the results are shown as a composite picture in Exhibit 6, which consists of the following graphs:

- The time series baseline
- Frequency distribution showing two modes
- A scatter plot between size and productivity

163

The time series baseline gives a first-order picture of the process, which is centered on mean and sigma. The probability curve projects the most common behavior. The scatter plot finds a governing relationship showing how size influences productivity. These three graphs present the process capability, the goal, and a process constraint, respectively. Seeing the three graphs together and comparing the messages we detect a hidden process problem.

The frequency diagram shows a tendency, the dominant one looks worthy of becoming an aggressive goal. Without seeing the frequency diagram, if one sets productivity goal there could be a critical error of setting inferior goals because the mean of baseline is very much lower than the dominant mode.

The productivity metric is decomposed, and the relationship patterns between the elemental factors are exposed. Scatter plots can be drawn between chosen pairs. Here the goal (productivity) and a driver (size) are studied.

The scatter diagram reveals a more-basic constraint: it shows a nonlinear dependency of productivity on size. The productivity initially increases with size, reaches a saturation point, and then drops beyond imagination. Perhaps the productivity goal depends on size.

Viewed independently, the graphs would not have highlighted the problem — and educated the viewer. Visual synthesis helps in discovering unseen problems.

In this example, problem discovery can lead to the following benefits:

- Perfection in goals setting
- Precision in metrics data collection
- More effective resource allocation

Process decisions are best taken from a composite view of all three dimensions. Thus visual synthesis of the graphical analysis is easy and effective in achieving a balanced judgment of the process under study.

Process Diagnostic Panel

Analytical views, lower-level models, and graphs all can be combined to form a diagnostic panel — a super model to represent complex processes, such as the support process illustrated in Exhibit 7.

Where Mathematical Solutions Are Messy

Creating a mathematical model for the entire collection of support processes is very complicated. The support processes constitute the environment in which core processes function, a systems model for the environment has to cope up with two difficult tasks:

	Training Cost / Employee	Downtime of Assets (Hours)	Attrition %	Metrics Effort (PM / Q)	Process Improve-ments/Q
Metric					
Three Analytical Dimensions	TREND CHART	TREND CHART	TREND CHART	TREND CHART	TREND CHART
	HISTO-GRAM	HISTO-GRAM	HISTO-GRAM	HISTO-GRAM	HISTO-GRAM
	SCATTER PLOT	SCATTER PLOT	SCATTER PLOT	SCATTER PLOT	SCATTER PLOT
Multiple Metrics From Same Data	CTRL CHART I	CTRL CHART I	CTRL CHART I	CTRL CHART I	CTRL CHART I
	CTRL CHART II	CTRL CHART II	CTRL CHART II	CTRL CHART II	CTRL CHART II

Exhibit 7. Diagnostic panel for support processes.

- Developing an objective function
- Integrating exclusive elements

Formulating an osmosis model for influence of the environment on the core function; this model depends on very abstract factors that shape the organizational climate as well.

Erecting constraint equations for this model poses additional difficulties. The boundary value functions are blurred with statistical uncertainty terms. It will turn out that the support process is, in scientific terms, an ill-defined problem that defies classical solutions. An approach is to use discrete modeling of a continuous process and use finite element methods to solve the simultaneous equations. Instead of a rigorous effort first to formulate a scientific problem and then to solve the same by finite element methods or neural networks, we propose the construction of a diagnostic panel, as illustrated in Exhibit 7.

Heuristic Run

The diagnostic panel can be designed to provide dynamically changing views when different metrics are chosen. Given the fact that each of the

Exhibit 8. Analytical summary of single metrics.

Analysis Methods	Analysis Statistics	Baseline Value	Inferences
Control chart	Mean		
	UCL (1 sigma)		Outliers....
	LCL (1 sigma)		Outliers....
Linear trend	Equation		Forecast (next event)
	(R^2)		Confidence Level 80 percent
Moving average	Window:5		Forecast (next event)
Frequency	Mode		(Assigning the goal, capability, and risk percentage)
	Capability (percent)		
	Risk (percent)		

support processes may run a dozen metrics or more, dynamic choice makes the panel interactive. Using the five-element panel shown in Exhibit 7 and by making heuristic displays by dynamic changes in metrics choice, we can analyze the whole, frame by frame. Each run results in a frame. And one can go through several runs until we succeed in generating a mental model.

Exploratory Data Analysis (EDA)

A diagnostic panel, as a super model, requires an intelligent design of metrics database and use of exploratory data analysis (EDA) methods to present dynamic views.

Analytical Summary of Single Metric

Analytical summary tables are models that reduce large numbers in statistical analysis to a brief table. These summaries reduce the amount of detail one has to go through, and avoid problems of interpretation due to information overload. The table uses agreed upon and familiar symbols and statistical terms to summarize findings.

The summary table, as a process model, allows us to focus on crisp messages that have been distilled from data. Results without messages have already been excluded from the table in the preparatory rounds of message filtering.

In Exhibit 8, we present this tabular model with two dimensions of process perception. If the metric happens to be complex and needs to be

166

decomposed, then the third dimension of relationship can be added. The table can be suitably expanded.

The process model template is meant to establish baselines in pertinent dimensions, and keeps interpretation as a model element (may be subjective element). This model of representing processes is ideally suited for the following type processes:

- Core processes
- Critical processes
- Cost management

Sometimes messages drawn could show signs of inconsistency. A unique final message may not appear in the table. The summary table is not a final model and certainly not a conclusive summary. It is a convenient compilation of scattered messages.

Global Summary

We now attempt to reduce the entire project management scenario to a single tabular model. A global summary table of core metrics, as shown in Exhibit 9, would achieve just that. Each row in the table is dedicated to a local model seen through one metric. All the core metrics are covered, row by row. When we are through with all the rows, we would have scanned the entire situation. It may be noticed that each row in the global summary in Exhibit 9 represents the entire analytical summary of the single metric shown in Exhibit 8.

The global model also includes goals that drive the process in the last column. The model is now very rich and very comprehensive, by juxtaposing statistical behavior with management intent. The global summary table includes SPC models, risk models, capability models, forecasts, trends, and process tendencies, all seen in the light of goals.

This tabular model is a worthy addition to process baseline reports published every quarter by Software Engineering Process Group (SEPG) in organizations. The global summary helps in seeing the following at a glance:

- Process performance summary in three dimensions
- Goal tracking
- Internal benchmarking
- Performance trends and forecasting

Above all, the global summary table will perform as a fact finder to the CEO, and can also provide objective vision.

Exhibit 9. Global summary.

Sl. No.	Metric	Control Chart				Trend Chart			Frequency Analysis			Goal
		Mean	UCL	LCL	R^2	Forecast (Linear)	Forecast Mov. Avg.	Mode	Capability (percent)	Risk (percent)		
1	M1											
2	M2											
3	M3											
4	M4											
5	M5											
6	M6											
7	M7											
8	M8											
9	M9											
10	M10											

Exhibit 10. Correlation matrix.

	M1	M2	M3	M4	M5	M6	M7	M8	M9
M1	r^{11}	r^{12}	r^{13}	r^{14}	r^{15}	r^{16}	r^{17}	r^{18}	r^{19}
M2		r^{22}	r^{23}	r^{24}	r^{25}	r^{26}	r^{27}	r^{28}	r^{29}
M3			r^{33}	r^{34}	r^{35}	r^{36}	r^{37}	r^{38}	r^{39}
M4				r^{44}	r^{45}	r^{46}	r^{47}	r^{48}	r^{49}
M5					r^{55}	r^{56}	r^{57}	r^{58}	r^{59}
M6						r^{66}	r^{67}	r^{68}	r^{69}
M7							r^{77}	r^{78}	r^{79}
M8								r^{88}	r^{89}
M9									r^{99}

Process Correlations

Correlation studies, as seen in Chapter 7, help us to study the relationship between metrics, taken two by two. But process results are influenced simultaneously by several process variables, and hence, by several metrics. Multivariate analysis pending, we can have a bird's eye view of process relationships by analyzing correlation between pairs of metrics and arranging them in the form of a correlation matrix.

The correlation matrix is a relationship model, the values in each cell represent the strength (on a scale of 0 to 1) and type (positive or negative) of relationship. The format for correlation matrix is illustrated in Exhibit 10 for a set of nine chosen metrics. The cells are filled with correlation coefficients rmn, which define the relationship between associated metrics. Process correlation models of this kind have been used also as higher-level process diagnostic tool, as in quality function deployment (QFD) system. Basically, a correlation matrix reveals conflicts and connectedness that exist in the process. It also serves as a gap analysis, by exposing unexpected and unhealthy relationships.

The correlation matrix structure is quite elastic and can accommodate as many metrics as we choose, virtually allowing large degrees of freedom in model building.

Multiple Scatter Plots

More than capturing strengths of relationships in the process, we may have to establish mathematical relationships involving all the metrics. Multivariate model building perhaps requires special efforts and budget not generally available in project environment. However, a nearly equivalent model can be composed using scatter plots using the structure illustrated in Exhibit 11. Four metrics are considered in the multiple scatter plot model:

DEFECT DENSITY

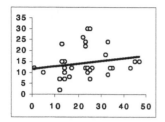

EFFORT VARIANCE %

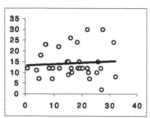

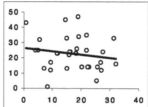

SCHEDULE VARIANCE %

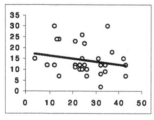

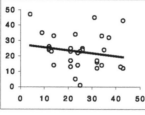

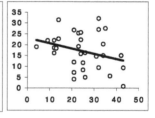

SIZE

Exhibit 11. Multiple scatter plots.

1. Defect density
2. Effort variance
3. Schedule variance
4. Size

The purpose of this model is to establish defect drivers in the process and see defect correlations with the core metrics. The standard search algorithms seek out to establish dependencies and associations between the ordered pairs of metrics, as shown in Exhibit 12. Six regression models have been constructed and made as a composite model in Exhibit 11.

Multiple scatter plot facility is available in many data analysis tools and can be easily built into the spreadsheet. Using the drop-and-drag facility, the dataset can be changed to view different scatter plots. By iterative

Exhibit 12. Dependencies and associations between ordered pairs of metrics.

Dependent Variable	Independent Variable
Defect density	Effort variance
Defect density	Schedule variance
Defect density	Size
Effort variance	Size
Effort variance	Schedule variance
Schedule variance	Size

interactions, we can understand relationship patterns in the process. These plots provide insight into the process chemistry.

Design of Experiment (DOE)

Building Models from Experimental Data

The models we have seen thus far are based on data collected by an ongoing metric system from natural observation posts. The data comes from an economically designed system, perhaps to suit the broader needs of the organization.

When we take up process studies that are specials tasks — temporary tasks, from the project view — that have been announced to solve a special problem, we may find that the available data may not be enough. Instead of changing the metrics system to acquire this data, suggesting permanent cost burden, we will resort to doing experiments to collect the data to meet the purpose at hand.

Experiments are also done under controlled conditions, assuring better quality and consistency in data. Scientifically designed, these experiments will help to build capable models.

The models built from DOE are expressions of relationship, which can be plotted and visually interpreted.

Design of Experiments

An experimental design is the set of plans and instructions by which the data in an experiment is collected. A design of experiments is a standard statistical technique used for simultaneous evaluation of two or more parameters that influence the resultant system performance and variability.

The design of experiment technique is especially useful when there is the need to optimize a process that can involve interactions and effects of several variables at several levels and an absence of concrete information.

Design of experiment gives fast and pragmatic approach to the optimization of processes.

Approach to Experiments

- State the problem or area of concern.
- State the objective of the experiment.
- Select the quality characteristic and measurement system.
- Identify control and noise factors.
- Select levels for the factors.
- Select interactions that may influence the selected quality characteristics.
- Analyze and interpret results of the experimental trials.
- Conduct confirmation experiment.

Models from DOE

DOE yields process models that have considered the simultaneous influence of several factors. These models capture process behavior more exactly than the models we have seen. What is more, DOE offers economical ways of doing the experiment, without losing quality of results.

Such models can be easily created for products. For modeling processes in a project, experiments are not always feasible. A project is a one-shot process, repetition is rare. Perhaps DOE can be used when new processes go through pilot runs — which can be thought of as experimental runs. During these runs, a temporary metrics plan must be drafted to support DOE.

While we take pains to make sure that factors are changed simultaneously in DOE, not one at a time, we must realize that in practical situations factors change in a similar way, naturally. Hence, natural observations yield truer pictures than simulated environments.

The wealth of naturally collected metrics data is awaiting model building, before we jump to experiments.

Chapter 9
Estimation Models

Estimation Process

Estimation is a process that uses prediction systems and intuition for cost and resource planning. Estimation is controlled by "cost realism," which does not always insist on exactness but lays equal emphasis on logic as much on the mathematical form of the prediction system. It is concerned about assumptions regarding the future and the relevance of history. It is concerned about bias in prediction.

On one hand, estimation models use rigorous statistics for generating the prediction equation. On the other hand, common sense rules several choices and assumptions made en route.

Estimation is as much art as science.

There are useful techniques available for time and effort estimation. Process and project metrics can provide historical perspective and powerful input for the generation of quantitative estimates. Past experience of all people involved can provide immeasurably as estimates are developed and reviewed. Estimation lays a foundation for all other project planning activities and project planning provides the road map for successful execution of the project.

Size, effort, schedule, and the cost of the project are estimated in parallel with the requirements definition phase. As requirements get clearer and refined, the estimates also get refined in parallel. Size estimation involves predicting "how big" the software will be. This is done by counting the number of features, functions, lines of code, or objects and applying appropriate weights to arrive at one or two numbers that represent the size of the software. Based on the size of the software, productivity-related data, and experience from past projects; the size is converted into effort. Effort is usually estimated in terms of person-hours, person-days, or person-months that need to be consumed to create the software. Schedule is derived from the effort estimate, the number of team members, and the extent to which project life cycle activities are independent of each other. Estimated costs are calculated based on the effort that needs to be put in and other elements of cost such as travel, hardware, software, infrastructure, training specific to the project, and expected usage of communication facilities. Though estimation is an intense activity during and at the end of the requirements stage, tracking of estimates and reestimation continues throughout the project at a reduced intensity.

Exhibit 1. Why do we estimate size, cost, and schedule?

- To scope proposed tasks
- To explore alternative system concepts
- To design to cost/budget
- To explore alternative design concepts
- To explore alternative proposals for enhancements and upgrades
- To identify key design elements
- To identify key process parameters
- To prioritize needs vs. wants
- To identify key assumptions
- To identify and quantify uncertainties
- To identify tasks and their relationships
- To assess schedule feasibility
- To identify, allocate, and schedule resources
- To assess an organization's ability to perform within targeted costs
- To evaluate the consequences of internal and external constraints
- To establish achievable objectives
- To establish a basis for quality service
- To establish commitments
- To bound the risk against customer needs
- To balance levels of risk against customer needs
- To provide a basis of successful risk management
- To do build vs. buy analysis
- To prepare successful proposals
- To evaluate proposals from competing bidders
- To establish baselines for project tracking
- To do enhance/reuse vs. redesign analysis
- To predict life cycle costs
- To predict returns on investments
- To provide information for establishing business and investment strategies

The mathematical side of estimation requires a higher degree of precision and dependability than general regression needs. To win a place in the estimation model, the prediction equations are built using validated data, more precise measurements, and even experiments (Exhibit 1 through Exhibit 3).

Software Estimation Risks

The effects of inaccurate software estimation and schedule overruns are well known. Software estimation errors generally result from four major risk areas:

1. The inability to accurately size the software project
2. The inability to accurately specify a development environment that reflects reality

Exhibit 2. Elements of good estimating practice.

- Written objectives
- Product description
- Task identification
- Involvement of different project people into the estimating process
- Use of more than one cost model or estimating approach
- Estimating potential cost and schedules impacts for all identified tasks
- Identification and quantification of uncertainties in descriptive parameters values
- Estimates updated with changes
- Method for organizing and retaining information on completed projects
- Analyze dictated schedules for impacts on cost

Exhibit 3. Estimating capability indicators.

- Management acknowledges its indicators of estimating capability
- Estimators equipped with the tools and training needed for reliable estimating
- Experienced and capable people assigned as estimators
- Quantify, track, and evaluate estimating capability of the organization

3. The improper assessment of staff skills
4. The lack of well-defined objectives, requirements, and specifications during the software development life cycle

Estimation Methodologies

Analogy Method

Estimating by analogy means comparing the proposed project to previously completed similar projects where project development information is known. Actual data from the completed projects are extrapolated to estimate the proposed project. Estimating by analogy can be done either at the system level or the component level.

Bottom-Up Method

Bottom-up estimation involves identifying and estimating each individual component separately, then combining the results to produce an estimate of the entire project.

Top-Down Method

The top-down method of estimation is based on overall characteristics of the software project. This method is more applicable to early cost estimates when only global properties are known. The focus is on system-level activities such as integration, documentation, project control, configuration management, etc. The top-down method is faster, easier to implement, and requires minimal project detail.

Expert Judgment Method

Expert judgment involves consulting with human experts to use their experience and understanding of a proposed project to provide an estimate for the cost of the project.

Two Variables Algorithmic Method (Parametric Method)

The algorithmic or parametric method involves the use of equations to perform software estimates. The equations are based on research and historical data and use one input as source lines of code (SLOC) or number of functions to perform to predict cost. The limitation of these models is that they are two-dimensional snapshots of reality (which has several dimensions).

Multiple Variables Algorithmic Method

These models employ several parameters or factors as cost drivers. The estimation process considers the simultaneous influence of all these factors, and hence are considered more realistic and dependable.

Thumb Rules

In first-order estimations, we use our personal rules of thumb. These rules come from experience. The danger is that these are subjective. The strength is that before final acceptance each of the estimations requires a sanity check from the rules of thumb. If there is gross difference between the estimate and the rules of thumb, we need to reconsider the estimate and evaluate the assumptions that have been made. Rules of thumb are important; they provide rough order of magnitude (ROM) estimates.

Delphi Estimate

The wideband Delphi technique is a structured way of estimating based on collective expertise. It is used for first-cut estimation in situations where the expertise in estimating is particularly valuable. It is also used to complement other estimation techniques. In the context of software sizing, the wideband Delphi technique can be used to arrive at the LOC estimates for the proposed system.

It is a group forecasting technique, generally used for future events such as technological developments, that uses estimates from experts and feedback summaries of these estimates for additional estimates by these experts until a reasonable consensus occurs. Wideband Delphi technique is based on recognition of the fact that when many experts independently come to the same estimate based on the same assumptions, the estimate is likely to be correct. Of course, the experts involved in the estimation should be working on the same and correct assumptions. It has been used in various software cost-estimating activities, including estimation of factors influencing software costs.

Golden Rule

Without the collective knowledge of a group and its multifaceted analysis of the situation, we can still achieve dependable results by using the golden rule of estimation. The rule suggests a process of inquiry, either in the mind or using a PERT chart, to study the optimistic, pessimistic, and most-likely values, and then take a pragmatic view that combines all the three estimates using Equation 9.1. There is logic behind this calculation, which is based on the illustration.

$$\text{Estimate} = \frac{t_o + t_p + 4t_m}{6} \qquad (9.1)$$

where:

t_o = optimistic value
t_p = pessimistic value
t_m = most-likely value

The golden rule estimate takes into account the entire range of possible variation, based on the experience of the estimator. Specifically, it removes bias from the estimate, and hence gives a safe and more dependable basis for project planning.

Prediction Capability

A critical step in software project management is estimation. Essentially, estimation is a predictive exercise. We aspire to build "prediction capabilities" in projects to strengthen the planning and management systems. Projects begin with size estimation based on requirements analysis; for budgeting and resource planning, we try to predict cost, schedule, and defects from size. These are the most visible and widely discussed prediction applications at the business level.

At the micro level, prediction is used as a decision tool in numerous areas: to set process goals, fix threshold levels for decision making, and define control limits. In mature organizations, at the end of every phase the next phase process parameters are predicted. This prediction is seen as a refinement over the baseline predictions because fresh data has come in from the completed phase to improve the prediction.

To predict an expected value in the work center is now recognized as the beginning of process innovation; almost all improvement initiatives are anchored to this moment of prediction.

Prediction capability is also regarded as the ultimate contribution from a metrics system.

For prediction, the dependent variables (responses) and the independent variables (predictors) must be selected and defined. The associated data must be gathered; from these empirical data statistical prediction models can be built. While the most popular prediction models are based on regression and probabilistic models, time series models have also been used for prediction.

Prediction Equations

At the heart of a prediction is a prediction equation that translates project experience into a mathematical form. Attributes of experience are transferred to the legacy equations; limited experiences produce equations with limited potential. The broader the experience, the broader the application range of the prediction equations.

From regression analysis of metrics data that capture experiences from project clusters, we can build useful prediction equations. Besides the experience-based limitations, the following data-dependent restrictions apply to these prediction equations:

- Inconsistency of data
- Errors in data
- Inadequate sampling
- Misrepresentations
- Bias

The regression equations cannot easily be applied to ranges beyond that of parent data. Even within the range, the equations may operate at undesirably low confidence levels.

Despite all these limitations, these prediction equations can be called "prediction models" and can be used in the decision-making process.

A collection of prediction models from the empirical analysis illustrated in Chapter 7 is presented in Exhibit 4. The table contains the equations of the prediction models and their confidence levels. Each equation represents some practical experience seen from a metrics window. The source data consists of natural observations picked from log sheets and metrics databases, not from special data collection exercises or specially designed experiments.

Estimation Algorithms

Since the 1950s, attempts have been made to arrive at estimation algorithms or cost estimation relationships (CERs) for project budgeting. The problem was attacked by different schools of thought, and diverse solutions came up in the form of equations, defended seriously by the authors but viewed skeptically by practitioners. Each algorithm represented an approach and gave an answer different from the others. The answers varied, making common sense the better judge. But the busy project manager liked to have different models on which he would sit in judgment, rather than figuring out all for himself right from scratch. With the help of such algorithms wherever they were available, estimation turned out to be decision making — choosing among the alternatives.

The overall structure of such algorithms, in most cases, took the form shown in Equation 9.2.

$$\text{Effort} = a + b\left(EV\right)^c \tag{9.2}$$

where:

a, b, and c = empirically derived constants

Effort = measured in person-months

EV = estimation variable (LOC or FP)

The practice of using algorithms brought possibilities of automation into the estimation process, so far a "manual" process, now transforming into a tool-based process.

Estimation Science: The Early Models

During the past few decades, a large number of estimation equations have come into existence. While the science of estimation was pursued by researchers, practitioners with a pioneering spirit started creating their own local models similar to the 12 presented in Exhibit 4.

Growing dissatisfaction with LOC as an estimator led to the invention of FP and other scientific size measures. Equations used in some of the well-known estimation models are presented here.

Bailey–Basili Model

$$\text{Effort} = 5.5 + 0.73 * \left(\text{KLOC}^{1.16}\right) \tag{9.3}$$

Exhibit 4. Prediction equations from limited data.

S. No.	y Dependent Variable	x Independent Variable	Prediction Model	%R2
1	Effort Variance%	Requirement Effort%	$y = 0.84\,x^2 - 21.22x + 147.57$	86.75
2	In-Process Defect Density (KLOC)	Design Effort%	$y = -1.31x + 36.62$	53.42
3	Customer Reported Defects	In-Process Defects	$y = 0.35x + 4.13$	91.32
4	Productivity FP/PM	Requirement Effort%	$y = 8.14\mathrm{Ln}(x) + 1.38$	64.34
5	Post Delivery Density (Def/100FP)	Review Effort%	$y = 8.24x^{0.90}$	73.38
6	Defect Density (Def/100FP)	Productivity (FP/PM)	$y = 0.05\,x^2 - 1.04x + 6.59$	49.38
7	Bad Fixes	Productivity (FP/PM)	$y = 0.09\,x^2 - 0.47x + 8.06$	26.1
8	Productivity LOC/day	Team Size	$y = 99.30x^{-0.59}$	42.28
9	Defect Density (Def/KLOC)	Size (KLOC)	$y = 20.16\,x^{-0.38}$	44.18
10	Cost of Bug Fixing (Normalized)	Review Effectiveness%	$y = -17.03\mathrm{Ln}(x) + 120.4$	46.27
11	Effort (Hrs)	Size (FP)	$y = 19.93x - 183.5$	39.75
12	Actual Days	Estimated Days	$y = 1.24x$	80.58

Doty Model

$$\text{Effort} = 5.288 * \left(\text{KLOC}^{1.047}\right) \qquad (9.4)$$

Albrecht and Gaffney Model

$$\text{Effort} = -13.39 + 0.0545 * \text{FP} \qquad (9.5)$$

Kemerer Model

$$\text{Effort} = 60.62 * 7.728 * 10^{-8} * \text{FP}^3 \qquad (9.6)$$

Matson, Barnett, and Mellichamp Model

$$\text{Effort} = 585.7 + 15.12 * \text{FP} \qquad (9.7)$$

Watson and Felix Model

$$\text{Effort} = 5.2 * \left(\text{KLOC}^{0.91}\right) \qquad (9.8)$$

$$\text{Duration} = 4.1 * \left(\text{KLOC}^{0.36}\right) \text{ months} \qquad (9.9)$$

Halstead Model

Halstead predicts effort from program volume, a software complexity measure, seen in terms of operators and operands of a program. The effort equation is as follows:

$$\text{Effort} = \left(n_1 * N_2 * V\right) / \left(36 * n_2\right) \qquad (9.10)$$

where:

V = $(N_1 + N_2) \log_2 (n_1 + n_2)$
n_1 = number of unique operators in the program
n_2 = number of unique operands in the program
N_1 = number of operator occurrences in the program
N_2 = number of operand occurrences in the program

Putnam's Model

Putnam's model is one of the first algorithmic cost models. It is based on the Norden-Rayleigh function and generally known as a macro estimation model for large projects. The Putnam software equation is of the form:

$$L = C_k K^{1/3} t_d^{4/3} \qquad (9.11)$$

where:

K = effort in years
L = the size delivered (SLOC)
C_k = constant that is a function of local conditions
t_d = development calendar time in years

Barry Boehm's COCOMO (Constructive Cost Model)

In 1981, Dr. Barry Boehm announced the basic equations:

$$\text{Effort} = 3.2 \left(\text{Size} \right)^{1.05} \tag{9.12}$$

$$\text{Time} = 2.5 \left(\text{Effort} \right)^{0.38} \tag{9.13}$$

Several empirical estimation models relating effort to size have been published. These models have been derived from experience but are not universal. Before applying them we must calibrate them and prepare a "calibration curve."

The estimation models have grown in scope along with time, having the emerging benefit of a large number of product databases.

The scientific models vied for universal application and aroused keen interest in many tool developers who gobbled up such equations to generate prediction systems. However, the empirically derived "local" models rarely made it to the core of management conscience.

Advent of Parametric Models

The estimation methods discussed so far, from ROM to the scientific equations, have their own uses but are not as reliable as we would like them to be. The need for more-reliable estimates is becoming important.

For this reason, software parametric cost estimating tools have been developed since the late 1970s to provide a better defined and more consistent software estimating process.

In these models, a process is seen from different angles or dimensions. Each dimension is represented by one parameter. Hence, with the help of multiple parameters we get a fuller picture of the process. These parametric models relate the individual parameters to cost. Hence, the cost model becomes naturally more realistic. In addition, the models consider the interactions between the parameters and process nonlinearity, making the model more reliable. These models can be seen as extensions of the simple two-variable models.

Calibration

The calibration procedure is theoretically very simple. Calibration is the process of comparing the output of the model with the actual values. The difficulty or the errors are noted down, from which correction factors can be derived. After calibration, with the help of the correction factors, the model will reach a higher level of accuracy. Every estimation model requires calibration before use. Calibration is in a sense customizing a generic model.

The calibration factor obtained is considered good only if the type of inputs that were used in the calibration runs. For a general total model calibration, a wide range of components with actual costs need to be used. Numerous calibrations should be performed with different types of components in order to obtain a set of calibration factors for the possible expected estimating situations. An example of this is shown in Chapter 7 applications.

An estimation model is as good as calibration. Even the best model is unreliable if it is not calibrated.

COCOMO

One of the most successful estimation models is COCOMO (constructive cost model) from Barry Boehm. The model has been revised and improved in the past 20 years and recently has been published as COCOMO II.2000. This is a model, Dr. Barry Boehm notes, "to help you reason about the cost and schedule implications of software decisions you may need to make." The primary objectives of the COCOMO II.2000 are to

- Provide accurate cost and schedule estimates for both current and likely future software projects
- Enable organizations to easily recalibrate, tailor, or extend COCOMO II to better fit their unique situations
- Provide careful, easy-to-understand definitions of the model's inputs, outputs, and assumptions
- Provide a constructive model
- Provide a normative model
- Provide an evolving model

Here is a list of the major decision situations we have determined that you might want to use COCOMO II for in the future:

- Making investment or other financial decisions involving a software development effort
- Setting project budgets and schedules as a basis for planning and control

- Deciding on or negotiating trade-offs among software cost, schedule, functional, performance, or quality factors
- Making software cost and schedule risk management decisions.
- Deciding which parts of a software system to develop, reuse, lease, or purchase
- Making legacy software inventory decisions about what to modify, phase out, outsource, etc.
- Setting mixed investment strategies to improve your organization's software capability, via reuse, tools, process maturity, outsourcing, etc.
- Deciding how to implement a process improvement strategy

COCOMO II.2000 Parameters

This model still uses the original 1980s equation but cleverly incorporates the influence of several process variables into the equation, without escalating the complexity of Equation 9.12. A significant contribution from the model is the definition of the following parameters or cost drivers.

COCOMO II handles 22 such cost drivers and uses the basic equation (see Exhibit 5).

Levels

The cost drivers need to be recognized by the user and mapped to his project scenario. After recognizing the applicable cost drivers, the impact levels of these drivers must be adjudged. COCOMO II.2000 uses six levels for each driver:

1. VL = Very Low
2. L = Low
3. N = Normal
4. H = High
5. VH = Very High
6. XH = Extra High

Lookup Table

The model proposes impact levels, as given in Exhibit 6, based on the best fit to empirical data. Our intention here is not to cover application scenarios of the model, which will vary according to life cycle phase of the project (even the cost drivers might change accordingly). Rather, we wish to present one example of the lookup table, as given in Exhibit 6, to consider the application of the model for typical decision making.

Exhibit 5. COCOMO II cost drivers.

Scale Factors
1. Precedentedness (PREC)
2. Development flexibility (FLEX)
3. Risk resolution (RESL)
4. Team cohesion (TEAM)
5. Process maturity (PMAT)

Effort Multipliers
6. Required software reliability (RELY)
7. Database size (DATA)
8. Product complexity (CPLX)
9. Developed for reusability (RUSE)
10. Documentation match to life cycle needs (DOCU)
11. Execution time constraint (TIME)
12. Main storage constraint (STOR)
13. Platform volatility (PVOL)
14. Analysis capability (ACAP)
15. Programmer capability (PCAP)
16. Personnel continuity (PCON)
17. Applications experience (APEX)
18. Platform experience (PLEX)
19. Language and tool experience (LTEX)
20. Use of software tools (TOOL)
21. Multisite development (SITE)
22. Required development schedule (SCED)

Equations

After selecting the cost drivers and choosing from the lookup table the appropriate levels, they may be substituted in the Equation 9.14 and Equation 9.15.

Effort Equation

$$PM = A * Size^E * \Pi_{i=1}^{n} EM_i \qquad (9.14)$$

where:

PM = effort in person month
A = multiplicative constant, 2.94
E = $B + 0.01 * \Sigma_{j=1}^{5} SF_j$
B = exponential constant, 0.91
Size = software size in KLOC
EM_i = effort multiplier
SF_j = scale factor

Exhibit 6. The COCOMO II.2000.

Drivers	VL	L	N	H	VH	XH
Scale factors						
Precedentedness	6.20	4.96	3.72	2.48	1.24	0.00
Development flexibility	5.07	4.05	3.04	2.03	1.01	0.00
Risk resolution	7.07	5.65	4.24	2.83	1.41	0.00
Team cohesion	5.48	4.38	3.29	2.19	1.10	0.00
Process maturity	6.24	6.24	4.68	3.12	1.56	0.00
Effort Multipliers						
Required software reliability	0.82	0.92	1.00	1.10	1.26	
Database size		0.90	1.00	1.14	1.28	
Product complexity	0.73	0.87	1.00	1.17	1.34	1.74
Developed for reusability		0.95	1.00	1.07	1.15	1.24
Document match to life cycle needs	0.81	0.91	1.00	1.11	1.23	
Execution time constraint			1.00	1.11	1.29	1.63
Main storage constraint			1.00	1.05	1.17	1.46
Platform volatility		0.87	1.00	1.15	1.30	
Analysis capability	1.41	1.19	1.00	0.85	0.71	
Programmer capability	1.34	1.15	1.00	0.88	0.76	
Personnel continuity	1.29	1.12	1.00	0.90	0.81	
Applications experience	1.22	1.10	1.00	0.88	0.81	
Platform experience	1.19	1.09	1.00	0.91	0.85	
Language and tool experience	1.20	1.09	1.00	0.91	0.84	
Use of software tools	1.17	1.09	1.00	0.90	0.78	
Multisite development	1.22	1.09	1.00	0.93	0.86	0.80
Required development schedule	1.43	1.14	1.00	1.00	1.00	

Schedule Equation

$$TDEV = C * \left(PM\right)^{F}$$
(9.15)

where:

C = multiplicative constant, 3.67

$F = D + 0.2 * 0.01 * \Sigma^{5}_{j=1} SF_{j}$

or

F $= D + 0.2 * (E - B)$
D $=$ exponential constant, 0.28
PM $=$ effort in person month

It may be observed that while filling in the equations, we find the sum of all the scale factor influences and the product of all the effort multiplier

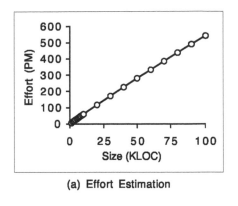

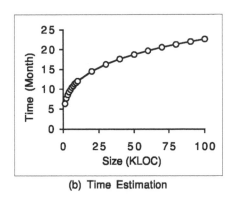

(a) Effort Estimation   (b) Time Estimation

Exhibit 7. COCOMO models.

influences. The scale factor sum together with the exponential constant B controls nonlinearity of the model. Because B is equal to 0.91, when the scale factor sum is equal to 0.09 the combination of both becomes unity (0.91 + 0.09 = 1.00). This represents a transaction point called economy of scales. If the scale factor sum is larger, the model predicts high cost for big projects. If the scale factor sum is smaller, the model predicts benefits of size in terms of cost reduction.

COCOMO II.2000 Applications

The COCOMO estimation model can be used for decision making in all business processes. Some of them are explained in the following discussion.

Financial Decisions

The first application of the model is to run it for the range of sizes and predict the cost and time behavior, as illustrated in Exhibit 7.

These graphs are dependent on the assumption made in selecting the cost drivers and their influence levels. There is a possibility that when different people run the model, they might come out with different graphs, each representing a scenario. We can ask the "what if" question and explore a wide range of possibilities, especially while preparing budgets and proposals. This also helps in negotiating cost and time requirements with the customers and stakeholders. It also helps in refining our project assumptions.

Trade-Off Decisions

An important decision in projects is to balance conflicting factors. For example, high reliability may be a customer requirement, but the cost and time implication of offering higher reliability might not be objectively

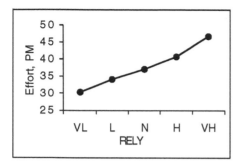 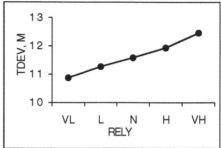

Exhibit 8. Trade-off decisions with COCOMO.

assessed and discussed during the contract negotiations. While it is commonly known that reliability costs money, translating this knowledge into a cost function is tricky. Some people use a rule-of-thumb that doubling the reliability level would cost 50 percent more. But these are wage generalizations. What we need is a specific answer to the additional cost required to achieve an increasing reliability level, taking into account all the associated cost drivers. Another problem we face in this exercise is to quantify the required hike in reliability. Using the COCOMO model, we can simulate the impact of reliability on cost and time, as illustrated in Exhibit 8.

It may be observed that using the simulation run we can predict for a given increment in reliability the corresponding escalation in time in months and escalation of cost in present months.

If constraints exist on cost and time, they can be projected on the simulation run and the feasible level of reliability can be read off from the graph. At this time if the feasible level and the required level are far apart, we encounter a trade-off situation. Either additional cost must be provided or reliability must be traded off, both according to the model forecasts.

COCOMO provides for such trade-off analysis against several product constraints and process realities. Such trade-off calculations help in some of the most critical decision-making movements in the projects.

Risk Management Decisions

Risk perception is yet another critical step in project management. Although risk more often arises from external forces, its impact on cost and schedule have to be known with some level of credibility. Many risk perception tools such as the Risk Exposure Matrix depend on subject assessment and give volatile results. COCOMO allows us to perform risk analysis with reasonable levels of objectivity. For example, let us consider the risk of attrition, because of which programmers with lower capabilities fill in vacancies when experienced programmers leave. Assuming that the drop

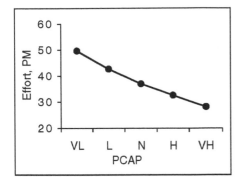 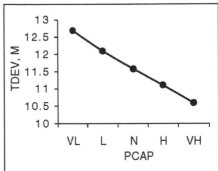

Exhibit 9. Estimating the impact of attrition.

in programmer capability (PCAP) levels is from high (H) to low (L), the corresponding cost risk and schedule risk can be estimated, as illustrated in Exhibit 9.

It is also possible from the model to create worst-risk scenarios such as simultaneous drop in all human capabilities affecting at least more than five cost drivers. COCOMO predicts very steep rises in cost and time when capabilities drop. It must be kept in mind that the worst scenarios may have lower probability of occurrence. COCOMO does not deal with the probability issue but only computes the impact. It is left to the user to use other methods for assessing probabilities.

We can perceive risk through almost all the cost drivers and build suitable risk scenarios on COCOMO.

Sensitivity Analysis Decisions

Sensitivity analysis is the study of changes in the results due to small variations in the cost. A small perturbation in the x variable gives rise to a change in the y variable. The ratio y/x is the sensitivity factor.

The cost function is more sensitive to certain cost drivers than others; also, in the case of a nonlinear relationship such as between cost and size, sensitivity varies.

Sensitivity of cost and time on platform volatility (PVOL) is illustrated in Exhibit 10. In this case, the relationship is almost linear and has a static sensitivity factor.

Understanding sensitivity in cost behavior gives a special insight into the economic system and is highly informative input to the project staff.

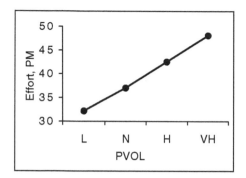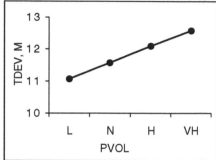

Exhibit 10. Effect of platform volatility.

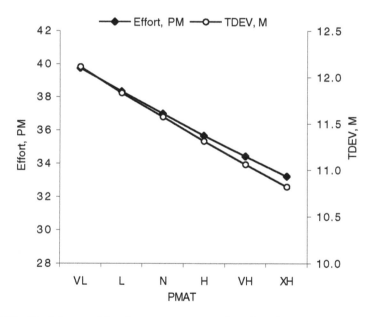

Exhibit 11. Decision making for process maturity planning.

Strategic Decision Making with COCOMO

In planning for the long term, we may face questions such as: "what will be the cost benefit if we move from CMM level two to level three in process maturity?" or we may ask ourselves the question: "what are the cost benefits in having prior experience?" Except for a feeling that all will go well when capability improves, we do not have dependable numbers to make a decision on investment. COCOMO helps with such strategic decisions. An example is shown in Exhibit 11, which indicates cost benefits from process maturity.

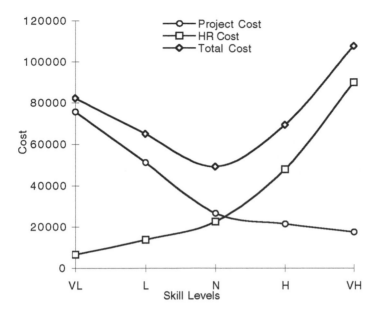

Exhibit 12. Applying COCOMO for HR decisions.

Optimization of Support Processes

A judicious use of estimation models is to combine them with other quantitative results and take an integrated view. For example, COCOMO can be used to estimate the cost advantage of skills. This can be shown as project cost curve. This may be seen together with the cost of hiring skilled people, as shown in Exhibit 12. The two cost trends are in opposite directions, presenting a conflict. If you plot the total cost of both, you may get an optimization curve. Depending on project constraints, we can choose the appropriate point.

Tailoring COCOMO

COCOMO can be tailored to a particular organization in various ways. It can be calibrated to existing project data by adjusting constants A and B; even the impact levels can be readjusted if the data supports. The redundant parameters can be identified for a given project situation and its life cycle phase. This redundancy can be eliminated. The strength of COCOMO is in the fact that it can absorb additional cost drivers into the framework without affecting mathematical formulations. Hence, the user can expand the model to map greater complexities.

COCOMO has all the benefits of a good estimation model. It further demonstrates how an estimation model can be applied to decision making. It allows us to see entire processes in a unified cost perceptive. The model is

191

flexible and adoptive. The model is so transparent that it has inspired the development of several estimation tools.

Estimation System

The estimation model has emerged as a management thinktank. The scope of the models has increased from simple cost estimation to higher-level project concerns. Some of the models combine the basic prediction equations with constraint equations that represent project goals and attempts to solve the total project management system. This breed of estimation models, for example, predicts not only costs but defects as well. They are useful to track and control projects. One such example is SLIM.

SLIM (Software Life Cycle Management)

The estimation system SLIM was developed by Larry Putnam based on the Rayleigh-Norden model given in Equation 9.11. It draws on a database of over 5000 projects. This has been developed as a suite that consists of three modules:

1. *SLIM-Estimate:* This tool can be used for estimation of effort required for software and for deciding on the strategy for the design and implementation in terms of suitable trade-off factors such as cycle time, team size, cost, quality, and risk.
2. *SLIM-Control:* This tool is meant for project tracking and control using statistical process control to assess project status and highlight areas that need attention.
3. *SLIM-Metrics:* This tool builds the repository of projects and performs benchmarking, to use for future estimation and better management of future projects.

SLIM-Estimate

SLIM requires three primary inputs. The first input is the proposed size of the application. SLIM is flexible enough so that any of the popular sizing metrics can be used.

- Source lines of code
- Function points
- Objects
- Windows
- Screens
- Diagrams

The second input is productivity and complexity in three levels of detail. SLIM also determines an appropriate productivity level based on answers to the detailed questions.

The final input is the project constraints, including:

- The desired schedule
- The desired budget limit
- The desired reliability (acceptable mean time to defect) at delivery
- The minimum staffing required to have the skill mix to get the job done
- The maximum practical staffing possible

SLIM uses this input information to determine an "optimum" estimate. The optimum estimate is a solution that gives you the highest probability of developing the system within the management constraints that you have specified. If the constraints are too tight, then the optimum estimate will exceed one or a number of your goals. If this is the case, you must evaluate other practical alternatives. These might include scenarios for reduced function products, increased staffing, or improved efficiency. Variations of the basic estimate can be logged so that you can compare the merits of each alternative and make a decision about which estimate is the best.

SLIM presents the results of estimate in an effective and persuasive way. There are 181 different reports and graphs that SLIM can generate. We can select the right ones for presentation from the following major categories:

- Project description
- Estimation analysis views
- Schedule section
- Risk analysis section
- Staffing and skill breakout section
- Effort and cost section
- Reliability estimate section
- Documentation section

SLIM can be calibrated with minimum metrics: project size, development time, and effort. Until maintenance and enhancement releases, SLIM covers the complete life cycle. SLIM estimates are extremely sensitive to the technology factor.

Software Sizing Tools

While using estimation models a key input is size. If size estimation tools are available, they would save a lot of time and effort in preparing size data for running the estimation models. Some of the size estimation tools are:

- ASSET-R
- CA-FPXpert
- CEIS
- SIZEEXPERT
- SEER-M

Estimation Tools

Many of the estimation models have been computerized and brought out as tools with many useful features. Use of tools makes it easier to run these models and generate reports. Some tools provide special support on calibration as well. Following is a representative list of tools for estimation models:

- PRICE-S
- REVIC
- SASET
- SEER-SEM
- SOFTCOST-R and SOFTCOST-ADA
- The ANGEL Project
- CoCoPro
- Construx Estimate 2.0
- COOLSoft
- COSMOS
- Costar
- SLIM

Chapter 10
Metrics for Defect Management

Defect Measurement

Measuring defects is one of the most difficult tasks. It requires an approach that is wide and comprehensive. It involves all the measurement scales, from cognitive to quantitative. It involves collecting defect data and using it to understand and characterize defects. The data is also used to understand, in great detail, the processes associated with defect, from injection through discovery to fix. From this understanding, models can be developed for causal analysis and forecasting.

Metamorphosis of Defects

There are three expressions for product anomalies: error, defect, and failure. Mistakes that happen during creation are errors. When these affect the next process, they are termed defects. When the defects reach the customer and cause operational problems, they are known as failure. The life cycle of a defect begins as error and ends as a failure, going through a series of value changes. As errors propagate into the product, they get more intricate, more difficult to find, costlier to fix. When errors migrate into future, the degree of impact they are likely to exert on the users increases. As time moves on, defects sink to unfathomable layers. With time, the cloud of uncertainty that is characteristic of defect discovery grows thicker and thicker, making defects invisible. When we measure defects, what we get to see about defects depends on the metamorphic phase defects have reached.

Seeing Defects

Scrutiny of products and processes and seeing defects is at the core of defect measurement. Seeing is measurement, more so in the case of defects. Propelled by delivery pressures and a need to succeed, people see more perfection, less problems. There exists a bias in our perspective when we are seeing what we want to see. We are just being optimistic. But to see defects, we need the opposite perspective. Balancing business positivism with an ability to see failure modes is a management trait emerging strong at the turn of the century. Seeing defects gives a competitive advantage; it helps us build robust processes and prevent defects. Not seeing defects leads to customer complaints after which we fix problems aggressively but often too late.

Counting Defects

In order to measure product defect, we need to count the number of defects that have been detected in a work product and normalize by the product size. Because there are many different ways of measuring size, there are as many ways of measuring defects. This metric is known as defect density and is expressed in units such as defects/KLOC, defects/FP, and defects/page. If the work product size is taken proportional to the effort that has gone into making the same, then defect counts are normalized by effort and expressed in the unit defect/person hour. If the work product size is measured in terms of the number of opportunities or micro level work elements, then defect is normalized by the number of opportunities and expressed in the unit DPMO (defect per million opportunities).

Process Defects

Products tend to be defective when the processes tend to be defective. Process defects become visible when the outcome of the process deviates from expectations. Defective processes inject defects into work products. Process defects are measured through metrics by comparing them to process goals and by seeing anomalous patterns from model predictions. The measurement of process defects however is not direct.

Defect Classification

Attributes

We recognize defects by their attributes such as severity, phase, priority, impact, and trigger. Additional details related to defects are cost of fixing, the method of fixing, cause, preventive action, previous detection stage where the defect might have been found, and defect lifetime. By analyzing these data we understand the characteristics of defect. Defining attributes amount to measuring defects in the nominal scale.

Types

For better management and analysis, defects have to be categorized or classified. It may be recalled that classification is a measurement in the typological scale. Cem Kaner has grouped software errors into a four-level taxonomy; the first level types are:

- User interface errors
- Error handling
- Boundary-related errors
- Calculation errors

- Initial and later states
- Control flow errors
- Errors in handling and interpreting data
- Race conditions
- Load conditions
- Hardware
- Source, version, and ID control
- Testing errors

Defect Database

A key factor in defect management is the defect database. It is a common practice to log every defect and keep the following fields in a defect record:

- Defect ID
- Description
- Type
- Open date
- Close date
- Software component reference
- When found (life cycle phase)
- How found (method used)
- Priority
- Assigned to
- Severity
- Origin (phase)
- Could have been found at
- Effort to fix
- Effort to detect
- Cause
- Possible preventive action

This record structure includes elements for defect control, defect management, and defect prevention. Also, defect classification is built into the structure by means of the field type, severity, origin, etc. When enough defect history is available and their causes have been determined, a standard list of causes can be published and the defect logger can select the nearest cause from a menu and record it. Similarly with rich experience and preventive actions, a menu can be attached to the database. One can do a quarry on the database and analyze defects from different perspectives. A good database will permit useful applications in defect management. In this case defect measurement and defect database are intimately related.

Exhibit 1. Summary of defect analysis.

	Req.	Des.	Cod.	Tes.
Start date of defect discovery process				
Defect density				
Defect count: critical				
Defect count: major				
Defect count: minor				
Total defects found				
Total defects closed				
Total defects open				
Defects open beyond time limits				
Estimated reliability level				
Cum. total cost of defects				
Review effectiveness				
Review efficiency				
Process capability on review				
Rework				
Bad fixes				
End date of defect discovery process				

Analysis of Defect Data

Summary Information

The defect database contains a wealth of information. A summary table as shown in Exhibit 1 can be prepared after defect data analysis.

The 80/20 Analysis

The widely used analysis of defects for better management is the 80/20 principle or variations of the same. A good example is provided by Barry Boehm and Victor Basili, who have discovered rules for defect management based on 30 years of research on defect data. A few are presented here:

- About 80 percent of the avoidable rework comes from 20 percent of the defects (80/20 rule).
- About 80 percent of the defects come from 20 percent of the modules (80/20 rule).
- About half the modules are defect free (50/50 rule).
- About 90 percent of the downtime comes from at most 10 percent of the defects (90/10 rule).

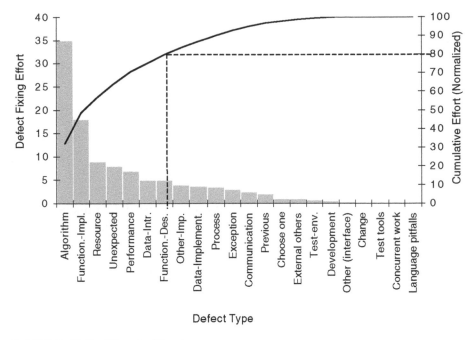

Defect Type

Exhibit 2. Defect Pareto Chart.

In a similar vein, from the defect database, the following Pareto analyses can be made:

- Pareto Chart on defect type (to understand the defect types that occur more often)
- Pareto Chart on defect severity (to understand the severity levels that occur most often)
- Pareto Chart on cause (to find common causes)
- Pareto Chart on proposed preventive actions (to find most effective preventive actions)
- Pareto Chart on origin (to model defect injection)

Example of Defect Pareto Chart

The Pareto Chart has been used as a problem-solving tool and plays a principle role in defect analysis. In the example shown in Exhibit 2, postdelivery defects in telecom software are analyzed in a Pareto Chart where the prioritization rule is based on cost of fixing defects. This chart was used in a root cause defect analysis by a cross-functional team as reported in a case study. The chart consists of bars that represent individual cost and a line that represents cumulative cost. The slope of the cumulative line rises steeply in the beginning and soon tends to be flat, resembling the law of diminishing returns. We can seek the 80 percent impact point on the cumulative graph

199

and drop a partition line through that. This line divides the problem space into two compartments — the vital few on one side and trivial many on the other. After this analysis the team was able to focus on the vital few defect types, namely, algorithm and functionality, throughout the rest of the analysis.

Also the case study shows how signature analysis was done using just these two significant defect types (in the four dimensions identified). After the Pareto reduction, the problems space diminished and became manageable.

Defect Management Graphs

The defect database can be exploited and several defect management graphs can be automatically generated. The following graphs may be included in the list:

- Defect Life Time (control chart, prioritywise)
- Defect Review Effort (control chart)
- Detection Effort (control chart)
- Cost of Defect (control chart)
- Cost (histogram)
- Defect Life Time (histogram)
- Review Effort (histogram)
- Cost of Defect (histogram)
- Defect Injection Profile
- Defect Detection Profile
- Detection Cost (fix cost, regression line)
- Severity (detection effort, regression line)
- Severity (fix effort, regression line)
- Defect (fix cost, cumulative graph)
- Defect Arrival Graph
- Defect Closure Graph
- Reliability Growth Graph
- Defect Severity (reliability bias bar graph)

Defect Correlation

There is a belief that defects are correlated. Field defects, a study shows, are correlated to defects found in system testing; the correlation coefficient is reported to be 0.711. Such correlation supports the satire "for every bug found, one more is hiding." This is not always the case, as Exhibit 3 demonstrates. It is good to perceive defect correlation and derive support from data to minimize in-process defects. Despite criticism regarding the application of such correlation to defect forecasting, defect correlation studies reinforce the need for early removal of defects. Correlation

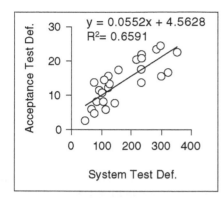 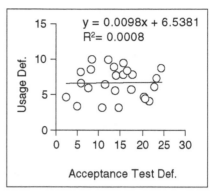

Exhibit 3. Defects correlation study.

Exhibit 4. Defect driver matrix.

Defect Drivers	DD: Review Defects	DD: Test Defects	DD: Usage Defects
Design effort	r_{de1}	r_{de2}	r_{de3}
Effort variance	r_{ev1}	r_{ev2}	r_{ev3}
Productivity	r_{pr1}	r_{pr2}	r_{pr3}
Req effort	r_{re1}	r_{re2}	r_{re3}
Requirements volatility	r_{rv1}	r_{rv2}	r_{rv3}
Review effectiveness	r_{re1}	r_{re2}	r_{re3}
Review time	r_{rt1}	r_{rt2}	r_{rt3}
Schedule variance	r_{sc1}	r_{sc2}	r_{sc3}
Size variance	r_{sv1}	r_{sv2}	r_{sv3}
Skill level	r_{sl1}	r_{sl2}	r_{sl3}
Test cases	r_{tc1}	r_{tc2}	r_{tc3}
Test coverage	r_{cv1}	r_{cv2}	r_{cv3}
Training fulfillment ratio	r_{tr1}	r_{tr2}	r_{tr3}

also gives a broad indication of testing process and the ever changing, dynamic behavior of defect removal mechanisms.

Defect Driver Matrix

A defect driver matrix such as shown in Exhibit 4 helps in identifying potential drivers of defects. All available process metrics are scanned for any correlation with defect density. To improve the effectiveness of the search, defect density values at different stages are used as separate metrics:

- *Defect density (review defects):* DDR
- *Defect density (test defects):* DDT
- *Defect density (postdelivery):* DDP

The process metrics choices are directed by logical reasoning and can include metrics such as:

- Effort variance
- Schedule variance
- Skill level
- Requirements volatility
- Training fulfillment ratio
- Productivity

A correlation matrix can be generated, as shown in Exhibit 5, relating these two sets of metrics, defect metrics and process metrics.

Looking for Consistency

Defect Control Chart

A straightforward control chart on defect density could be a powerful indicator for the project manager. In such a chart we look for a learning curve. Experience in development can have some major consequences: learning and defect reduction. If the defect control chart does not show a decreasing trend, we have a problem that is larger than defect management. In this case it is true that defects are mirror images of processes. Defect control results from process control.

The 1:10:100 Rule

It is now established that the cost of fixing defects increases in the later phases of the project. If it costs $1 to find and fix a defect in the review stage, it may cost $10 to do so at the system testing stage and $100 during the alpha stage. This economics trend is commonly referred to as the 1:10:100 rule. In many projects, people have discovered more linear patterns.

This rule makes one thing very clear: fix defects early. But instead of accepting the published trend, each organization must discover its own trend. The very relation of the economic impact of delayed discovery provides strong reasons for shift in inspection approaches. This is seen as a direct move toward cost management.

Defect Filter Matrix

A key concern in defect management is tracking defect origin and defect propagation across the several inspection gates or defect filters. Defect detection is an uncertain process, and hence we refer to defect detection probabilities for each filter. In simpler terms this is also referred to as defect removal effectiveness.

Exhibit 5. Defect correlation matrix.

	Req. Defects	Des. Defects	Code Review Defects	Unit Test Defects	System Test Defects	Acceptance Tests Defects	Usage Defects
Req. defects	r_{11}	r_{12}	r_{13}	r_{14}	r_{15}	r_{16}	r_{17}
Des. defects		r_{22}	r_{23}	r_{24}	r_{25}	r_{26}	r_{27}
Code review defects			r_{33}	r_{34}	r_{35}	r_{36}	r_{37}
Unit test defects				r_{44}	r_{45}	r_{46}	r_{47}
System test defects					r_{55}	r_{56}	r_{57}
Acceptance tests defects						r_{66}	r_{67}
Usage defects							r_{77}

A defect filter is a matrix structure shown in Exhibit 6. From the defect database we extract information such as:

- Number of defects discovered by each defect filter
- Distribution of defects among the origins

Once we compile defect data in the form of a defect filter matrix, we can perform some simple yet very useful analyses:

- Defect removal effectiveness
- Defect profile
- Influence of review on cost
- Dynamic value of requirement review effectiveness
- Reliability growth curve

Analysis 1: Defect Removal Effectiveness (DRE)

The matrix DRE, defect removal effectiveness, can be computed by the following formula given in Equation 10.1.

$$\text{DRE} = \left(\left(\left(\text{Defects found by the filter} \middle/ \begin{array}{c}(\text{defects found}) \\ +(\text{defect leaped})\end{array}\right)\right) * 1\right) \quad (10.1)$$

The DRE estimates for all the defect filters. It may be noted that the actual value of DRE depends on the inspection or testing methods used by the filter. There are different ways of inspecting a product but often we strike a balance between inspection effectiveness and inspection cost. But we should know quantitatively the DRE values to understand defect propagation.

Analysis 2: Dynamic Model for DRE

It is commonly felt that the true value of DRE for any filter will be known only after the product goes to field use and all field complaints are received and locked. By this time we get to know the complete picture of defects leaked. Hence DRE is taken as a postmortem analysis.

Dynamic modeling helps in overcoming this setback. For example, let us try to determine the DRE of the first filter, namely, the requirement review filter. When the inspection report arrives from this filter, all we know is the number of defects found and we are not to know the number of defects that might have leaked. When the second filter operates, it might capture the defects that have leaked from the first filter. At this gesture, we can compute DRE based on this information. The truthfulness of this information is questionable because there is always a possibility that the subsequent filters might detect additional leakages from filter one. However, we now think of a dynamic value of DRE for filter one that will be continuously

Exhibit 6. Defect filter.

Defect Injected At	Defect Filter								
	Req. Rev.	HLD Rev.	LLD Rev.	Code Rev.	Mod. Test	Int. Test	Alpha	Beta	Def. Inj.
Req.	5	1	0	1	0	0	0	1	8
HLD		2	3	1	0	0	1	0	7
LLD			2	1	1	0	0	0	4
Cod.				25	20	20	3	1	69
Bug Fix					1	4	2	2	9
Def. Found	5	3	5	28	22	24	6	4	97

updated as other filters enter into operation. The value of DRE will steadily fall as more leakages are discovered. This fall is usually an asymptotic that settles down on a plateau in the final stages. The drop in the value of DRE of filter one is known as the dynamic model of DRE. Applying this model one can react to the first but partial calculation of DRE and take necessary action early enough in the project instead of waiting for the complete truth to be known after project conclusion. By using pattern recognition methods one can even forecast the expected final value of DRE from the initial estimates.

Analysis 3: Defect Profile

By plotting a graph of defect discovered against life cycle phases we can infer a lot about the process. This graph is known as defect profile. One can connect the tops of the bar and create a continuous profile. Such defect profiles have been known to follow the Rayleigh distribution model. Studies show that the peak of defect profile shifts to the left when the process maturity increases. With practice one can judge the maturity level of the development process by looking at the defect profile.

Analysis 4: Influence of DRE on Cost

If we have in the defect database information about the effort required to fix a defect, then one can compute the cost of fixing defects and relate it to defect discovery phase. Normally discovery at later phases attracts more cost for defect fixing. With this cost input, one can now compute an economics of review effectiveness.

Analysis 5: Forecasting Hidden Defects

We can plot a defect discovery trend line and derive a ballpark figure for the latent defects in the product. This is only a crude approximation. A more complete and dependable forecasting of defects requires more complicated defect models, which are beyond the reach of a project member. If our aim is to make use of the naturally available data and construct a model, however approximate it may be, then the trend line can be used for strategic decisions. At least these trend lines will differentiate an extremely bad product from an extremely good one. Hence, before launching the product, if you want to certify the goodness of the project in gross terms such as excellent, good, and bad (class A, class B, class C), then we can use the trend line as an input. Surely the project managers have the other evidences and additional factors to help in making this judgment; all we are saying is that the trend line contains critical information.

Analysis 6: RGC

A perfect reliability growth graph can be drawn using cumulative defects found with time. The construction of such RGCs makes use of detail information of defect discovery on a daily and sometimes even on an hourly basis. Such a graph will be a coarse version of RGC where defect dictation events are not caught in full detail but summarized for each filter. The x-axis will be the defect filter number and the y-axis, the cumulative defects found. The graph, despite its obvious limitations, helps us in judging the completeness of defect discovery and hence is deciding whether to shift the product or not. It is safer to release the product after the curve becomes flat. It is dangerous to shift the product when the curve is climbing steep. Visually, the graph indicates the risk of defect leakage at the time release.

We have seen that by reorganizing the defect data in the form of defect filter matrix, we benefit from the six defect analyses and the associated decision support.

Defect Detection Probability

Defect detection is an uncertain process, showing large variation. We can ascribe a defect detection probability to the detection process, and characterization is based on probabilistic models. Comparing effectiveness of detection methods presents problems, because the ranges of result overlap. The baselines are blurred and overlapping discrimination is almost impossible.

We illustrate a defect detection model that makes it easier to see the probabilistic behavior by taking an example from the review process. The review process has come under rigorous studies after the industry started realizing the beneficial influences of review in reducing costs and increasing reliability. Team reviews have been favored by many, and practiced by many after Fagan presented their usefulness. But they are costly. Reviews without real meeting, on the other hand, are known to be less effective. Porter and Norman have compared experimental studies and presented the data that we have studied and fitted to normal distributions.

The experimental study involves two types of reviews. The first type is without meeting, and reviewers inspect the software individually. They perform a preliminary inspection and then do a final one, named the detection–detection method. In the second type, inspection is done through meetings, though the participants go through some kind of preliminary study before they attend the meeting.

The distributions are shown in Exhibit 7 as normal curves. The data spread represents the presence of variable factors in the process. Review without meeting has a bias toward higher performance levels; the process

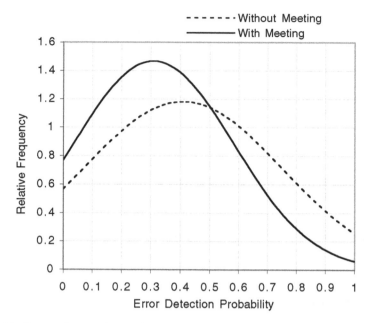

Exhibit 7. Comparing review effectiveness.

peak shows a 10 percent advantage. The team performance shows more capability by controlling variation.

Rayleigh Defect Discovery Model

Putnam has proposed an elegant solution to reliability modeling: defects follow a Rayleigh pattern. The Rayleigh equation has been calibrated to represent defect discovery pattern in a project, as defined by the Equation 10.2.

$$E_m = 6\left(\left(E_r/t_d^2\right)t\exp\left(-3t^2/t_d^2\right)\right)$$
(10.2)

where:

E_m = errors per month
E_r = total number of errors expected over the life of the project
t = instantaneous elapsed time
T_d = elapsed time at 95 percent reliability level

The cumulative values of errors discovered, expressed as a percentage, indicate the reliability level of delivered software. The defect discovery pattern and the reliability curve are shown in Exhibit 8.

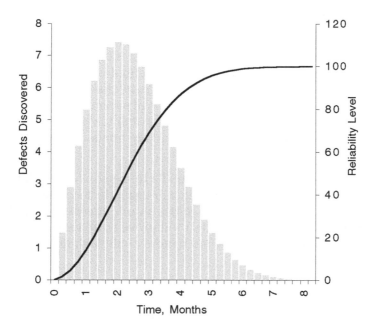

Exhibit 8. Putnam's Rayleigh model.

Three Phases of Reliability Measurement

Reliability measurements are categorized into three phases:

1. Requirements reliability
2. Design and code reliability
3. Test reliability

Defect behavior in the three phases is different, and the model required to characterize defect also differs. Requirements are analyzed using checklists and, as in NASA, by a semantic model. Design and code reliability metrics involve size (or complexity) measurements and defect normalization. Test (and inspection) reliability depends on the rate at which defects are found and fixed.

Reliability Enhancement

Software failure rates decrease as more defects are found fixed. The more software is used, the more it is exposed to failure triggers. Each failure exposes a defect and immediate defect fixing enhances reliability. In a bug-fixing environment, occurrence of one defect means detection and removal of the defect. In this case, reliability improves with execution time. Experience shows that the failure rate thus decreases exponentially. The reliability metric MTBF (mean time between failure) increases accordingly.

Home-Grown Model

Statistical models are not totally successful in defect forecasting, and hence statistically based reliability models do not fare so well. Causal models and other approaches may be required to understand defect behavior in more detail. It is rare to find a reliability model that can be used as a universal tool. Each model is limited to the type of parent projects from whose data the model was built. Statistical models fail to deal with personality issues, uncertainty in the environment, and the human factor where cognitive models fare well.

When a project team attempts to build a home-grown reliability model, many of the inadequacies are removed. For example, a combination of failure tree diagram (a causal model) and a simple regression model from quantitative data (a statistical model) will prove to be very effective when used by a decision maker; he will find it more credible than borrowed models with unfamiliar history.

Broad-Based Approach

In home-grown modeling, dependability may be achieved by a broad-based approach that exploits all the measurement scales and supports three types of models:

1. Cognitive models (trees, maps)
2. Semantic models (classification, signature)
3. Statistical models (time series, regression, probabilistic)

The cementing force that integrates all these models is human intuition.

Use Defect Models, Stay Proactive

Managing defects using defect models such as those mentioned in this chapter involves a paradigm shift, from fixing problems in response to customers to finding problems and fixing them. Making use of models to find problems has a special advantage: the same models that helped to find problems also help to fix problems. By iterative runs we can diagnose the problems and derive clues for solution.

Quantitative Defect Management

Using defect metrics and defect models for decision making is a process that needs leadership for nourishment. When the leader shows the way, these quantitative defect management practices percolate to all levels of the organizations. At the team level, process capability studies are made. The process behavior is modeled to perceive defects. At the individual level, the movement shifts gear to continuous improvement. In both the modes, defect metrics data enables causal analysis and creation of causal maps.

Managing Process Defects

Process defects are indicated by anomalous behavior or by departure from expected behavior. Seeing both these types of process defects requires process analysis and model building. A control chart will reveal process outliers. A frequency diagram shows process risk. Regression models examine the aberration in process relationship. With the help of these models, process defects can be diagnosed and quantified. Without depending on product defects to reveal potential process defects, we can use process models well ahead in time to foresee defects. Managing process defects involves detection of problems and prompt and corrective action. It is well known that corrective action on a process is equal to prevention of product defects.

Creating Product Health Report

Based on the defect database, we can generate a product health report that contains defect metrics, defect models, defect arrival and closure patterns, and a variety of statistical models. Such a comprehensive report will help in tracking the health of the product from several angles and provide an excellent early warning system with which we can control defects and prevent them from reaching the customer.

Chapter 11
Online Use of Metrics

The Challenge

The need for online application of metrics is a sharply felt one, but remains a hard nut to crack. Metrics data is more customarily viewed as historical data and brings benefits from offline analysis. We need to be taking metrics from the world of history to present reality. The reluctance in thinking on one's feet with metrics arises due to several factors:

- Not having the right metrics
- Fear of data errors
- Information overload and paralysis
- Slow and lengthy process of metrics data collection and analysis
- Difficult interpretation rules

It is also true that metrics data may catch us unaware and challenge our assumptions in the critical moment when we are about to present our summary information to top management. The psychic cost of having to cope with this sudden imposition is so high that metrics data may be suppressed from entering into our conscience and in the reports.

Having online metrics systems makes one feel under a microscope and continuously watched. With wrong metrics in place, this could bring in extraordinary stress. No one wants to be exposed by online metrics without having had a chance to digest the situation, assess the consequences, and verify the data.

Metrics Intelligence

Application of metrics begins with addressing a basic intellectual need. Metrics can correct a fundamentally human problem. The human mind suffers from an impaired, fragmented, and prejudiced vision. The data analysis products implanted in the human brain can lead one to a new vision, which is objective and real. Metrics data must be applied to enlighten human intelligence. The purpose of metrics here is to help us perceive reality very clearly.

When it comes to decision making, the nemesis of metrics is intuition, which overrules observed data. Metrics get rejected by the inner layers of the mind and relegated to the outermost tentative layers with skepticism. The war between intuition and metrics arises from the polarization of their weaknesses: intuition is unreliable, while data is incomplete. The strong

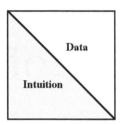

Exhibit 1. A creative collaboration.

points of both — data is objective and intuition can reach realms where data does not even exist — have failed to ignite a fusion of the two.

We have to build a creative collaboration between metrics data and human intuition, as represented in Exhibit 1. The weakness of intuition is compensated by the strengths of data and vice versa. We need both for excellence in decision making. Plugging the holes, the coming together of intuition and data can do something more significant. Each can help to enhance the other. Data refreshes the human consciousness, if we allow. In the long run, data feeds intuition and shapes our minds. Intuition gives data a sense of direction, tenders context, and supports data interpretation.

The question then is not how many metrics we use, but how we use them. This is the application we need to start with. And this application calls for inner change — a silent transformation — in the way we look at real life and results in the achievement of "metric intelligence."

Metrics Synchronization

Timeliness in metrics enhances the chance of metrics entry into decision making. Untimely information is of less value and faces rejection. Ideally, it has to be like clock-work. In fact, it is a race: metrics data must move to the decision centers ahead of its rival, human judgment. When metrics data does not keep pace with the organization's information needs, it indicates a problem. The problem could be traced to causes such as having too many metrics, poor definition of metrics, measurement noise, lack of motivation, inefficient analysis, procrastination in report generation, ineffective communication, and poor automation. But the root causes may lie in the very design of systems in the organization. Achieving "metrics synchronization" is a vital requirement for integration of metrics with the organization.

Milestone Diary (MSD)

A milestone diary is a planning and tracking tool that captures management metrics at the conclusion of each milestone. A comparison is made directly between the observed and planned, and the project status is determined. This is different from task-level tracking of projects. Milestones

214

Exhibit 2. Milestone diary format.

Task		Start Date		End Date		Duration	
ID	Description	Planned	Actual	Planned	Actual	Planned	Actual

represent production of tangible and measurable results, and hence is a convenient way of tracking projects. MSD enjoys support from practitioners because of its simplicity and focus on results; it is a handy tool. MSD easily takes metrics into management structure. The basic MSD format is shown in Exhibit 2. MSD provides a framework for measurement at chosen intervals of time within a project life cycle, and enables continual monitoring of the project using metrics.

Measuring at milestone levels, instead of task levels, has some natural benefits. In projects where progress follows the nonlinear S curve, measuring earlier than milestones are achieved yields artificial values. A good deal of progress in these cases takes place in the last 10 percent of the milestone period. Also, economy in metrics is achieved because of fewer numbers of metrics and less data collection effort. In maintenance assignments, which follow linear progress trends, task elements are combined to form "work packages," completion of which can be equated to milestones.

Earned Value Model

From MSD we can develop the Earned Value Model (EVM) and benefit from EVM's forecasting and cost control capabilities. In EVM, progress is measured not in terms of number of tasks completed, but in terms of economic value generated or earned value.

A typical EVM table is built around the work breakdown structure (WBS) of projects. Each WBS element is assigned a budgeted cost and a schedule.

Key EVM Parameters

- *Budgeted Cost of Work Scheduled (Planned Value):* BCWS is the cumulative budgeted cost of work scheduled up to the status date.
- *Budgeted Cost of Work Performed (Earned Value):* BCWP is the cumulative budgeted cost of work completed.

- *Actual Cost of Work Performed (Cost):* ACWP is the actual cost to date including fixed costs and variable costs.
- *Schedule Variance:* Normally, Schedule Variance indicates the difference in the actual and planned schedule of a project calculated at a given point of time. Schedule variance of a project can also be found in terms of earned value at any given point of time as the difference between Earned Value and the planned budget.
- *Cost Variance:* Cost Variance is the difference between the planned cost and the actual cost of a project calculated at any given point of time. In EVM terms, Cost Variance is defined as the difference between the earned value and the actual cost of work.
- *Cost at Completion:* The cost with which the project is completed.
- *Schedule at Completion:* The time by which the project gets completed.

Earned Value Model Table

Generating an EVM table for a typical software project from MSD is illustrated in Exhibit 3. The milestones are identified; schedule and resources are allocated to each. A weightage factor is determined and attached to each resource. Then an economic value indicator is calculated based on the effort of all associated resources taking into consideration the weightage factors. The last three columns contain BCWS, BSWP, and ACWP.

Earned Value Graph

The three EVM parameters can be plotted in what has come to be known as an Earned Value Graph, a powerful graphical tool for progress monitoring, risk assessment, and forecasting.

Baseline Plot. BCWS or earned value for the entire project can be plotted right in the beginning of the project, based on the plan. This graph is known as the baseline graph, shown in Exhibit 4. In projects following the waterfall cycle, the baseline would typically be an S curve or a nonlinear variation of the same. Where incremental models are followed, the baseline tends to be more linear, as illustrated. From experience, one can judge from the shape of the baseline the hidden risks. Hence, the plan can be corrected to avoid or minimize risky planning patterns such as steep climbs, untenable bursts of concentrated deliveries.

Tracking. When the BCWP and ACWP are plotted against the backdrop of the baseline, as illustrated in Exhibit 5, we are able to track the project by observing the following:

- Progress made in terms of earned value, as of today
- Gap between value and cost
- Cost escalation from the budget

Exhibit 3. Milestone diary.

	Ms No	Ms ID	Start	End	Staff	Rate	Effort	BCWS	BCWP	ACWP
Plan	1	KICK OFF	1-Jan-02	2-Jan-02	4	10	40	40		
	2	SRS	2-Jan-02	31-Jan-02	3	10	870	910		
	3	HLD # 1	1-Feb-02	2-Mar-02	2	8	464	1374		
	4	GUI PROTO	3-Mar-02	17-Mar-02	4	8	448	1822		
	5	LLD # 2	18-Mar-02	26-Apr-02	2	8	624	2446		
	6	BUILD # 1	27-Apr-02	26-May-02	4	8	928	3374		
	7	HLD # 2	27-May-02	25-Jun-02	2	8	464	3838		
	8	LLD # 2	26-Jun-02	15-Jul-02	2	8	304	4142		
	9	BUILD # 2	16-Jul-02	14-Aug-02	4	8	928	5070		
	10	INT TESTS	15-Aug-02	23-Sep-02	2	9	702	5772		
	11	BUILD # 3	24-Sep-02	2-Nov-02	4	8	1248	7020		
	12	BUILD # 4	3-Nov-02	22-Nov-02	4	8	608	7628		
	13	SYS TEST	23-Nov-02	17-Dec-02	2	9	432	8060		
	14	CAT	18-Dec-02	16-Jan-03	2	9	522	8582		
	15	ALPHA	17-Jan-03	5-Feb-03	1	9	171	8753		
	16	BETA	6-Feb-03	2-Mar-03	1	10	240	8993		
	17	LAUNCH	3-Mar-03	7-Mar-03	2	10	80	9073		
Actual	1	KICK OFF	24-Jan-02	27-Jan-02	6	10	180		40	180
	2	SRS	27-Jan-02	13-Mar-02	4	10	1800		910	1980
	3	HLD # 1	14-Mar-02	27-Apr-02	3	10	1320		1374	3300
	4	GUI PROTO	28-Apr-02	22-May-02	6	10	1440		1822	4740
	5	LLD # 2	23-May-02	1-Jul-02	3	8	936		2446	5676
	6	BUILD # 1	2-Jul-02	4-Aug-02	5	8	1320		3374	6996
	7	HLD # 2	5-Aug-02	7-Sep-02	3	8	792		3838	7788
	8	LLD # 2	8-Sep-02	17-Oct-02	2	8	624		4142	8412
	9	BUILD # 2	18-Oct-02	29-Nov-02	4	8	1344		5070	9756
	10	INT TESTS	30-Nov-02	18-Jan-03	2	9	882		5772	10638
	11	BUILD # 3	19-Jan-03	15-Mar-03	4	8	1760		7020	12398
	12	BUILD # 4	16-Mar-03	14-Apr-03	4	8	928		7628	13326
	13	SYS TEST	15-Apr-03	27-May-03	2	9	756		8060	14082
	14	CAT	28-May-03	11-Jul-03	2	12	1056		8582	15138
	15	ALPHA	12-Jul-03	23-Aug-03	3	12	1512		8753	16650
	16	BETA	24-Aug-03	22-Oct-03	3	12	2124		8993	18774
	17	LAUNCH	23-Oct-03	27-Oct-03	5	10	200		9073	18974

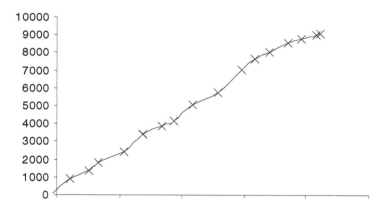

Exhibit 4. Baseline EVG.

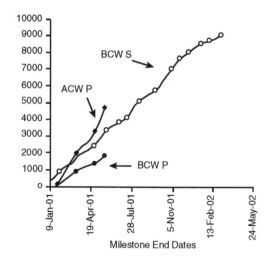

Exhibit 5. Tracking using EVG.

- Schedule slippage (as time)
- Schedule variance (as cost)
- Estimated cost at project completion
- Estimated time to complete the project
- Cost risk
- Schedule risk

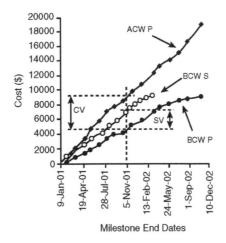

Exhibit 6. EVG of a completed project.

EVG is an early warning system of risk (cost and schedule). Also, by extrapolating the BCWP line we can estimate the schedule at completion, and by extrapolating ACWP we can estimate the cost at completion. In Exhibit 5, linear extrapolation has been employed because of the more or less linear shape of the baseline. In the case of nonlinear models, appropriate extrapolation techniques may be used.

Complete Earned Value Graph

The EVG of a completed project is shown in Exhibit 6 for a quick reference. The EVG now is a historical record of project implementation. One can annotate anomalous behavior, as in control charts; lessons learned can be reused in the next project planning. EVG is equally effective in small projects, as it is with huge projects. In one single window, the entire project life cycle is represented. This simple tool focuses on value.

Extended Milestone Diary

The basic milestone diary captures time and effort data, the primary concern in meeting project deadlines. People are understandably reluctant to include additional metrics to the basic milestone diary. It costs more money to collect more data, and it also causes more stress by adding to the number of problems one has to handle. Including additional metrics in this milestone framework can give substantial benefits. MSD as structure allows easy extension as shown in Exhibit 7. One can choose any other metric critical to business success and include the same in MSD. For example, if the MSD includes defects detected, product quality gets reviewed at each milestone. In reality, defect data is collected by other tools and is kept in separate databases not readily available in a simple form to the project

219

Exhibit 7. Extended milestone diary.

Milestone ID	Standard Metrics Columns		Newly Added Metrics Columns	
	Effort	Schedule	Defects	Rework
1				
2				
3				
4				
5				
6				
7				
8				
9				
10				
11				
12				
13				
14				

team. By bringing defect data into the MSD, we bring "quality concern" into the mainstream of project management.

Responding to Metrics

Having created a credible metrics system, creating a metrics-sensitive organization is necessary. Online use of metrics amounts to responding to metrics data. Responding to the threat signals, risk clues, and the multitude of messages that may issue forth from the metrics system needs a responsive organization that "thinks on its feet."

The Decision Point

Responding to metrics data involves a series of intermediate stages. From metrics to responsive action is a long journey. A milestone in the journey is the moment of decision making using data — a moment that shows trust in data and the empirical truth it carries. Two streams of influences compete at this turning point in the mind of the decision maker. Data asserts a statistical perspective of reality, while past experiences present time-proven strategies in a style very familiar and hence very acceptable. If the two influences point to two different directions, there arises a decision dilemma. The alternatives are evaluated by the decision maker, unfortunately in this case, based on the principle of least resistance and the laws of convenience. The agreeable and culturally stimulating option is preferred. The

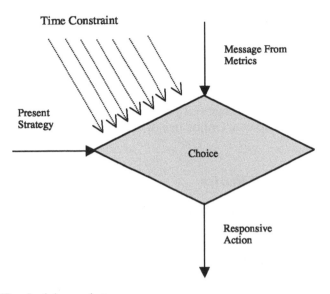

Exhibit 8. The decision point.

chance of metrics-based vision being selected depends to a large extent on how well metrics appeals to the mind. One lesson is worth recalling now: raw metrics data is the least appealing. Higher-level presentations, continuous modeling, and data visualization will maximize the chance of metrics being considered. Exhibit 8 illustrates the turning point.

High-Speed Decision Making

Using metrics online does not have the time advantage. Given larger timescales, objectivity would flourish. Under time constraint, pushed by milestones, speed prevails. Time applies enormous pressure on projects and the behavioral dynamics changes inside the chamber. The need for high speed makes people adopt high-speed data acquisition and high-speed analysis. The fastest known data acquisition method is the way the brain recalls experiences; the fastest analysis is the way the subconscious mind processes the recalled information. To top the speed, the brain offers a variety of highly efficient data selection and problem-solving algorithms. The metrics database, analysis, and delivery systems must improve capability in order to participate in online metrics use in decision making. And, as a prerequisite, data must be transformed into visual elements.

Responsive Action

The final stage in responding to metrics is taking action. An orientation toward action — the bias for action — is required to consider messages from metrics data. Where there is no motivation for action, the messages from metrics data are irrelevant and of no consequence. Action upon metrics can happen in three levels: individual response, team response, and organizational response. The response patterns are unique, instantaneous for the individual, milestone-driven for teams, and much slower for the organization. The nature of responses also varies, from attitudinal changes to breakthroughs. Performance expectations of online metrics must be based on the action dynamics of process owners. Metrics cannot make people act, leadership can. Online use of metrics therefore requires leadership support.

Cultural Induction of Metrics

Online use of metrics can happen after the establishment of metrics culture. With limited time, people resort to shorter forms of communications. When metrics are freshly introduced, the definitions, symbols, and icons are new to people, and they do not have time to process these cultural artifacts. With use and gaining familiarity, these artifacts gain acceptability and acquire the power to communicate effectively. Metrics are to be culturally inducted into management thinking. It requires great preparation and practice.

Discovering "the Factory within the Factory"

The purpose of online metrics is to help project teams to see the details within each project phase — the natural milestone. The metrics system for this purpose is specially designed and owned by the project team. The close views are required first for the project staff. Each milestone is a miniature project, a scaled-down version of the big business. It is generally believed that the milestones only become visible with process maturity, and metrics are required to characterize the sub-processes and unmask "the factory within the factory." Process owners discover knowledge from online metrics instead of centralized agencies. Learning while doing — best done with the use of metrics — is the new discipline.

Phasewise Reestimation

In the evolutionary life cycle models, the favorite choice of many, conclusion of each phase or work package proffers a chance for correcting the baseline plans and estimations. This requires field calibration of estimation models and working out increasingly better forecasts and estimates as milestones are crossed. As the fundamental metrics would bear out, estimation is where the highest contribution from metrics happens. Online metrics help to map the emerging customer needs, as well as the evolving process capability. They also help to refine the decision models continually, and keep them bound to changing realities.

Managing New Technology

The role of metrics in software engineering has always been used as a weapon to deal with new technologies. From online creation of a small estimation model for fixing bugs to the development of suitable size metrics, metrics have been used innovatively to solve technical problems. Technology life cycles are getting shorter and shorter and projects are gearing up to cope with changes within project life cycles. The engineering rules are being rewritten, a process to which metrics naturally belong.

Few Data: Sharp Focus

One thing is certain. Online metrics will be fewer in number and sharper in focus. Time constraints and the consequent drive for economy will see to it. Metrics choices converge for online application, and the fittest survive. Every observation is precious, more so here. The extreme focus elevates metrics to higher levels of business processes, adding value to data each time. What follows is a need to extract maximum information from minimum data. This may be achieved by modern forms of exploratory data analysis, equipped with the power of dynamic data visualization. Moreover, the precious few data points may be used to calibrate known models instead of attempting to build new. It is good to begin online data analysis with a library of theoretical models and use data as clues.

Data Connections

Use of legacy models in conjunction with online metrics data helps in integration of software engineering with other processes. Models are embodiments of interrelationships between process variables. Hence, they bridge the few data points from one process with the rest of the processes, using established mapping rules. Behavior of one process, as revealed by the sample data, can reflect the behavior of other processes. In the integrated environment well represented by models, sample data points would do. Limited data can still provide unlimited perspectives. Few metrics can cover the entire process network.

Early Warning

Within the project span, early risk resolution is an emerging good practice. A clever design of online metrics, along with the use of appropriate extrapolation techniques, will provide for early warning and risk forecasting. Even with limited metrics, early warning is possible. Detection of outliers, anomalous process behavior, process drift, and transgressions of limits in one phase are potential warnings for the subsequent phases. The responsive corrective action in one phase is proactive preventive action for the subsequent phases. If there is trouble hiding, metrics analysis in the first phase will certainly expose the same and provide early warning.

Choice of Online Metrics

Representative Metric

Metrics, which qualify to have a place on the project dashboard, also qualify to become online metrics. If we believe that just one key metric in a process would somehow contain the necessary clues or information about the process, we can settle for one representative metric from each process, as in the following examples:

- *Project Management Process:* Earned Value Metrics
- *Process Management Process:* Defect Metrics (Just One)
- Support Process
  - *HR:* Absenteeism%
  - *Facilities:* Downtime
  - *Training:* Cost of Training per Employee
  - *QA:* Cost of Poor Quality
  - *Measurement:* Cost/Benefit Ratio
- *Engineering Process:* Design/Code Ratio

The Magical Seven

If we wish to collect metrics for characterizing a process, more metrics may be required. As many metrics as the process owner feels necessary can be collected. Perhaps the number of factors in the proposed process would dictate data collection. But there is an age-old wisdom regarding human limits in managing complexity: keep the number of alternatives to fewer than seven. Hence, process characterization with online metrics should limit the number of metrics to a seven. Less is better.

Critical Metrics

While choosing online metrics, critical metrics are given a special place. This means that we should first identify critical characteristics of major processes within the project and then map them to the smallest metric set. Correlation matrix format could be used to analyze the mapping and to reduce the metrics count.

Benefits of Online Metrics

Online metrics have all the benefits that can be ascribed generally to all metrics, of course. However, there are special benefits resulting from the deployment method, including:

- Because the primary user is the process owner, effective use is guaranteed.
- Because the best metrics make it online, we get good return on investment on metrics data collection.
- Analysis and application of metrics data reaches its heights.
- Results from metrics application are quick to see and tangible.
- Application-oriented metrics culture sets in.

Chapter 12
Metrics-Based Decision Support Systems

Two Systems

Business information systems and metrics systems are interrelated but manifest a testy relationship. The metrics system attempts to address all the processes, while the archetypal information system focuses on short-term business results. The former provides a fertile ground for process research; the latter is anchored to issues related to delivery.

The two types of systems evolve with time and cut parallel inroads in the organization. It takes several cycles of experience and realization to bring them to unison. Until such time, the project information system is in better circulation. The fact that metrics has the potential of being a primary source of information is often missed.

As organizations mature and achieve integration, automated project dashboards are set up. These tools issue forth stereotyped reports, month after month, beating a track for metrics application, which will stifle other avenues.

The most natural environment for metrics is one of decision making. This involves creating alternative scenarios, doing what-if analysis, and generating models for simulation. Such features are beyond the scope of conventional project information systems. We need, therefore, to develop a metrics-based decision support system.

The Humble Beginning

In the beginning of the evolutionary history of metrics, the metrics system was regarded with skepticism and caution, and was considered an untrustworthy supplier of information. In those early times, the organization could not take a risk by depending on information from metrics systems that suffered from delinquencies. The business information system, which we denote by MIS, existed in any of its many forms as a strong protagonist. The business tolerated inadequacies in MIS, the familiar buddy but

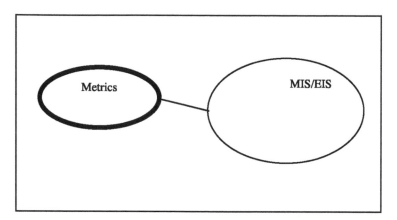

Exhibit 1. A simple information environment.

quenched metrics system, the newcomer. The information scenario (Exhibit 1) was simple, with just these two elements, one well imbibed and the other awaiting admission.

In those beginning days, strangely, there was no next to automation in MIS. The project manager personally created MIS reports, collecting information from memory and through various sources.

Metrics systems, quite understandably, were handled by Quality Assurance (QA) or SEPG who furnished the periodical product health reports and, in tune with CMM, published process capability baseline reports.

MIS was instantly associated with the direct execution of business, and commanded utmost respect and attention. The metrics reports were put in circulation and were studied with detached interest but failed to excite energetic managerial action.

Advent of Software Management Tools

The information scene changed continually as more tools were introduced in the organization.

Defect tracking tools have total control of defects data and produce standard reports. Some defect tracking tools focus on software testing and maintain complete history since testing, while some start from the first review. The defect tracking tools also support certain defect metrics; the list could vary from just a few numbers to several scores. Defect data analysis likewise could vary from elementary control charts to sophisticated pattern recognition.

Project management tools help in planning and tracking the project using core metrics such as cost and schedule. They also contain vital data related

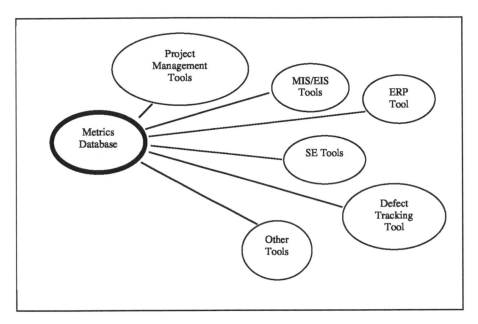

Exhibit 2. Heterogeneous information environments.

to work breakdown structure, task dependencies, responsibility allocation, critical tasks, completed tasks, earned value, and resource balancing.

Each tool operates from its own design philosophy, collects its own data, and generates very specific metrics. The organizational metrics database now has to gather data from a heterogeneous set of tools and their captive databases. Exhibit 2 illustrates the scenario.

Software Management Tools that Focus on Engineering

Some software management tools place emphasis on software engineering, support, and control, and cover the life cycle processes from requirements management to testing. These tools come as a suite of products or modules, each devoted to a life cycle phase and generate metrics for control and management.

The requirements management tools use case development, business modeling, and data modeling. They maintain a requirements repository and address the problem of communicating customer requirements to all stakeholders in the enterprise. They help in analyzing and tracing requirements.

Development toolkits include visual modeling, design, and runtime analysis. These tools provide support in automatic code generation and simulation. They provide the environment for development.

227

Software configuration management tools help in managing software changes through comprehensive version control and defect and change tracking.

Software Management Tools that Focus on Estimation

Another class of software management tools focus on estimating, tracking, benchmarking, and metrics analysis. These tools support quantitative approaches in software management and some of them enable statistical process control and forecasting. A more visible metrics plan is used by such tools. Metrics analysis, therefore, becomes a management tool for tracking the critical aspects of the project.

Software Management Tools that Focus on Testing

The third type of software management tools centers on testing. These tools help to measure product quality and manage defects. They quite naturally track defects in all life cycle phases and exercise a firm control on defect fixing and change management.

Dashboard

The three categories of tools support a management dashboard. Although the structure and the contents of the dashboard vary, this attempt to connect to management is an attractive and desirable feature of these products.

Software Management Tool Vendors

Following is a representative list of vendors who provide software management tools:

- www.rational.com
- www.telelogic.com
- www.qsm.com
- www.compuware.com
- www.softlanding.com
- www.mccabe.com

Birth of Process Databases

Measurement is an inseparable part of process; hence, there is a logical need for maintaining process metrics data in cognitive, semantic, and quantitative forms. The process owners — individuals or teams — are rich storehouses of metrics data. Certainly they commit the data to memory. Data entrenched in human memory needs to be gathered and archived before it evaporates. Discipline in personal and team processes, as envisioned by

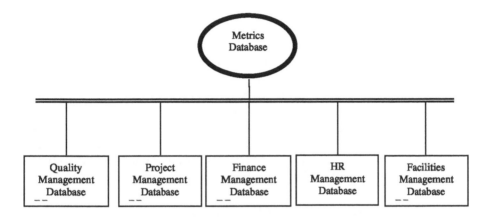

Exhibit 3. Metrics in distributed information environment.

Humphrey, makes this happen. People record their experiences as numbers or notes, thus creating a process database.

The newfound metrics culture is responsible for the creation of a multitude of process databases across the organization. These metrics databases are highly localized, each denoting an individual style. To understand and later integrate them, we can group these diverse databases under some broader titles according to organization structure. To manage diversity in location, we can think of a distributed database, as indicated in Exhibit 3. The organizational metrics database is not an isolated information system but, by being seamlessly connected to the several process databases, is a network.

With optimum choice of the following elements, it is possible to overcome distribution difficulties and ensure a metrics database that is safe and consistent:

- Data structure
- Partitions
- Replication
- Redundancy
- Access rights

Proper distribution solves technical problems in sustaining process databases in different locations, making it possible to reap some inherent benefits of having local databases. As authors of data as well as the database, process owners tend to become metric owners. In them, metrics data analysis is an inspired activity.

Enterprise Integration

Intelligence Integration

A remarkable benefit of metrics systems is that they achieve integration of intelligence by creating a network of the decision centers. In the name of metrics data collection, analysis, and research, we really look into process behaviors from a single window. Study of interrelationships between metrics is indeed a study of possibilities of process integration. Publishing capability baselines all together in one edition brings to a common platform several business issues, from goals to performances. Enterprisewide intelligence integration through metrics is an easy win, a most natural, often unintended result replete with benefits.

Enterprise Resource Planning (ERP) and Metrics

Integrating the enterprise at the operational and tactical levels of management is achieved by enterprise resource planning (ERP) solutions. ERP enables the integration of data and business processes throughout an organization. Modern ERP solutions are supported by new technologies in information processing and networking. Internet technology has brought in further capabilities to the ERP and has made decision making possible at lower levels of management.

With enterprisewide IT solutions in place, metrics must be seen as an information product, one of the several beneficial results of IT implementation. The job of metrics data collection is totally replaced by metrics extraction from the operational databases. This scenario provides an ideal opportunity for automatic metrics creation and application.

When ERP and metrics system coexist, special attention must be paid to data collection. The data gathering processes may compete or duplicate, with unpleasant consequences. People may find they feed the same data to both the ERP software and the metrics system in two different points of time; or, essentially the same data may be collected in two different formats by the two systems. Sometimes, without being aware that the ERP modules generate some metrics, people work separately and generate metrics, perhaps because those ERP-generated metrics are hidden within the ERP system.

In classical software development projects, where software products are designed from basic concepts, the challenge of enterprise integration has been overwhelmed by problems in software engineering. Software development tools dominated the scene, and ERP implementation began tentatively in the Finance Department and expanded to human resource management (HRM). In this scenario, software development tools bred automated software metrics.

In the new generation of high-volume software projects focused on build, enhancement, and maintenance, the challenge has shifted from engineering to service, quality, and speed. The need has arisen for defining new business models and extending ERP to service management, supply chain management, project management, performance management, and quality management. When a complete suite of ERP modules is implemented, almost all metrics including the core ones can be extracted from the ERP databases.

By integrating business functions, ERP solution gives several benefits to the organization, including the few mentioned here:

- A single system to support rather than several small and different systems
- A single applications architecture with limited interfaces
- Access to management information unavailable across a mix of applications
- Access to best practice systems and procedures
- More integration hence lower costs
- More automation of tasks
- Increased flexibility
- Reduction of lead time
- Better customer satisfaction
- Improved performance
- Improved resource utility

On the other hand, when managers see the organization through ERP and its well-structured reports, they may soon recognize a problem: the system lacks an organic feel, tends to make things look more routine, and reduces sensitivity. Because of the richness of functionality, the "toy box effect" can take over.

A well-designed metrics system is an elegant and fitting complement to the ERP solution. The metrics system can make use of the ERP data and provide higher-level decision analysis, and function as an add-on decision module. The inherent nimbleness of such decision modules alleviates the stiffness of ERP. Metrics systems can be used to consolidate many benefits of ERP, and more importantly, avert some of the undesirable traits of ERP.

Enterprise Metrics

The goal of bringing a metrics culture in all business functions is strengthened by seeing metrics with ERP, where possible. When the metrics system involves a progression of values adding transformations of data into wisdom, ERP provides the raw material — data — which can be accessed using a single application from all kinds of business functions including the following:

- Finance
- Treasury
- HRM
- Enterprise controlling
- Investment management
- Production planning
- Manufacturing and production planning
- Sales and distribution
- Plant maintenance
- Quality management
- Materials management
- Project management
- Supply chain management
- Front office
- Performance measurement
- Service management
- Procurement management
- Payroll
- Utility

In all these functions, metrics and models can be created, establishing quantitative process management. Applying metrics in an ERP environment benefits from the groundwork already done by the organization in implementing ERP. Implementing IT in all these business functions lays the foundation for implementing metrics in these functions.

ERP Vendors

There are ERP solutions available that offer a wide range of capabilities to address a variety of business segments. There are also a host of ERP consultants who offer support in implementing ERP. Following is a partial list of ERP vendors:

- SAP AG
- Oracle
- JD Edwards
- Peoplesoft
- Baan
- SSA
- JBA
- Marcam
- Intentia
- QAD
- Ramco

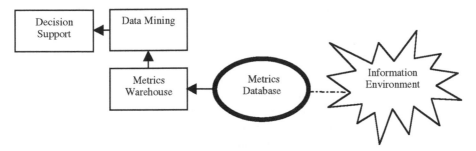

Exhibit 4. Metrics and the information environment.

Process Intelligence

A new dimension emerges in the use of metrics databases when it is well fed by a rich information environment, as shown in Exhibit 4. The metrics database now becomes a large storehouse of assorted data pouring in from the various sources. The value of this data goes beyond providing information. The data contains intelligence that needs to be extracted for the benefit of decision makers. Extraction of this intelligence is a very delicate process and usually involves pattern recognition techniques and other sophisticated statistical methods. All these approaches are bundled into a methodology known as data mining.

Metrics Warehouse

The metrics database in its original form cannot be easily used for data mining. We have to create a data warehouse where the raw data is cleaned and structured to facilitate advanced treatment. Setting up a data warehouse is in fact preparing for the knowledge discovery process. It involves selection of data from various databases, cleaning the data, and removing erroneous and false data. Inconsistency and duplication of data will also be similarly removed. As a data warehouse is designed for decision-support queries, data that is needed for decision support is extracted from the operational data and stored in the warehouse.

The metrics warehouse structure should be time dependent, nonvolatile, subject oriented and integrated. The data will also be regularly enriched; new information will be continually added to the old, regardless of the sources. Thus the data warehouse can handle heterogeneous data inflow.

It may be noted that we are not recommending a data warehouse because of the volume of data involved. We need to use the data warehouse structure for its well-known benefits. Many SEPG members who have analyzed metrics data for publishing process capability baselines recall that they have manually cleaned, validated, and enriched data, the same way as the data warehouse does. It makes practical sense to adopt data warehousing methodologies.

Metrics Data Mining

In data mining, we use computers to look at data and analyze it as the human brain does. Data mining is one of the forms of artificial intelligence that uses perception models, analytical models, and several algorithms to simulate the methods of the human brain. This would suggest that data mining helps machines to take human decisions and make human choices. The user of the data mining tools will have to teach the machine rules, preferences, and even experiences in order to get decision support.

With a metrics warehouse in place, we can install data mining algorithms, such as:

- Query tools
- Statistical techniques
- Visualization
- Online analytical processing
- k-Nearest neighbor
- Decision trees
- Association rules
- Neural networks
- Genetic algorithms

However, it is almost impossible to design universally applicable data mining algorithms. But we select from a large number of commercially available data mining tools to suit the purpose at hand.

Applying Business Intelligence Tools to Metrics

These tools (such as from www.spss.com) analyze data and create business intelligence using data mining techniques. These tools offer an impressive array of features, including:

- Event detection
- Scorecard creation
- *Ad hoc* queries
- Creation of data marts
- Model building
- Model exploration
- Experiments with models
- Iterative learning

When applied to metrics data, these tools create process intelligence. Metrics applications now become automated and fast.

Enterprise Intelligence Systems and Metrics

The new generation of ERP solutions provide interfaces to related technologies such as the following:

- Business process reengineering (BPR)
- Decision support systems (DSS)
- Executive information systems (EIS)
- Data warehousing
- Data mining
- Analytic intelligence
- Online analytical processing (OLAP)
- Supply chain management
- Customer relationship management
- Balanced scorecard
- Value chain
- Activity-based management
- Human capital management
- Operations management
- Knowledge management
- Risk management

These applications may be from different vendors and may not mesh. Integrating all these applications may require some effort and the use of enterprise application integration (EAI) techniques.

Some vendors offer product suites (such as www.sas.com) with many of the applications we have listed, from which we can easily build integrated intelligence systems. Equipped with such power, metrics data analysis and generating process intelligence become very simple tasks.

A Symbiotic Dependence

With the usage of software management tools, process databases, ERP solutions, and enterprise intelligence systems, the organization generates large volumes of data. The metrics system faces a new problem of having to cope with a complex information environment, comprising assorted data generators and their prolific creations. With time, the captive databases attached to various tools grow in size. This explosive growth of enterprise data might not proportionately enrich the metrics database of the organization.

Until the enterprise data reaches a common metrics database, the usage of data happens to be isolated attempts in narrow areas. But the organization fails to gain global perspectives or benefit from internal benchmarking. Integrated project management using quantitative methods remains an even more difficult proposition.

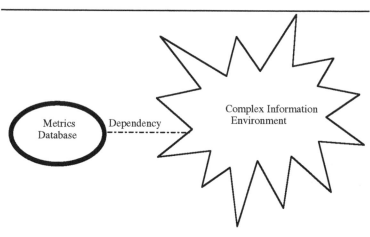

Exhibit 5. Metrics and automated DSS.

The relationship between the metrics system and its complex information environment, indicated in Exhibit 5, is symbiotic with mutual advantages. The metrics system should be made more organic and flexible, and should be in a position to adapt itself to fit into the complex environment.

Being organically coupled to a complex information environment offers new and changing roles to the metrics system. As information provider, the metrics system furnishes data; as a "rider," it extracts data, although partially, from the several databases. A metrics system operates, in this context, as an information exchange bureau, providing opportunities for metrics data conduits across the organization.

The structure of a metrics system must closely follow the evolution of the IT environment in an organization. The interaction between metrics and information systems is so complex that IT strategies will shape metrics strategies.

An Economic Alternative: Metrics-Based Decision Support Systems (DSS)

Metrics-Based DSS

The IT approach to DSS involves complex tools and sophisticated statistical techniques. A simpler approach is to build DSS from metrics. The architecture of a metrics system is conceived around decision centers, and directly addresses the question of quality of decision making.

Constructing a metrics system, well balanced in its metrics choice and equipped with analytical capabilities, amounts to construction of a metrics-based DSS (MBDSS).

Human-Centric Approach

A metrics system provides a low-cost DSS by sustaining process models, permitting analysis of models, and forecasting. By extending metrics to support processes, the scope of model-based analysis is also extended to other than the core processes.

To create process intelligence from metrics is a "human" activity. From available metrics, by human inquiry and creativity, we can generate meaningful models and carry out decision analysis. Human analysis allows higher-level decision analysis in "unstructured" modes, whereas analysis by common tools can solve only structured problems. Human analysis possesses strategic decision-making capability.

Manual Analysis

MBDSS provides decision support using simple and manual methods. The first is a process capability baseline, extracted from a metrics database. Other simple tools, which can work from either a metrics database or more efficiently from a metrics warehouse, are:

- Data visualization techniques
- Frequency domain analysis
- Time domain analysis
- Relationship domain analysis
- Process synthesis

These data analysis methods are described in Chapter 4 through Chapter 8. Using these, we can build a library of process models, each supporting the decision-making process.

Simple Tools

MBDSS requires some minimum IT support. The least is an RDBMS. Then we need some spreadsheet tools for statistical analysis.

MBDSS can be improved by adding a metrics warehouse and a statistical analysis package. There are a large number of data analysis tools that provide basic statistical analysis. We have listed in Exhibit 6 a few tools that support process control. Typical features of these tools are:

- Process capability analysis
- SPC
- Design of experiments
- Business intelligence options
- Real-time monitoring
- Report generation

Exhibit 6. Data analysis tools.

S.No.	Tool	Vendor	Address
1	Analytica	Lumina	www.lumina.com
2	XLReporter	SyTech	www.sytech.com
3	origin, origin pro	OriginLab	www.originlab.com
4	DADISP/2000	DSP	www.dadisp.com
5	QI Analyst4.2	wonderware	www.wonderware.com
6	DT Analyst2.0	wonderware	www.wonderware.com
7	SPSS Exact Tests	SPSS	www.spss.com
8	Minitab	Minitab	www.minitab.com

Web Enabling

MBDSS requires an intranet for effective communication. The analysis tools can be made available in the network and accessed by the user for a "do-it-yourself" kind of analysis.

Knowledge Management

Creating process intelligence goes hand in hand with knowledge management initiatives in the organization. Experimenting with process models is a knowledge-generating game. Knowledge is in fact a byproduct of the metrics system in its natural course. In this context, a metrics system is a virtual process learning center (VPLC).

Human Inquiry

At the center of MBDSS is human inquiry, as shown in Exhibit 7. The process of human inquiry can have "boundary-less" access to all tools, databases, and knowledge management systems for decision making. If automated decision-making tools are installed, human inquiry would consider the decision prompts from such tools as inputs.

The final decision is human.

Metrics Dashboard

We can construct a simple metrics dashboard that presents pictorially the details about a chosen project or product. The dashboard can be designed using the drill-down approach and can have links to relevant applications.

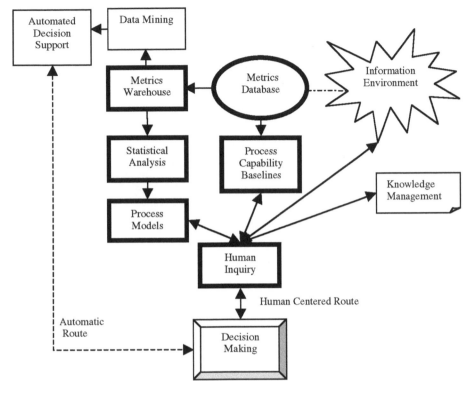

Exhibit 7. Proposed metrics-based DSS solution.

MBDSS: Information, Intelligence, and Strategy

MBDSS contains all the necessary elements, connectivity, and human insight to help organizations develop strategies from data. It also gives practical alternative, less-costly approaches for intelligence creation. Above all, it makes the best use of metrics.

Chapter 13
Metrics for Strategic Vision

Beyond the Obvious

Making use of metrics to look beyond the obvious is quite important. Metrics have been seen as a tool to look at the details, a costly research microscope. Metrics can be equally powerful in looking into the future, viewing beyond the immediate neighborhood. This kind of application of metrics is in tune with proactive management initiatives. When the management process changes its approach from merely responding to a situation to working with vision, from myopic schemes to strategic vision, the predictive abilities of metrics will be in vogue.

Model-Based Approach

A step in the direction of building strategic vision from metrics is to build models, as many of them as possible, and use these models in management thinking. The agenda for models is prediction, forecasting, and estimation. We have seen in the previous chapters how we can build empirical models from metrics and apply them for decision analysis. In almost each of such applications, the objective has been to predict future from the several perspectives provided by those models.

Seeing the future through metrics-based models is like making two-dimensional drawings of a three-dimensional object. Several views such as the front view, the top view, the side views, isometric views, and cross-sectional views are required to understand the true object. We have to apply our imagination while looking at drawings. Likewise, we have to apply innovation while running models. We build vision by running these models iteratively, scanning frame after frame of the scenario.

The Vision Called Integration

The metrics system integrates an organization in a manner not very different from how information technology integrates enterprises. The very establishment of metrics, from definition to deployment, is based on an integrated point of view of processes. The empirical formulas that use multiple variables also integrate, conceptually, the corresponding process

241

variables, allowing us to see process as a system. Metrics are champions of integration, constantly bringing together those ideas, parameters, and process indicators.

Integration of process indicators, from data fusion to process modeling, presents a new outlook and an enduring vision, which becomes the cornerstone of postmodern management.

In this chapter, we will see a few applications of metrics in vision building. These are complementary to similar applications that lie scattered in the earlier chapters.

Metrics in Project Management

Applying metrics to the project amounts to scaling down the organization's metrics plan to the project requirements. Such a tailoring is based on a focus on the project goals, which are relatively short term. Also metrics can play a crucial role in capturing customer requirements quantitatively. A much-acclaimed use of metrics is in risk analysis and forecasting. Goals, customers, and risk represent three critical factors that a project must reckon with.

Tailoring Metrics for the Project

From the larger list of metrics proposed in the metrics system, the project manager selects those that correlate with the project goals. Hence, the selection rule has to resolve the problem of clearly defining and articulating the project goals, and also positioning them with the relevant organization goals. In matured projects even process goals can be added to this list.

Then the goals must be quantified and prioritized. In framing the goals it is possible to set directly measurable goals such as timely delivery. Sometimes the goals do not have a direct measure. But they can be related to a metric with affinity. For example, optimum resource utilization can be a goal; many find it difficult to measure it directly, whereas a simple metric such as effort variance points to resource utilization. Schedule variance along with effort variance can provide information about resource utilization.

For each goal a weighting factor or rank can be ascribed and the goal list can now be rearranged according to its significance. Setting measurable goals in a structured way such as this brings vision and clarity to the project. And this remains among the finest contributions of metrics.

Setting Quantitative Goals: Goal–Metrics Correlation (GMC)

Vision is expressed through goals. Vision building and goal setting are interdependent. Goals, for better understanding and application, must be

Exhibit 1. Goal/metrics correlation table.

	Goals	Rank	SV	EV	DD	RE	P	REN	A	DT
						Metrics				
Corporate Goals	CS	1	1	0.3	0.7	0.2	0.2	0	0	0	2.4
	PFT	1	0	0.7	0.8	0.5	1	0.6	0.7	0.7	5
	MS	1	0.5	0	0.5	0	0	0	0	0	1
Project Goals	TD	1	1	0	0.3	0.3	0.3	0.5	0.8	0.2	3.4
	REL	2	0	0	1	0.7	0	0	0	0	1.7
Process Goals	CMM	3	0	0	0	0	0	0	1	0	1
	REV	2	0	0	0	1	0	0	0.2	0	1.2
			2.5	1	3.3	2.7	1.5	1.1	2.7	0.9	

expressed quantitatively. The metrics system in the organization, initially an offspring of goals, eventually supports in giving a quantitative expression to goals.

In principle, any goal can be measured directly. Some goals are easily measurable; some are abstract and can be measured through survey forms and rather elaborate procedures. Economy in quantifying goals is achieved by the GMC method.

As the name suggests, goal–metrics correlation is a matrix structure, as shown in Exhibit 1. The GMC structure has goals in the columns and metrics in the rows. The weightage factor is also indicated along with the goals in a separate column.

Metrics
SV = Schedule Variance%
EV = Effort Variance%
DD = Defect Density (Defect/KLOC)
RE = Review Effectiveness%
P = Productivity LOC/Month
REN = Risk Exposure Number
A = Attrition
DT = Downtime of Assets, Hours/Month

Goals
CS = Customer Satisfaction
PFT = Profit
MS = Market Share
TD = Deliver in 3 Months
REL = 97% Reliability
CMM = SEI CMM Level 5
REV = Better Reviews

The goal list is carefully prepared. The organizational goals, the project level goals, and whatever goals the teams are required to follow, need to be brought in the list. Conflict between goals, if any, is resolved. The project manager, who is going to use the GMC as a planning tool, will ensure that accepted goals appear in the table.

Every cell in the matrix bears a correlation coefficient, which measures the strength of the relationship between the associated goal and metric. Instead of directly quantifying a goal, we are going to be satisfied if they correlate well with a metric. We are transferring numeric quality from metrics to goals by association.

By examining the GMC matrix we can easily find and pick those metrics that fit into the goal system. They are the ones that post correlation figures. We know that only such metrics will survive in the goal-dominated project environment. Hence, after the GMC study the fittest metrics are selected for the project and a practical metrics system is deigned (other metrics are spotted and isolated for study). This way, the metrics plan gets tailored to the project plan and the commonly felt problem of the gap between planned metrics and actually used metrics is preempted.

Following is a list of the overall benefits of GMC:

- Setting measurable goals
- Tailoring metrics plan
- Firm foundation for project plan
- Good communication tool for goals and metrics to project team
- Overview of entire goals and metrics system at a glance

GMC Analysis

Metrics Effectiveness

In the GMC matrix, we first add the columns and with the resultant values we can plot a bar graph with the metric name in the x-axis and the sum in the y-axis. This is known as the effectiveness profile of metrics. This profile is shown in Exhibit 2.

Effectiveness of metrics can be defined, in predictive style, as the association it has with goals. A metric that has scored high has a high association with the defined goal. Lower scores indicate poor association.

Metrics that do not connect with any known goals are "lone rangers" and must be taken away from the active list.

The metric effectiveness profile also provides strategic information about the most effective metrics in the project that need to be supported at any cost.

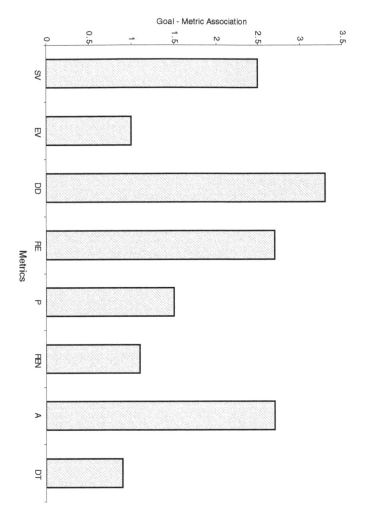

Exhibit 2. Metrics effectiveness map.

Goal Deployment

The row totals indicate a measure of metric support to the goals. The profile of goals scores is shown in Exhibit 3. Larger scores indicate that the goals stand a good chance of being interpreted in measurable terms. The larger the score, the larger the degree of effective goal deployment in the project.

If this profile has large imbalances, we normally revisit the choice of goals and metrics. Maybe we will have to improve the metric system (if the profile scores match the ranking ascribed to goals, then the metrics system already reflects goal preferences).

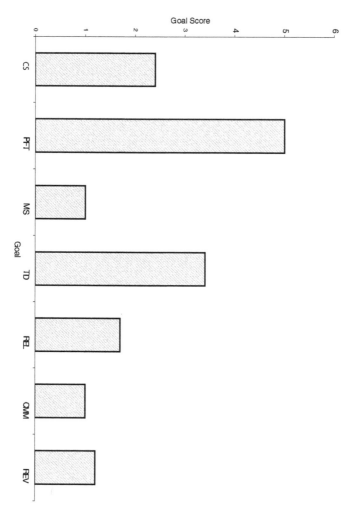

Exhibit 3. Goal deployment profile.

Iterative Process

GMC matrix analysis is iterative. The first analysis may show incongruities that will have to be ironed out and refined before the second run. For example, as is a common experience GMC may reveal the absence of a goal but still have metric that addresses the goal. Conceptually, people put metrics in place first, and then define goals.

After a couple of iterations one can expect a refinement in a metrics system for the project.

Exhibit 4. Customer requirements topology.

What		
Customer Requirements		
Category	Requirements	Rank
A		
B		
C		

Quality Function Deployment (QFD)

Metrics can be applied to capture the customer's voice using the well-known quality function deployment (QFD) structure. The complete QFD known as the house of quality can be built in four stages.

Stage 1: Defining Customer Requirements

Customer requirements are defined and prioritized in this stage. These definitions must use a minimum number of words, almost encoding the quintessence of customer requirements. The precision involved in this exercise makes it the measurement of requirements in linguistic scale, as shown in Exhibit 4.

Stage 2: What–How Analysis

Next, the process capabilities and facilities available in the project are identified and listed in a row. A correlation mapping is done between the requirements and capabilities using a WHAT-HOW matrix, as illustrated in Exhibit 5. The WHAT column represents the voice of the customer and HOW column represents the organization's ability to respond to the voice.

This mapping will expose the weaknesses in the organization's ability to meet the customer needs. Sometimes we also come across the capabilities and facilities that do not relate to customer requirements. This also acts as a resource planning tool. A mismatch between resources and requirements forewarns process risk.

Exhibit 5. What/how matrix.

What			How (Features, Capabilities)							
Customer Requirements			Group 1		Group 2		Group 3			
Category	Requirements	Rank	F1	F2	F3	F4	F5	F6	F7	F8
A										
B										
C										

Exhibit 6. Correlation matrix.

	F1	F2	F3	F4	F5	F6	F7	F8
F8								1
F7							1	
F6						1		
F5					1			
F4				1				
F3			1					
F2		1						
F1	1							
	F1	F2	F3	F4	F5	F6	F7	F8

Stage 3: Process Analysis

In Stage 3, a relationship study is made between the process capabilities, and the target values for each capability are expressed quantitatively, as illustrated in Exhibit 6.

This stage involves a scientific study of correlation between processes and meticulous determination of capability baselines and process goals. Such a study will bring an in-depth understanding of the interline between process elements and help to detect and solve some hidden problems in the process.

Exhibit 7. House of quality.

			Correlation Matrix								
		F8									1
		F7								1	
		F6							1		
		F5						1			
		F4				1					
		F3			1						
		F2		1							
		F1	1								
			F1	F2	F3	F4	F5	F6	F7	F8	
What			How (Features, Capabilities)								
Customer Requirements			Group 1		Group 2		Group 3				
Category	Req.	Rank	F1	F2	F3	F4	F5	F6	F7	F8	
A											Benchmark I
B											
C											
	Benchmark II										

Stage 4: Benchmarking

In this stage, two benchmarking studies are conducted. The first is to compare how our best three competitors fail in meeting customer requirements. The second is to compare our process capabilities with the best three competitors.

Comparison with the market condition gives major input to strategic planning. It is quite likely that different organizations may employ different measurement scales to measure the process parameter. Care must be taken to arrive at a common scale. See Exhibit 7 for illustration. By benchmarking we measure the market scenario to which the customer is going to be exposed. Today's competition is tomorrow's customer requirement. Hence, we measure indirectly the future requirements of the customer.

Thus, QFD is a business survival tool. It measures the most important parts of business: customer and market. QFD maps all processes to the market and exposes mismatches. QFD can be applied to all processes right from marketing to maintenance. This series of applications will translate the customer's voice to the process.

Risk Estimation

Most software metrics activities are carried out for the purpose of risk analysis of some form or another. Forecasting risk by the traditional analysis of metrics has been found to be insufficient. Special techniques are required. We are presenting two simple methods for measuring and forecasting risk. One is simulating schedule risk by a computerized planning tool and the other is mapping risk using a risk exposure number (REN) matrix.

Simulating Schedule Risk

Risk arises from unexpected variations in deliveries. There is a finite probability that the schedule may vary, which is customarily computed from probabilistic models derived from data. In the absence of historical data construction of models from data is not possible. Instead we simulate the project scenarios on a computerized planning tool and trigger variations by altering the project elements.

Variations in the project duration can be traced to three project elements:

1. The work breakdown structure (WBS)
2. The schedule estimations of individual tasks
3. Network architecture (sequential, concurrent, or a combination of both)

The WBS can have different tasks lists based on the planner's experience and approach. Schedule estimation for each task may vary in similar fashion from person to person. For a given task list and set of estimates one can think of a variety of task networks with a combination of sequential and concurrent arrangements. All three elements could vary simultaneously and give rise to a large number of project scenarios, each having its own duration. Creation of scenario is running a simulation run in the software. It can be a series of simulations and capture all possible schedules. In Exhibit 8 and Exhibit 9, two scenarios are presented for illustration.

The results of all simulation runs can be summarized in the format given in Exhibit 10.

From this table one can arrive at the first-order estimate of risk by computing descriptive statistics as minimum duration, maximum duration, mean, median, mode, and standard deviation. If the number of simulation

Exhibit 8. Scenario 1.

	W1	W2	W3	W4	W5	W6	W7	W8	W9	W10	W11	W12	W13	W14	W15	W16	W17	W18
Start	■																	
Fix scope		■	■															
Meeting with customer				■														
Req. analysis					■	■	■											
Prototype						■	■	■	■									
Prepare SRS								■	■	■								
End										■								

Exhibit 9. Scenario 2.

	W1	W2	W3	W4	W5	W6	W7	W8	W9	W10	W11	W12	W13	W14	W15	W16	W17	W18
Start	■																	
Interview customer		■	■															
Document				■														
Internal review						■	■											
Document						■												
Risk analysis			■					■	■									
Document										■								
GUI prototype						■				■	■							
Meet customer													■					
Final draft SRS														■				
End															■			

251

Exhibit 10. Format: summary of simulation runs.

Scenario Number	Duration Weeks

runs is sufficiently large, from this data we can create probability distribution of schedule, as illustrated in Exhibit 11. Perceiving risk from the probability distribution is discussed in Chapter 5.

Mapping Risk Using Risk Exposure Number

Mapping risk in a project involves first recognizing risk elements. To a large extent, recognition depends on past experience of the analyst. Each recognition must be defined without ambiguity and expressed in a concise form. Some even give IDs for each risk so that they are traceable.

For each risk element we estimate the likelihood of occurrence and the magnitude of damage that would be caused if the risks were to be attacked. Both the likelihood and damage are expressed in convenient quantitative scales. One possibility is to express likelihood on a probability scale of 0 to 10 and the damage on a scale of 0 to 10. Risk exposure is now computed by multiplying these two, as illustrated in Exhibit 12.

Analysis of REN

The first-cut analysis is to sort out the table according to risk exposure number. This will give a focus on critical risks.

One can also generate the risk Pareto chart, as shown in Exhibit 13. Apply the 80/20 principle and identify the 20 percent of risk elements that account for 80 percent of the damage.

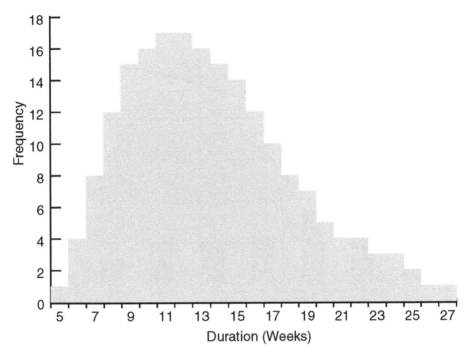

Exhibit 11. Frequency distribution of simulation output.

Exhibit 12. Risk exposure number.

Risk Exposure Matrix
LEVEL: SM

Risk	Probability	Loss	REN	CREN	CREN%
Price cut	9	6	54	54.0	600.0
Order cancel	2	10	20	74.0	822.2
Review failure	4	4	16	90.0	1000.0
Wrong requirements	2	5	10	100.0	1111.1
Attrition	1	9	9	109.0	1211.1
Defect leakage	3	3	9	118.0	1311.1
Delivery slippage	1	5	5	123.0	1366.7
Technology change	0.5	3	1.5	124.5	1383.3

Having short-listed risk elements, we can arrive at a mitigation plan to cut down probability and a contingency plan to minimize damage.

The sum total of REN count is taken as overall measure of risk, which can be tracked from time to time in the project.

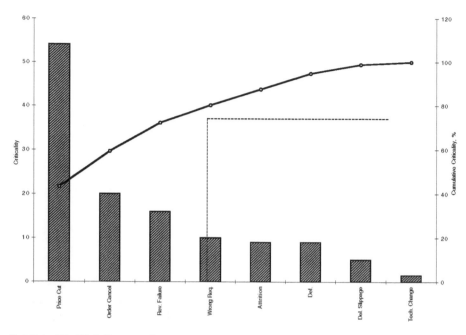

Exhibit 13. Risk Pareto chart.

Six Sigma Renaissance

Six Sigma Vision

At the core of the Six Sigma movement is a new vision that combines quantitative methods with leadership. This powerful combination has achieved breakthrough improvements. It has also brought all the tools for improvement developed in the past five decades to focused use.

The Six Sigma cycle uses metrics to advantage in almost all the phases in recognizing, defining, measuring, analyzing, improving, and controlling; the Define, Measure, Analyze, Improve, Control (DMAIC) model revolves around measurement and analysis.

Metrics in the Boardroom

The magic of Six Sigma has its origin in the boardroom and happens when top management believes in data and is willing to train people to look at and analyze data and apply the knowledge gained to improve the situation. Top management has taken this training a bit seriously and enlisted support from all. All Six Sigma case studies are case studies of leadership faith in numbers. The Six Sigma breakthroughs start with achieving quantitative understanding of processes, as Bill Smith, the originator of the Six Sigma concept, did in Motorola.

When the metrics system is taken seriously by the board, the organization takes a new shape, perhaps in the name of Six Sigma.

Money, the Greatest Metric

Perhaps Six Sigma succeeds where other initiatives have failed; it is because Six Sigma uses financial benefits as the criteria. Profits and bottom lines are the watchwords.

Money seems to be the greatest metric ever. Crosby knew it when he insisted that cost of failures must be measured in monetary terms. Now sigma improvement is judged by cost savings. On the surface it looks like a short-sighted business drive. But there is a lot of wisdom behind this choice. Modeling process behavior in terms of cost functions is an established scientific approach (used widely in optimization algorithms). Defining a cost function or a profit function enables one to see performance clearly and relate the result to influences now called cost drivers. Converting process variables into cost variables helps to combine several processes for modeling.

And, in the organizational context, money represents great value, health of the projects, and a very communicative indicator.

In money, Six Sigma has achieved the great convergence.

Metrics Black Belts

Six Sigma Black Belts (application experts, as they were called in yesteryear) take professional training on measurement and analysis of metrics data and changing the organization through a series of improvement projects. The body of knowledge (as in the ASQ Black Belt certification curriculum) that the Black Belts are expected to master includes several data analysis methods:

- Measurement Scales
- Metrology
- Types of Data
- Methods of Data Collection
- Descriptive Statistics
- Inferential Statistics
- Probability
- Graphical Methods
- Frequency Distributions
- Process Capability
- Exploratory Data Analysis
- Simple Linear Regression
- Multiple Linear Regressions
- Design of Experiments

Metrics data analysis is a basic Black Belt skill. Metrics application for improvement is the very purpose of Black Belt learning. For Black Belts, application is the key.

Measurement Capability

As defects are reduced to part-per-million levels, process measurement capability must improve to match. A normal measurement system has the ability to detect one tenth the variation it tries to measure. The ability to detect even the smallest process drift or deviation is not easily achieved in software projects. The organization "sees" what it measures. Where measurement capability is less, many process problems are buried beneath the carpet. Where measurement practice is absent, even larger problems are not seen; they do not exist for all practical purposes, and hence there is no perceived need for process improvement!

Six Sigma programs realize this early in their project phases. Attempts to build models from metrics data will reveal such inadequacies related to precision of measurements.

Consummate Vision

We have presented in this chapter four components of vision. The first is related to goals, seeing them, defining them, and deploying them. Goals are expressions of vision. Then comes a vision that covers market forces and the customer; QFD is good way of consolidating this vision. Risk perception is next, seeing well ahead what could fail later is what this is about. Finally, the combination of data analysis and leadership offers a unique vision with great power; it could transform organizations.

The purpose of metrics, ultimately, is to build a consummate vision and give the user strategic benefits.

Chapter 14
Metrics System Implementation

Toward Truth

The metrics journey is a movement toward truth. We implement metrics because we wish to deal with true values, to see the true picture, and to arrive at true solutions. This is the foundation on which metrics implementation seems to rest. This quest lies dormant, subdued by business pressures, and waits to be invoked. Implementation of metrics is invocation of this spirit.

No Universal Method

There is no universal technique when it comes to implementing metrics. Every organization must build its own method. Of course, there are lessons learned which are to be found in the references cited from which one can work out a system of avoiding the pitfalls. Advice such as "do not begin by measuring performance" and "start small" could be certainly useful but, by themselves, are not prescriptions for success.

One can also pick up clues from the ERP (enterprise resource planning) implementation experience of the last decade; from the well-publicized business process reengineering (BPR) problems and how some have solved them; from Six Sigma project initiatives and the eventful stories of Black Belts who changed organizations. Implementing metrics is not too different from these experiences of change management. As these stories would testify, there is no "off the shelf" solution, no ready-to-use strategy.

Roadmap?

Successful implementation of metrics could be the result of a long chain of preparatory events, from designing an appropriate metrics system to creating the right applications. The whole process begins with a desire to have a new culture that accepts transparency and statistical thinking. Then it evolves, fuelled by an emphasis on humanism, which asserts mastery of the human mind over environment. It is very difficult to trace evolutionary paths of metrics, much less to prescribe roadmaps.

The tree of metrics taxonomy can really branch into an intricate network, covering the deep fathoms of software engineering on the one hand, and penetrating process layers on the other. It could be a simple study of project management effectiveness or an elaborate research on product architecture. There is no single track to pick or beaten track to follow.

But perhaps, if one gathers the field experiences of metrics champions, one can collect some key concepts, clear principles, and some fundamentals, which help metrics implementation. We attempt to give a modest compilation of such ideas in this chapter.

Effective Use of Metrics

The central point of implementation is effective use of metrics. Implementation begins with showing results from metrics, however modest they may be. In fact, it is recommended to begin the metrics system in a low key but execute an improvement cycle in a key business area. It could be, for example, developing a simple metric called cost of poor quality and using the findings to reduce cost — a tangible benefit that everyone appreciates. In an organization such a positive and result-oriented move creates interest and orientation toward metrics implementation.

Metrics are mirrors that reflect realities. Fear of exposure inhibits the mind from accepting metrics. When the mind becomes ready to see change and reality, effective use of metrics is possible.

Effective use is possible with "bias for action," which has the power to overcome ambiguity inherent in software metrics. Let us not use metrics to motivate people. Metrics produces results in the hands of motivated people.

Looking at Metrics Data

Goal Activation

Perhaps implementation starts when people "look" at data. Looking at data is a process that is influenced by "goals" and we see what we want to see. Also we see that part of data alone that is related to the problem at hand. Thus, a problem-solving culture and heightened sense of goals are required for recognizing data. Goals need to be refreshed periodically, otherwise they rise to their peak and fade away in the organization preview. Correspondingly, the context set by goals by metrics interpretation could also rise and fall. To keep metrics alive, therefore, the goals and metrics context must be activated periodically.

Knowledge Discovery from Data

Metrics systems contain meaning in several layers and one has to mine meaning through the knowledge discovery process. Implementation here means extracting knowledge and putting it to use. Extraction of knowledge can be done through a simple method that makes use of the power of pictorial representation.

Data Visualization. There are numerous ways of analyzing data statistically. Any process behavior can be represented in three dimensions, namely, time, frequency, and relationship. There is no process behavioral pattern that cannot be captured in these three dimensions. Accordingly, looking at process data involves three fundamental analytical views:

1. Time domain analysis
2. Frequency domain analysis
3. Relationship domain analysis

Each analysis by itself can result in great understanding of the process. It is a diagnostic tool. Also, the analytical framework can simultaneously be a "process model" helping in forecasting.

A synthesis of these three analytical results could prove to be more useful and comprehensive than many sophisticated analysis using rigorous statistical methodologies. To implement metrics, we must keep the analysis as simple as possible.

It is a mistake to collect a lot of data but not analyze it adequately. A better ROI comes about when we collect minimum data and perform maximum analysis. Successful implementation of metrics has one cardinal principle: cut down the data collection cost.

Applying Metrics

The purpose of having metrics, interpreting them, and discovering knowledge is to apply them to the business. All applications must be well integrated with the business process flow. Other applications, even if technically feasible and very attractive, must be rejected.

Applications can promote metrics better than procedures, guidelines, and instructions. Applications could be infectious; one breeds another.

Application Categories

Metrics have been put to a lot of applications, from business to science. The applications are as numerous as the management approaches that prevail. The applications are as numerous as the number of problems waiting to be solved. All these applications fall under six categories:

1. *Creating estimation models:* Having estimation models builds a capability to foresee problems and supports planning, a must for excellence in software engineering.
2. *Creating process models:* Process models are process assets, knowledge capsules that pave the way for innovation in the workplace.

3. *Online use of metrics:* Selecting core metrics and responding to them online makes one "vigilant" and "intelligent" regarding work progress.
4. *Using metrics for managing defects:* Defect is a telling manifestation of process characteristic. Managing defects is managing process.
5. *Building a decision support system (DSS) from metrics:* In the final analysis, metrics provide intelligence. Building a decision support using metrics will establish a modern "nerve center" for the organization.
6. *Creating strategic vision:* Metrics can help in seeing the intangible and in quantifying the abstract; hence, a great support for building a strategic vision.

These are possible directions of applying metrics; one need not travel in all the directions to implement metrics. Substantial benefits of metrics can be realized even in one category of applications.

For example, an organization that is not comfortable with IT innovations may skip DSS and instead choose the well-established process modeling, or one can transform the organization just from defect metrics. There have been instances when strict adherence to project discipline and online application of project metrics has led projects to outperform others. And of course, it is well known how foresight (derived by using metrics) could give competitive advantage.

Value Generation

Every successful application, whatever its direction, creates value. So waves of application in an organization will create a new value system that may compete with existing values. Those who implement metrics must be prepared for this.

Application of metrics also results in creation of intellectual assets, knowledge units, and process assets. Therefore, application of metrics amounts to creation, protection, and utilization of this wealth.

Deconstruction

Metrics play as symbols, heralding a new culture. The established thought system is often destroyed, and a new system slowly comes into being. The suspension of existing symbols and assumption leaves the scenario empty.

The series of models that issue forth from metrics analysis create a strong set of higher-level symbols of a different kind. The old symbols conveyed meaning by operating as referential icons. The new symbols allow one to think and construct one's own meaning. The former is "stock response," the latter "intelligent creation."

Implementing metrics involves a transition from mechanical application of decision rules to "decision analysis" and optimal construction of meaning. This is seen as a painful transition that the organization fights involuntarily.

In one instance, trying to measure goals and track their progress changed the goals themselves. In another, measurement of size led to radically new concepts about software size. In both these examples, it turned out to be a case of self discovery and deconstruction. Prefabricated notions were examined and discarded in favor of more valid ones.

Creating Decision Centers

Metrics could eventually bring about changes in the way the organization thinks. By sharing data with people and making them see and think, we will be creating knowledge centers in the work area. By allowing them to analyze the situation and solve problems, we will be taking those knowledge centers to a higher level of organizational culture. These will evolve into decision centers that are empowered to act upon knowledge.

Creating an organization with decision centers is a postmodern trend in management. Most likely those who apply metrics will find themselves facing the emergence of this new organization. This encounter could lead to problems if the top management is not willing to create such a new organization. Unwittingly, metrics champions meet with a conflict of which they never dreamed. Therefore, it is up to the top management to prepare itself and others for the organizational changes before implementing metrics.

The full use of metrics can be realized only through decision centers. This could bring in sweeping improvements across the organization.

Equip People with Knowledge at Less Cost

Implementation of metrics involves data analysis, as well as decision making — an essentially human process that cannot be mechanized and automated completely. Human involvement and the human ability to deal with complex, real-life situations alone can lead to success with metrics.

Tools can be made use of, for a price, to support the human initiative. It is recommended with the pick-and-choose, low-cost tools that perform selected functions and install them in the decision centers. With some training on the basic statistics and on the use of tools, the decision centers are well equipped.

Attempts at using tools providing global solutions and possessing higher levels of intelligence failed in implementing metrics. These solutions are prohibitively expensive. For the high cost they have serious limitations.

Exhibit 1. Statistical functions.

AVEDEV	COVAR	HARMEAN	NEGBINOMDIST	STDEVA
AVERAGE	CRITBINOM	HYPGEOMDIST	NORMDIST	STDEVP
AVERAGEA	DEVSQ	INTERCEPT	NORMINV	STDEVPA
BETADIST	EXPONDIST	KURT	NORMSDIST	STEYX
BETAINV	FDIST	LARGE	NORMSINV	TDIST
BINOMDIST	FINV	LINEST	PEARSON	TINV
CHIDIST	FISHER	LOGEST	PERCENTILE	TREND
CHIINV	FISHERINV	LOGINV	PERCENTRANK	TRIMMEAN
CHITEST	FORECAST	LOGNORMDIST	PERMUT	TTEST
CONFIDENCE	FREQUENCY	MAX	POISSON	VAR
CORREL	FTEST	MAXA	PROB	VARA
COUNT	GAMMADIST	MEDIAN	QUARTILE	VARP
COUNTA	GAMMALN	MIN	RANK	VARPA
COUNTBLANK	GEOMEAN	MINA	STANDARDIZE	WEIBULL
COUNTIF	GROWTH	MODE	STDEV	ZTEST

On balance, the cost of high-level tools is several times higher than the cost of equipping people with analytical skills.

Implementation is fundamentally the human process with or without tools. Human beings cannot effectively implement prefabricated decisions. Analysis, decision making, and action are organically embedded in human systems. Implementing metrics must draw from this inherent human potential. Any other technical "alternatives" fade in comparison. The only way to implement metrics is through invoking the human initiative.

The Marvelous Spreadsheet

The spreadsheet can be used to great advantage in making decisions using data. While implementing metrics, practice on Excel's analytical capabilities has been found supportive. There are more than 80 statistical functions available in Excel that will help in performing a wide variety of analysis (see Exhibit 1). For example, a simple function such as NORMDIST can be used to generate a Gaussian model of processes and estimate risk as a percentage.

Similarly, Excel has financial, logical, mathematical, and many other functions that will help in deeper analysis of metrics data.

Special macros are available for making complex data analysis easier. For signature analysis there is the Fourier transform macro. Similarly, powerful macros are available for ANOVA, t-Test, regression statistics, and frequency analysis. Excel allows a user to record personal macros to do repetitive tasks. Macro scripts can be edited and improved easily using Visual Basic.

Excel has very good graph-making capabilities. We can customize the graph styles to suit the business presentations. By selecting different datasets, we can generate dynamic views of graphs. This creates multiple scenarios quickly using the same data.

In addition to this, database management facilities including sort, filter, and pivot table are very useful in managing metrics data. Special tools such as Goal Seek, Scenarios, and Wizard will be very useful in decision-making applications. Excel also allows adding personal macros to the list to increase productivity of data processing and report generation. Implementation becomes easier with Excel.

Things to Remember during Implementation

- Before introducing a metrics plan, the project management systems and engineering processes must be well defined and documented. Without this foundation, metrics will end up with conflicting numbers.
- Project managers need some essential metrics: cost, schedule, resources, performance, and customer satisfaction. Add one for human assets and another for fixed assets. These seven areas are of concern. Each can have sub-areas and process areas.
- Goals first, metrics next. This rule may be applied to the sub-processes.
- Avoid information overload and "analysis paralysis."
- When analysis starts, strike a balance among EDA, SPC, and DOE.
- As much you wish to act upon, so much you measure.
- Human factor "perception to action." Do not underestimate the human power for interpretation of data. The metrics system should be agile and flexible and not overly mechanical.
- Define the core metrics and allow metrics to evolve.
- Diagnose the process defects using process models.
- Extract wealth from metrics using KDD (knowledge discovery in database).
- The metrics system is the brain of the organization.
- Measure market environment at a strategic level.

Lead with Numbers

Implement metrics beginning from the leadership zone. Let the highest decision makers in business and technological issues use the first metrics, and demonstrate that they respect the data. Implementation could mean the construction of a cost model for the project, a complexity model for the product, or customer satisfaction analysis for a market segment. Let the senior-most people lead the way with numbers. The others will find it easy to follow.

Integrated Management

Metrics integrate organizational processes. Gain from this natural advantage. History was made in fixed assets management by announcing a metric called OEE (overall equipment effectiveness), which measures equipment effectiveness by considering three factors: downtime, defect rate, and productivity (hitherto the concern of three separate departments). OEE was the ace metric used in the total productive maintenance movement, which brought in spectacular results in Japan and the rest of the world.

The discussion of metrics in one forum brings all the core concerns of the organization to that forum. We get the opportunity to relate the usually separately viewed factors: productivity and quality, effort escalation and delivery slippage, employee satisfaction index, and defect density.

Implementation of a metrics culture establishes integrated project management. Quantitative methods bring in great improvements in the planning process using aids such as Monte Carlo simulation, resource balancing, capability matching, and risk modeling. In a similar vein, the estimation process also gets reinforced by use of multivariate models, mathematical templates, and statistical techniques. Metrics create a new bondage — a synergy between planning and estimation.

Metrics data analysis produces analytical views — new symbols — which are integrated in the report. Persistent integration of symbols is a forerunner of integration of subcultures.

Mirror, Microscope, and Telescope

An analogy would help in getting the complexity of implementing metrics: implementation of metrics resembles installation of mirrors, microscopes, and telescopes.

Implement metrics and you install mirrors in the organization. Mirrors can be placed in vantage points.

The investigative power of metrics unfolds in two ways. The first is the way metrics provide details on selected key process areas. Metrics put the process under a microscope and reveal hidden details not seen by cursory glances. The universes within the universe — the processes within each process — emerge and appear in the eyepiece of the metrics microscope. Without this microscope, the primary research tool, new discoveries in software engineering are impossible. The second is how metrics are used as telescopes by surveyors, the explorer, the traveler who seeks to conquer new frontiers, and astronomers who reach out to the galaxies. Aided by the metrics telescope, we can see risks and opportunities more clearly. Market research, customer requirements research, competitor analysis, threats within the process network, defect production tendencies, failure patterns within the organization, and similar scientific studies are examples of how metrics can give foresight.

One can implement metrics as microscopes and as telescopes to suit the discovery agenda one has charted out. But microscopes and telescopes are mere tools. The user makes the difference.

Unlimited Scope

In this book, we presented a few simple and economic ideas for designing, analyzing, and implementing metrics. We have been extremely conscious of the constraints in organizations to make do with existing tools and cut costs. However, growth of technology such as artificial intelligence, data mining, and Bayesian Belief Nets (BBN) in recent times holds attractive promises for better analysis of metrics. Also, new directions in metrics application are continuously evolving, and correspondingly new discoveries will be made in metrics models. We have taken a human-centric approach that envisages the birth of decision centers in an organization in order to tap the best out of metrics. There could be other approaches to suit the emerging scenarios. Metrics have great potential; there are unlimited possibilities.

Bibliography

1. Adrian Burr and Mal Owen, *Statistical Methods for Software Quality*, Thomson Computer Press, 1996, 453 pp.
2. Alexis Leon, Enterprise Resource Planning .
3. Anderson, Sweeney, and Williams, *An Introduction To Management Science: Quantitative Approaches to Decision Making*, West Publishing Company, MN, 1994.
4. Andrew Webb, Statistical Pattern Recognition, Arnold Publishers.
5. Anita D. Carleton et al., Software measurement For DoD Systems; Recommendations For Initial Core Measures, Carnegie Mellon University, 1996.
6. Anita D. Carleton and Mark C. Paulk, Statistical Process Control for Software Tutorial, Carnegie Mellon University, 1997.
7. Armand V. Feigenbaum, *Total Quality Control*, McGraw-Hill International Editions, 1991.
8. Armstrong A. Takang and Penny A. Grubb, *Software Maintenance Concepts and Practice*, International Thomson Computer Press, London, 1996.
9. Barbara Kitchenham, *Software Metrics — Measurement for Software Process Improvement*, NCC Blackwell, 1996.
10. Barry W. Boehm et al., *Software Cost Estimation with COCOMO II*, Prentice Hall, Englewood Cliffs, New Jersey, 2000.
11. Bechtold T. Richard, *Improving the Software Process through Process Definition and Modeling*, International Thompson Computer Press, Boston, 1996.
12. Bruno, G., *Model-Based Software Engineering*, Chapman and Hall, 1995.
13. C. Stevenson, *Software Engineering Productivity: A Practical Guide*, Chapman & Hall, 1995.
14. Cem Kaner et al., *Testing Computer Software*, Comdex Computer Publishing Pvt. Ltd., New Delhi, 2000.
15. Chris Chapman and Stephen Ward, *Project Risk Management — Process, Techniques and Insights*, John Wiley & Sons Ltd., England,1997.
16. Crosby B. Philip, *Quality Is Free: The Art of Making Quality Certain*, McGraw-Hill, New York, 1979.
17. Dale H. Besterfield, Carol Besterfield-Michna, Glen H. Besterfield, and Mary Besterfield-Sacre, *Total Quality Management*, Prentice Hall, Englewood Cliffs, New Jersey, 1995.
18. David S. Linthicum, Enterprise Application Integration.
19. Edward Kit, *Software Testing in the Real World: Improving the Process*, Addison Wesley, England, 1995.
20. Elaine M. Hall, *Managing Risk: Methods For Software Systems Development*, Addison-Wesley Longman, Inc., Canada,1998.
21. Fenton E. Norman and Martin Niel, *Software Metrics: Road Map*, CSD QM&WC, London, August 2000.
22. Forrest W. Breyfogle III, *Implementing Six Sigma*, John Wiley and Sons, 1999.
23. Fowler, Roger, *Understanding Language: An Introduction To Linguistics*, Routledge & Kegan Paul, London, 1974.
24. G. Gordon Schulmeyer and James I. McManus, *Total Quality Management for Software*, International Thompson Publishing, 1997–98.
25. G. Winfield Treese and Lawrence C. Stewart, Designing Systems For Internet Commerce, Pearson Education Asia Pte. Ltd., UK, 2000.
26. Genichi Taguchi, Introduction to Quality Engineering: Designing Quality into Products and Processes, Asian Productivity Organization, Tokyo, 1986.
27. George D. Robson, *Continuous Process Improvement*, Macmillan, 1991.
28. George Eckes, *The Six Sigma Revolution*, John Wiley and Sons, New York, 2001.
29. Gerald V. Post and David L. Anderson, Management Information Systems, Solving Business Problems with Information Technology.

30. Gopal K. Kanji and Mike Asher, *100 Methods for Total Quality Management,* Response Books, New Delhi, 1996.
31. Gopal K. Kanji and Mike Asher, Total Quality Management Process, Productivity (India) Pvt. Ltd., Madras, 1995.
32. Ivar Jacobson et al., Software Reuse Architecture: Process and Organization for Business Success, Pearson Education Asia Pte. Ltd., 2000.
33. Ivar Jacobson et al., *The Unified Software Development Process,* Addison Wesley Longman Inc., USA, 2000.
34. J.M. Juran, *Juran on Quality by Design: The New Steps for Planning Quality into Goods and Services,* The Free Press, New York, 1992.
35. James A. O'Brien, Management Information Systems, Managing Information Technology in the E-Business Enterprise.
36. James F. Peters and Witold Pedrycz, *Software Engineering An Engineering Approach,* John Wiley & Sons, New York, 2000.
37. James Herzleb, Anita Carleton, James Rozum, Jane Siegel, and David Subrow, Benefits of CMM-Based Software Process Improvement: Initial results, Carnegie Mellon University, 1996.
38. Jeffrey A. Hoffer, Joey F. George, and Joseph S. Valacich, Modern System Analysis and Design.
39. Jennifer Gremba and Chuck Myers, The IDEALSM Model: A Practical Guide for Improvement, Bridge Issue 3, SEI Publication, 1997.
40. John A. McDermid, *Software Engineer's Reference Book,* Butterworth Heinemann, London, 1991.
41. John Gaffney et al., *Software Measurement Guidebook,* International Thompson Computer Press, Boston, 1995.
42. K. Ishikawa, *What Is Total Quality Control? The Japanese Way,* Prentice Hall, Englewood Cliffs, New Jersey, 1985.
43. Kaner Cem, Rethinking Software Metrics, *STQE,* March/April 2000.
44. Karl E. Wiegers, A Software Metrics Primer, *Software Development,* July 1999.
45. Karl E. Wiegers, *Software Requirements,* WP Publishers & Distributors Pvt. Ltd., Bangalore, 1999.
46. Kenny and Anthony, *Managing Software: The Businessman's Guide to Software Development,* Blackwell Scientific Publications, Oxford, 1989.
47. Kieron Conway, *Software Project Management,* Dreamtech Press, New Delhi, 2001.
48. Lawrence H. Putnam and Ware Myers, Expert Metrics Views, Cutter Information Group, 2000.
49. Mary Shaw et al., *Software Architecture — Perspectives on an Emerging Discipline,* Prentice Hall Inc., Englewood Cliffs, New Jersey, 1996.
50. Mordechai Ben-Menachem and Garry S. Marllis, *Software Quality,* International Thomson Publications, London, 1997.
51. NASA, Software Engineering Program — Software Measurement Guide Book, 1995.
52. Norman E. Fenton and Shari Lawrence Pfleeger, *Software Metrics — A Rigorous and Practical Approach,* Thomson Computer Press, 1996.
53. Pankaj Jalote, *An Integrated Approach To Software Engineering,* Springer-Verlag, New York, 1991.
54. Peter Kulik, Software Metrics: State of the Art — 2000, KLCI , December 2000.
55. Peter S. Pande, Robert P. Neuman, and Roland R. Cavanagh, *The Six Sigma Way,* McGraw-Hill, 2000.
56. Philip B. Crosby, *Quality without Tears: The Art of Hassle-Free Management,* McGraw-Hill, New York, 1984.
57. Pieter Adriaans and Dolf Zantinge, *Data Mining,* Addison-Wesley, 2000.
58. Ram Bansal 'Vigyacharya', Information System Analysis and Design, New Age International (P) Limited.

59. Richard I. Levin and David S. Rubin, Statistics for Management, Prentice Hall, Englewood Cliffs, New Jersey, 1997.
60. Rivkin and Ryan, Eds., *Literary Theory: An Anthology,* Blackwell Publishers, Massachusetts, 1998.
61. Robert E Park, Wolfhart B. Goethert, and William A. Florac, *Goal – Driven Software Measurement – A Guidebook,* SEI Publications, 1996.
62. Robert E. Park, Anita D. Carleton, and William A. Florac, *Practical Software Measurement: Measuring for Process Management and Improvement,* SEI Publications, 1997
63. Robert Schulthesis and Mary Sumner, Management Information Systems.
64. Robins, R.H., *General Linguistics: An Introductory Survey,* Longman, London, 1964.
65. Roger S. Pressman, *Software Engineering A Practitioner's Approach,* McGraw Hill International Edition, NY, 2001.
66. Ronald L. Iman, *A Data Based Approach to Statistics,* International Thomson Publishing, 1994.
67. S.C. Gupta and V.K. Kapoor, *Fundamentals of Mathematical Statistics,* Sultan Chand and Sons, New Delhi, 1970.
68. Sam Anahory et al., *Data Warehousing In The Real World a Practical Guide For Building Decision Support Systems,* Pearson Education Asia Pte. Ltd, UK, 2000.
69. Sami Zahran, Software Process Improvement, Addison-Wesley, Reading, MA, 1998
70. Saussure, Ferdinand de, *Cours de lingustique generale* (1916), translated by Wade Baskin as *Course In General Linguistics,* New York 1959.
71. Sim, Stuart, *The Routledge Companion to Postmodernism,* Routledge Taylor & Francis Group, London, 2001.
72. Software Productivity Consortium, *Improving The Software Process Through Process Definition and Modeling,* Thomson Computer Press, 1996.
73. Stephen Grey, *Practical Risk Assessment For Project Management,* John Wiley & Sons Ltd, England, 1995.
74. Swapna Kishore and Rajesh Naik, *Software Requirements Estimation,* Tata McGraw-Hill Publishing Company Ltd., New Delhi, 2001.
75. Thomas Pyzdek, *The Six Sigma Handbook – A Complete Guide for Greenbelts, Blackbelts, and Managers at All Levels,* McGraw-Hill, New York, 2001.
76. Thomas Thelin, Controlling quality in software inspections using Control Charts, 2000.
77. Trevor L Young, *The Handbook of Project Management – A Practical Guide to Effective Policies and Procedures,* Institute of Directors, 2002.
78. V.S. Janakiraman & K. Sarukesi, Decision Support System.
79. W.E. Deming, Out of the Crisis, Massachusetts Institute of Technology, Cambridge, 1986.
80. W.A. Shewhart, *Economic Control of Quality of Manufactured Product,* Van Norstrand Company, New York, 1931.
81. Walker Royce, *Software Project Management,* Addison Wesley Longman, Reading, MA, 1998.
82. Watts S. Humphrey, *A Discipline for Software Engineering,* SEI Series in Software Engineering, Addison-Wesley, 1995.
83. Watts S. Humphrey, *The Software Quality Profile,* Software Engineering Institute, CMU Pittsburgh, PA.
84. Wendir R. Bukowitz and Ruth L. Williams, The Knowledge Management Field Book.
85. William A. Florac, Software Quality Measurement: A Framework for Counting Problems and Defects, Carnegie Mellon University, 1996.
86. William E. Perry, *Effective Methods for Software Testing,* John Wiley & Sons, New York, 2000.
87. T.L. Woodings (1995) A Taxonomy of Software Metrics, Software Process Improvement Network (SPIN), Perth, Australia.

URLs

1. http://claymore.engineer.gvsu.edu
2. http://dec.bournemouth.ac.uk
3. http://home.uchicago.edu
4. http://members.aol.com
5. http://omlc.ogi.e.,du
6. http://sepo.spawar.navy.mil
7. http://support.microsoft.com
8. http://vtsoft.com
9. http://ww-cs-etsu.edu
10. http://wwitch.unl.edu
11. http://yunus.hun.edu.tr
12. www.adainc.com
13. www.adamssixsigma.com
14. www.alphaworks.ibm.com
15. www.analycorp.com
16. www.angoss.com
17. www.arlingsoft.com
18. www.baz.com
19. www.bell-labs.com
20. www.benchmark.com
21. www.checkpoint.com
22. www.chempute.com
23. www.circle4.com
24. www.cise.ufl.edu
25. www.computer.org
26. www.compuware.com
27. www.construx.com
28. www.corda.com
29. www.costxpert.com
30. www.cs.tamu.edu
31. www.cs.toronto.edu
32. www.cs.ttu.edu
33. www.curvefit.com
34. www.cutter.com
35. www.dadisp.com
36. www.datadesk.com
37. www.devicelink.com
38. www.distributive.com
39. www.dssresearch.com
40. www.econsys.com
41. www.elementool.com
42. www.etsu.edu
43. www.expertchoice.com
44. www.ficom.net
45. www.galorath.com
46. www.grove.co.uk
47. www.iconixsw.com
48. www.inet-sciences.com
49. www.infoharvest.com
50. www.insightful.com
51. www.iplbath.com
52. www.iseriesnetwork.com

53. www.isixsigma.com
54. www.itl.nist.gov
55. www.ivee.com
56. www.jmp.com
57. www.keypress.com
58. www.lumina.com
59. www.ncsu.edu
60. www.nnh.com
61. www.omegahat.org
62. www.originlab.com
63. www.ovum.com
64. www.pricesystems.com
65. www.processimpact.com
66. www.psmc.com
67. www.qsm.com
68. www.qualitydigest.com
69. www.radview.com
70. www.rational.com
71. www.risktrak.com
72. www.salford-systems.com
73. www.sas.com
74. www.seisage.com
75. www.sgi.com
76. www.sixsigmasystems.com
77. www.softlanding.com
78. www.softstarsystems.com
79. www.spc.ca
80. www.spr.com
81. www.spss.com
82. www.statsoftinc.com
83. www.sytech.com
84. www.telelogic.com
85. www.testingfaqs.org
86. www.treeage.com
87. www.visualstats.org
88. www.wonderware.com
89. www.wwk.com

Index